☆ JOHN ROBERT BAYLOR

☆ EDWARD CLARK

☆ RICHARD W. "DICK" DOWLING

☆ JOHN BELL HOOD

☆ FRANCIS RICHARD LUBBOCK

☆ JOHN BANKHEAD MAGRUDER

☆ PENDLETON MURRAH

☆ WILLIAMSON SIMPSON OLDHAM

☆ JOHN H. REAGAN

☆ LOUIS T. WIGFALL

W. C. NUNN
Editor

Published by
HILL JUNIOR COLLEGE PRESS

Library of Congress Catalog Card No.
68-58539

Printed by

Waco, Texas

Bound by
Library Binding Co.
Waco, Texas

Dedication

This book is dedicated to my former students at Hillsboro Junior College who made the supreme sacrifice for their country during World War II.

★ Ray Anglin — Hillsboro
★ Sam Baker — Itasca
★ Gene Campbell — Dallas
★ J. D. Gilliam — Corsicana
★ Jim Moody Williams — Clear Creek
★ Johnny Williams — Milford

and to

★ Zerk Robertson — Merkel
One of World War II's most decorated heroes who passed away from cancer in January 1966.

W. C. Nunn

Publisher's Preface

This volume may well be a first in publishing history—the publication of ten seminar papers written by selected graduate students and published in book form for nation-wide distribution.

The Board of Regents of Hill Junior College has obtained the services of Dr. W. C. Nunn, professor of history at Texas Christian University, in editing this volume and has also underwritten and elected to publish the work of ten of his graduate students. All too many times the college presses of the country are interested only in publishing the work of established authors or of senior faculty members, ignoring almost completely the work of the beginning or of the unknown writer. Thus, the writer who has never published finds himself in many cases without a means to break into the publishing field. Oftentimes it takes just one published work to start a young writer on his way—to encourage him to want to write more—to give him the one "break" that starts him on the road to a successful writing career. The Hill Junior College Press has given the contributing authors such an opportunity. It is hoped that this pioneer publication will encourage a few of the college presses scattered across the nation to underwrite the efforts of the graduate student, as well as the work of the established author or the senior faculty member.

Ten Texans in Gray is a step forward in filling a void that has long existed in Texas Confederate history. Little has been published on Texas Confederate civil and military leaders between the two or three paragraph biographical sketches found in the usual encyclopedic type work and the book length definitive life treatments. Numerous short biographical sketches concerning the men that Professor Nunn has selected for his book can be found. Too, several of the *Ten Texans* have been the subjects of full biographies. However, oftentimes the general reader and the scholar are seeking more than a multi-paragraph biographical sketch and, on the other hand, have not the desire nor the time to peruse a 300-page definitive work. The biographical study or essay as presented in Professor Nunn's compilation fills this void. While emphasis is on the Civil War phase of each subject's career, his pre- and post-war career has not been neglected.

This volume, understandably, is concerned with but a few of the outstanding Texans who made their mark during the Confederate era. It is hoped that another volume or two, using the same historical time period and the same approach will be forthcoming. The biographical studies are well researched, interestingly written and are a tribute to the editorial and teaching skill of Professor W. C. Nunn. Of particular importance to both the scholar and the writer are the extensive bibliographies compiled by the various authors.

The Hill Junior College Press is proud to present the work of ten of the senior graduate students majoring in history at Texas Christian University.

HILL JUNIOR COLLEGE PRESS

Author's Preface

"There is properly no history, only biography." Thus once wrote Ralph Waldo Emerson. Yet biographies except for the famed remain unwritten, and the knowledge of a person's life passes with the going of his contemporaries. Perhaps a few letters, a brief obituary notice in a newspaper, and possibly a mention in some document remain, and that is all.

Some but not all of the ten men whose biographies are treated here have, as far as the stories of their lives are concerned, been neglected. This is not true, however, of John Bell Hood, and John H. Reagan. It is true of most of the others. The battles of Galveston Island and of Sabine Pass have been told and retold, but John Bankhead Magruder and Dick Dowling, as individuals, have been lost sight of in the accounts of their achievements. General Magruder is included not because he was a Texan but for the reasons that he fought well there and served as commander of the area. John Robert Baylor, the man, has been all but forgotten. Obscured are the lives of the civilian leaders as well. The war governors Edward Clark and Pendleton Murrah have been so overlooked that they have become names only labeling their administrations. Williamson Simpson Oldham is scarcely remembered. Francis R. Lubbock wrote his own story, but it is familiar only to historians. As for Louis T. Wigfall, an extensive study of his life has been written, but it is as yet unpublished.

The authors of the ten biographies in this volume are graduate students in history at Texas Christian University, and it has been the privilege of the writer to have directed them in preparing these studies. Their combined purpose in writing these accounts is to cast more light not only upon the figures whose lives they narrate but upon the larger events of the Civil War in Texas as well.

A preface is an introduction and as such should present an apperceptive background so that one reading the book may better estimate what it contains. So it is for this reason that an historical background of the Civil War in Texas is incorporated in this preamble.

Had wisdom prevailed over the entire nation between 1850 and 1860 war could not have followed in 1861. However, too many people were not thinking but only feeling, so there was little place for wisdom North or South. Upon the election of Abraham Lincoln to the presidency in 1860, South Carolina led the Gulf states in secession from the Union, for neither the Palmetto State nor her sisters were willing to accept as chief executive a man who opposed the extension of slavery into the territories. Texas, through the affirmative actions of both a convention and a statewide vote, joined South Carolina in secession, becoming, in early 1861, a state in the newly formed Confederacy.

Governor Sam Houston was deposed for having refused to support secession. He was succeeded by Edward Clark, the lieutenant governor, who carried the military organization of Texas into effect as the war began in April with the fall of Fort Sumter in South Carolina. A gubernatorial election in November, 1861, brought Francis R. Lubbock into the state executive's chair, and his administration, lasting until November, 1863, would cover the climactic years of the war.

It was in Texas that General John R. Baylor's dream of an Arizona province of the Confederacy was conceived in 1861 and where early the next year, the expedition was begun of General H. H. Sibley as a part of the same Confederate program to conquer the West. Both men were to fail. As for Sibley, his expedition into New Mexico achieved temporary success with the capturing of Santa Fe and the surrounding area. However, the appearance of Union troops in superior numbers, combined with the great difficulty of operating far from a base of supplies, brought about his defeat which was followed by a retreat into Texas. General Baylor's futile story is told elsewhere.

Texans were most successful in Hood's Texas Brigade which was organized at Richmond, Virginia in 1861 with General Louis T. Wigfall as its commander. By the next year, General John B. Hood had succeeded in command. As narrated fully in another place, the brigade gained fame for its heroism during almost constant action in Virginia, Tennessee, North Carolina, and Georgia. Renowned also were Terry's Texas Rangers and Ross' Brigade. Terry's Texas Rangers were organized in 1861 as the 8th Texas Cavalry at Houston, and was named for its able leader Benjamin Franklin Terry who was killed at

Woodsonville, Kentucky in 1861. This body of men was involved in extensive combat at Shiloh, as well as Bardstown, Perryville, Murfreesboro, Chickamauga, and Knoxville. They surrendered to General William T. Sherman at Greensboro, North Carolina as the war was ending in April, 1865. Ross' Brigade bore the name of Lawrence Sullivan Ross who became its commander in 1863 and retained that position for two years. This brigade faced almost continual action in Mississippi, Alabama, and Tennessee, participating in battles at Lawrenceburg, Harpeth River, and Murfreesboro.

However, Texas too was to have fighting upon her soil. In fact, the coast of the state was blockaded from the beginning of the war, and Galveston, then the leading city in size in Texas, was captured by Union forces on October 4, 1862. Federal control of Galveston was temporary, for Confederate General John Bankhead Magruder recaptured the city, gaining his victory through attacking simultaneously by land and sea. Galveston was not retaken by the Federals.

Late in 1863, gunboats of the United States Navy, convoying a force of about 5,000 soldiers, attempted to invade Texas at Sabine Pass. At that place a Confederate force of less than fifty men who were commanded by Lieutenant Dick Dowling met the Federals and won a complete victory. This action as well as the fighting at Galveston are both recounted elsewhere.

Union soldiers continued to be active farther south along the coast in the Rio Grande Valley, and there were Federal troops in this area at the end of the war. They had come late in the struggle attempting to end for Texans the profitable business of exporting cotton into Mexico. The existence of the Union blockade of all Confederate ports long made this Mexican border trade lucrative to Texas.

The last attempt to invade Texas was stopped by a Confederate victory at the battle of Mansfield, Louisiana, in April, 1864. General Nathaniel P. Banks of the United States Army had planned an invasion by way of Red River only to meet defeat at the hands of General Richard Taylor and his Confederate forces. The indecisive battle of Pleasant Hill, shortly after and in the same area, ended the campaign entirely.

To the world, the Civil War ended on April 9, 1865 when General Robert E. Lee surrendered his depleted Confederate Army to General U. S. Grant at Appomattox, Virginia. However, a month later on May 13, 1865, the last battle was fought at Palmito Ranch near Brownsville. Colonel John S. Ford captured about eight hundred soldiers at this time.

The Confederate armies of the Trans-Mississippi had dissolved by the beginning of the summer, and General Kirby Smith surrendered that department at Galveston on June 2, 1865. Governor Pendleton Murrah fled to Mexico less than two weeks later, and stable government departed with him from defeated Texas.

W. C. NUNN

Contents

JOHN ROBERT BAYLOR 1
—Arthur Gilligan

EDWARD CLARK 18
—Tinsie Larison

RICHARD W. "DICK" DOWLING 36
—James Ward

JOHN BELL HOOD 55
—Harold B. Simpson

FRANCIS RICHARD LUBBOCK 76
—Le Anne Adams

JOHN BANKHEAD MAGRUDER 103
—Thomas Settles

PENDLETON MURRAH 122
—Bennie Deuson

WILLIAMSON SIMPSON OLDHAM 139
—Laura Harper

JOHN H. REAGAN 157
—S. W. Schuster

LOUIS TREZEVANT WIGFALL 175
—George Wirsdorfer

ILLUSTRATIONS .... following 194

BIBLIOGRAPHY 197

INDEX 223

List of Illustrations

Following 194

PORTRAITS

OF THE

TEN TEXANS IN GRAY

JOHN ROBERT BAYLOR (Soldier-Congressman) Plate No. 1

EDWARD CLARK (Governor) .... Plate No. 2

RICHARD W. "DICK" DOWLING (Soldier) .... Plate No 3

JOHN BELL HOOD (Soldier) .... Plate No. 4

FRANCIS RICHARD LUBBOCK (Governor) .... Plate No. 5

JOHN BANKHEAD MAGRUDER (Soldier) .... Plate No. 6

PENDLETON MURRAH (Governor) .... Plate No. 7

WILLIAMSON SIMPSON OLDHAM (Senator) .... Plate No. 8

JOHN H. REAGAN (Cabinet Officer, CSA) .... Plate No. 9

LOUIS T. WIGFALL (Soldier-Senator) .... Plate No. 10

TEN TEXANS IN GRAY

John Robert Baylor

by
ARTHUR E. GILLIGAN

The mission was difficult and fraught with danger. Colonel Earl Van Dorn, Confederate commander of the recently formed Department of Texas, pondered his meager troop resources and weighed this latest requirement against the many requisitions levied against his command. The war was little more than a month old, yet the demands for Texas soldiery were legion. Peril loomed large at the Mexican border. Forts Arbuckle, Cobb, and Washita, which buffered Texas from the Indian Territory, had drained 2,000 troops from the state. A Federal threat was developing in Missouri, and Texas hero Ben McCulloch, with a regiment of mounted rifles, sped to counter this situation. Then, too, there were the urgent appeals for levies received from the Confederate War Department now installed at Richmond. What could be spared for defenseless West Texas and the declared secessionists of the New Mexico Territory? Van Dorn decided, and thus it was that John Robert Baylor introduced himself to the chronicles of history.

May, 1861, found Lieutenant-Colonel Baylor in temporary command of the Second Regiment, Texas Mounted Rifles. The regular or elected commander, Colonel John S. Ford, was tending to the potentially explosive situation on the lower Rio Grande, where it was rumored that Mexico might try to regain Texas. Baylor was approaching thirty-nine years of age in the spring of 1861. A Kentuckian by birth, he had spent most of his youth and later years in the Southwest. His father, Doctor John Walker Baylor, was the assistant-surgeon of the Seventh U. S. Infantry regiment stationed at Fort Gibson in the Indian Territory. It was at this post that the younger Baylor first acquired his very definite opinions on the treatment of troublesome Indians. Savages, he maintained, should be dealt with as thieves when found with stolen animals or as murderers when they killed white settlers.[1] These opinions further crystalized after his arrival in Texas and with his participation in the campaign against the marauding Comanche Indians in 1840. Although Baylor managed to become successively a farmer, a lawyer, and a state legislator, his reputation before the war's outbreak was chiefly as an Indian fighter. His ability as a leader in this latter pursuit caused his neighbors to refer to him as Captain Baylor.

With secession's advent, Baylor was at San Antonio where he was instrumental in achieving the surrender of Major-General David Twiggs and what amounted to ten per cent of the United States army. In this major blow for the Confederacy, he was overshadowed by Mexican War hero and ranger Ben McCulloch. Actually, Baylor was responsible for the recruitment of nearly a thousand armed men—under the thinly disguised pretext of a buffalo hunt on the plains—who were used to coerce the San Antonio garrison into submission, and hence the surrender of all posts and camps in the state.[2] Now, General Order Number Eight directed the Second Regiment, Texas Mounted Rifles to proceed west and to man Forts Bliss, Quitman, Davis, Stockton, Clark, Inge, and Camp Wood. This line of forts traced out the nearly six hundred mile course of the San Antonio-El Paso stage road.[3] Colonel Baylor received his marching orders on May 24, and departed from San Antonio shortly thereafter at the head of seven hundred troopers. During the first week of July, the regiment arrived at Fort Bliss after a gruelling six hundred mile march through the scorching heat and dust of the Trans-Pecos region. When Baylor entered the confines of Fort Bliss his command had shrunk to four companies and one battery of artillery, amounting to approximately three hundred fifty effectives.

Fort Bliss was located on the ranch of James W. Magoffin, a Kentuckian who had achieved much wealth by maintaining a ranch and trading post opposite the Mexican town of El Paso del Norte. Magoffin, along with flour mill owner Simeon Hart and Judge Josiah F. Crosby, provided leadership for the secessionists of Franklin, Texas,[4] and the Mesilla Valley sixty miles north in the New Mexico Territory. These three men briefed the Colonel on the situation upriver.

Baylor, as a member of the Texas secession convention, knew the risks these men had taken in the formulation of plans to include the southern portion of the present day states of Arizona and New Mexico in the Confederacy. Hart had made the first overt move by communicating with a delegate to the secession convention, William R. Scurry. Hart proposed the convention appoint commissioners to urge the people of the territory to cast their lot with secession. Hart's proposal was seized upon by Scurry, for he submitted a resolution inviting the inhabitants to recognize the institution of slavery and to petition for admittance to the Confederacy. The resolution was speedily passed, and Hart was appointed as commissioner to treat with those New Mexicans of the northern reaches of the territory. A second commissioner, P. T. Herbert, convention delegate from El Paso, was selected to enter into negotiations with the population of the territory's southern region.[5] Herbert's task was accomplished before it was begun. When he arrived at Mesilla on March 19, 1861, he found that three days earlier, a convention had been held in response to a prior petition published in the *Mesilla Times.*[6] The convention proceeded to declare Arizona out of the Union and now a territory of the Confederacy. The citizens of Tucson, not to be outdone by their brethren at Mesilla, held a convention of their own on March 23, and they, too, proclaimed allegiance to the Confederacy. Commissioner Herbert could thus report that the southern region of Arizona was safely in the fold, and all that was needed was to set in motion the machinery of formal military occupation.[7] Simeon Hart reported that the northern area was also for the South, but in this he erred. Only a few of the wealthier class of Mexican extraction were ready to declare for the Confederacy. The remainder feared the Texans, and for the most part viewed slavery as odious.

Colonel Baylor made an astute appraisal of the Federal military concentrations, and evolved his opening gambit. From Simeon Hart he gleaned the information that the Federal troops at Santa Fe were on the verge of mutiny—they had not been paid for several months. Fort Craig, midway between El Paso and Santa Fe, and the keystone of the New Mexico defenses, was only lightly held. The garrison of Fort McLane near the Pinos Altos mines had been evacuated and combined with the troops stationed at Fort Fillmore. This last post thus posed the greatest threat to the Mesilla Valley secessionists as well as to West Texas. Fort Fillmore had been erected in 1851, on the east bank of the Rio Grande and six miles downstream from Mesilla. Its purpose was to protect communications with California, particularly the Butterfield stage route. Baylor learned that Fillmore was manned by nearly four hundred regular army troops under one Major Isaac Lynde. The fact that his command was slightly smaller than the Federal force daunted Baylor not in the least. He ordered his troops to prepare to march.

One chore remained for Baylor before his move against the Federals. In compliance with orders from General Earl Van Dorn, he summoned the principal chief of a large band of Mescalero Apaches into Fort Bliss for the purpose of drawing up a treaty. This chief was called Nicholas, and his band claimed the region around Fort Davis as their preserve. Baylor, anxious to keep his communication line with San Antonio unimpaired, had Nicholas brought from Fort Davis to Bliss by stage. The treaty was hastily drawn up. Nicholas was loaded down with presents. The chief was then placed aboard the stage which was to return him to Fort Davis. Nicholas had other plans. He left the coach before it reached the fort and with him went two pistols stolen from the Confederate escort. Within a week the Mescaleros would take the war trail.[8]

On July 23, 1861, the Texan force numbering two hundred fifty-eight men, began the march from Fort Bliss to the Mesilla Valley. Presumably, a hundred troopers were left at Bliss, including the necessary garrison and those reporting sick. At San Tomas, the Confederates captured seven Federal troops stationed in the town. Baylor learned that the Unionists outnumbered him by over a hundred men. This did not discourage the Texan, for he decided on a surprise assault on Fort Fillmore at dawn of the following day. On the night of July 24, Baylor brought his force within six hundred yards of the works. There his troops camped under arms and without benefit of fires.

Within the fort, Major Isaac Lynde was embroiled in a private war with his own officers. Lynde was old and ready for retirement, having completed thirty-five years in the military service. His officers were chagrined at Lynde's neglect of all military procedures necessary to protect a garrison in a wartime situation. Patrols had not been sent out. No screen of pickets lay outside the fort's perimeter. Only the few customary sentinels mounted guard within the fort. Lynde had been informed of Baylor's departure from Fort Bliss, according to his post surgeon Captain James C. McKee, and had refused the advice of his officers to send the post's women and children away to safety. To do so would only bring on the enemy, he argued. His officers urged that a detachment be sent up to Mesilla to haul down the Confederate flag flying there since that community had declared for secession several months before. Lynde twice ordered this mission, and twice rescinded the orders—the second time justifying his action by saying that to remove the insurgent banner would certainly bring on a collision with the Confederates.[9]

During the night of July 24, two Texans slipped into the fort. They indicated they were former United States soldiers and had deserted Baylor's command. They related the Confederate plan to attack the fort at daybreak and confirmed the number of troops Baylor had at his disposal. The long roll on the drum was beaten. The entire garrison manned the walls. There the troops stood throughout the entire summer night despite the knowledge the storming attempt would not come until dawn.

Colonel Baylor realized he had lost the element of surprise. At dawn, he ordered his disappointed men six miles upriver to Mesilla. His troops received a rousing welcome from the town's population. Shortly after noon a dust cloud was observed moving up from the south. Baylor immediately deduced the Federals were about to contest his possession of the town. Mesilla, which had a population of nearly twenty-five hundred in 1860, was composed of numerous adobe buildings clustered about the main plaza. These buildings were admirable for defensive purposes, and Baylor disposed most of his men inside or on the roof tops. The remainder were posted in the cornfields which surrounded the town. The women and children were evacuated, but the impending battle tempted them to climb a nearby sand hill from which they could view the entire proceedings.

The withdrawal of Colonel Baylor from Fort Fillmore environs that morning evidently stiffened Major Lynde for he ordered his entire command to prepare to march on Mesilla. His men were elated—despite their all-night vigil, they were anxious for action. It was afternoon, however, when the two companies of dragoons and seven infantry companies began the approach to the town. Once at the outskirts, Major Lynde sent his adjutant and Surgeon McKee into Mesilla under a white flag. They were met by Major Edwin Waller, Baylor's second-in-command. The Federal emissaries presented Waller with a demand for the immediate and unconditional surrender of the Confederate force. Waller answered that if Lynde wanted the town, he must of necessity come and take it. The two officers returned to Lynde with this defiant reply.

Lynde ordered Captain C. H. McNally and his cavalry units to charge the town—an assignment more appropriate for infantry. McNally plunged forward, waving his men toward the clustered adobe buildings. The Texans, from both town and cornfields, loosed a ragged volley at the advancing cavalrymen. This effort would not have been particularly damaging, except Captain McNally was hit in the chest, and fell from his horse. The cavalry charge braked at once. Three Federals were killed. Another officer, in addition to McNally, and four enlisted men were wounded. The Confederate fire continued though it was considerably ineffectual. Their armament included only a few rifled weapons as against a conglomeration of shotguns, muskets and pistols. The now static Federal cavalry thus sustained no further casualties. McNally kept his men deployed on the line waiting for the infantry supports to move up. When he fainted from loss of blood, a less resolute subordinate ordered the troopers to retire on the main body.[10]

After this demonstration, a white-faced Lynde ordered a howitzer fired, not at Baylor's positions, but at the clustered women and children watching from the sandhill. Fortunately the range was excessive for the short-range artillery piece. Suddenly Lynde ordered his command back to Fort Fillmore. His officers were appalled and begged the old man to allow them another charge. Lynde refused, arguing that night was approaching, and that they were outnumbered. The ignominious retreat commenced amidst considerable muttering.[11]

Colonel Baylor did not contest the withdrawal. In fact, he credited his opponent with using the retreat either as a feint to come in against the town from another direction or to lure him from his protected positions. When the puzzle finally unraveled, Lynde's command had reentered the fort, and Baylor found the situation exactly as it was the day before.[12]

The next morning brought a further surprise for the Texans. A column of dust was sighted moving toward the east and in the direction of the Fort Stanton trail. The implication was immediately apparent. The Federals had abandoned Fort Fillmore. Baylor quickly assembled his men. He directed Major Waller and a large detachment to take possession of the fort and salvage any material left intact. Waller was then to rendezvous with the main body. The whole Confederate force, at this juncture, would assail the Federals before they reached San Augustin Pass which broached the Organ Mountains—a wall of eroded brownstone pinnacles standing in close packed files and running in a north-south direction.

While Baylor organized his pursuit, the Federals found their situation rapidly developing into a nightmare. Early in the morning of July 27, Major Lynde directed his men to improve the defenses of Fort Fillmore and to man the firing steps to repel the attack Baylor was expected to launch. As the morning wore on, Lynde became exceedingly agitated. To the utter consternation of his command, he suddenly announced his intention to abandon Fillmore and march his force to Fort Stanton—one hundred fifty gruelling miles to the northeast. All equipment or supplies that could not be carried were to be destroyed. The fort was to be fired. In confusion, the troopers loaded the wagons of the command with those supplies and personal baggage that could be carried. While this was going on, a number of enlisted men broke into the whiskey rations and substituted this fiery broth for water in their canteens. With the fort in flames, a column of misery lurched out onto the desert, officers' dependents perched aboard wagons and buggies, the wounded bedded down in Captain McKee's ambulances.[13]

Colonel Baylor found his pursuit was not progressing as efficiently as he wished. Waller tarried at the fort, and more than a little time was lost before the two elements joined to resume the chase. Almost at once, the Confederates began to encounter numerous Federal stragglers. These men were suffering from heat exhaustion; nonetheless, the Texans must pause to disarm them and even care for them. This caused further delay. Baylor expected a fight at San Augustin Pass. There were springs at the mouth of the pass, and it appeared that more than half of the Federal force had reached these water sources. Also, the enemy had been reinforced. Thirty-five cavalrymen under Captain Alfred Gibbs had met Lynde's cavalry vanguard at the springs. Gibbs led his own men and a like number of Lynde's horsemen back along the wretched stream of infantry and laboring vehicles. Arriving at the tail of the column or at least that part not yet overtaken by the Texans, Gibbs deployed his men in battle formation. Here the Federal cavalry stood their ground until the Confederates began to mass for a charge. Gibbs retreated out of range, then re-deployed. In this manner, he kept the opposing force off balance. Several repetitions of this maneuver enabled most of the Federal infantry to gain the springs and temporary security.[14]

Colonel Baylor was prepared to wage a desperate fight for victory. He must win at this place or lose all. His situation was growing critical with each passing hour. Baylor knew that the Federal force from Fort Breckinridge was within sixty miles of Mesilla. A stand at San Augustin, if prolonged, could see him caught between two enemy concentrations.

Just as Baylor was about to order his men to the attack, there came a request for a parley. He sent Major Waller and Captain Peter Hardeman into the Federal lines. A few minutes later, Hardeman rode back. Major Lynde had requested a conference with Colonel Baylor himself. The Confederate leader, his apprehension yielding to optimism, cantered into the enemy perimeter.

Major Lynde sent Baylor's spirits a-soaring when he opened the parley by asking what surrender terms he could expect. The Colonel replied that the surrender must be unconditional. Lynde agreed, however, he asked that personal property be respected. This request was acceeded to without further discussion. Obviously, Baylor did not wish to delay the proceedings for the Fort Breckinridge Federals were now foremost in his mind. Lynde summoned his officers to witness the surrender. Both commanders then began dictating the surrender terms to Lynde's adjutant. Lynde's officers came up, clamoring against the surrender. So violent were their protests, Colonel Baylor sarcastically asked just who was the commander of the Federal force. Lynde finally had his way, and Baylor had his victory. He was quick to offer parole. He could not afford an engagement with the Fort

Breckinridge Federals with over four hundred prisoners on his hands. The parole list contained four hundred ten names. Sixteen men remained prisoners of war for some unexplained reason, while twenty-six deserted to the Confederates. A touch of irony—Baylor's father had served as assistant-surgeon in the Seventh Infantry which constituted most of Lynde's command. The paroled men made their way north to Santa Fe enduring many hardships. Lynde would be drummed out of the army for his "disgraceful abandonment of Fort Fillmore and the subsequent surrender of his command."[15]

The triumph belonged to Colonel Baylor because of his aggressive leadership and action. It had been cheaply purchased from a doddering, confused, old man, but this should not detract any credit from the Texans' exploit. They had eliminated one-sixth of the Federal military establishment in the New Mexico Territory. In addition, they had captured considerable booty including: cavalry remounts, various commissary stores, wagons, mules, and four hundred stand of small arms. Probably the most notable prize was $17,500 in Federal drafts which served to sustain Baylor's men during the fall and winter of 1861.

Colonel Baylor quickly sped a detachment west to the village of Picacho near Cook's Springs in the Mimbres Mountains. It was his intent to double his feat by subduing the other Federal force. The news of Lynde's surrender, however, had reached Captain Isaiah N. Moore who was leading his Union force through Cook's Canyon. He ordered the destruction of all excess baggage and managed to bring his four companies through to Fort Craig. The only fish caught in Baylor's net was Brigadier-General Albert Sydney Johnston, who was on his way from California to Richmond and eventual command of the Confederate armies in the West. Baylor had served under Johnston when the latter had been secretary of war during the days of the Texas Republic. Both men were Kentuckians and both were overjoyed at this chance meeting. Baylor, in a dramatic gesture, offered his command to his former chief for the duration of his stay. Johnston accepted this courtesy for the several days he spent with the Texans. He, then, resumed his journey at some loss to Colonel Baylor—George Wythe Baylor, the colonel's brother, volunteered to serve on Johnston's staff.[16]

On August 1, 1861, John Baylor published a sweeping proclamation:

> To the people of Arizona
>
> The social and political condition of Arizona being little short of general anarchy, and the people being destitute of law, order and protection, the said territory, from this date hereof, is hereby declared temporarily organized as a military government until such time as Congress may otherwise provide. I, John Baylor, Lieutenant Colonel, Confederate Army in the territory of Arizona, hereby take possession of said territory in the name, and behalf of the Confederate States of America.[17]

Baylor's legalistic and administrative talents were readily apparent in the proclamation. He decreed the new territory to include all of the New Mexico territory south of the thirty-fourth parallel, from Texas to California. He established Mesilla as the territorial capital. The colonel evolved a judicial system and also territorial officers. Finally, he appointed himself military governor.[18]

While solving the administrative needs of the new territory, Baylor still continued military operations against the enemy. He sent a force up into the Sacramento Mountains to occupy Fort Stanton. This post had been abandoned by the Federals as a result of the Lynde surrender. Another detachment was sent forty miles up the Rio Grande to reactivate Fort Thorn, abandoned in 1859, as an advanced base for operations against Fort Craig—the key to northern New Mexico. Baylor commented afterwards that he would have captured Fort Craig, but for the jaded condition of his horses. A glowing report was written to General Earl Van Dorn, in which Baylor not only cited his accomplishments in securing Arizona with its vast mineral wealth, but he stressed that the territory provided an outlet to the Pacific Ocean.[19]

Suddenly Colonel Baylor was beset with serious problems. The Mescalero Apaches nursed a tremendous hatred for the people of the Mesilla Valley. When the Federals abandoned Fort Stanton, this was a signal to ravish the scattered settlements near the Sacramento Mountains and as far south as Fort Davis. On August 11, 1861, Lieutenant R. E. Mays led fourteen troopers out of Fort Davis in pursuit of Chief Nicholas and his band. Nicholas had descended on the fort, killed a number of cattle, and driven off a large part of the horse herd. The trail led south into the Big Bend country. Nicholas, aware of the pursuit, realized he outnumbered the Texans six to one. He posted his warriors on the walls of a rock-strewn canyon. On August 12, the Mays detachment was wiped out. Only a Mexican guide escaped death to tell of the massacre. Colonel Baylor informed his superior of this engagement and bluntly stated he could not concentrate his force against Indians and Yankees at the same time. This was borne out by Apache attacks in the neighborhood of Forts Stanton and Inge, where depleted Confederate detachments suffered severe casualties. The situation was so critical, Baylor sanctioned the withdrawal of the Fort Stanton garrison.[20]

Baylor had other reasons for concern. Pestilence, in the form of smallpox and pneumonia, made an appearance in the Texans' camp. A rumor came to the colonel's ears that a powerful Federal expedition was departing from California for the Mexican fort of Guaymas. From there the Federals were to cross the Sierra Madre Mountains and move on to El Paso. Colonel Baylor urgently wrote to the newly-appointed commander of a New Mexico expeditionary force assembling in San Antonio. He indicated that unless he was reinforced, it might be necessary to retreat south to Fort Quitman, abandoning the Mesilla Valley and Fort Bliss. Baylor was also apprehensive over the increased Federal activity at Fort Craig. In anticipation of attacks from south and north, he directed the bulk of his supplies transported to Forts Quitman and Davis. Actually, the danger was not as acute as he imagined. The Guaymas threat was canceled since it was pure folly, and the Federal garrisons in the north were still on the verge of mutiny because of pay arrears.

In mid-December, relief came. Brigadier-General Henry Hopkins Sibley and the Confederate Army of New Mexico, three thousand strong, marched into Mesilla. General Sibley, hook-nosed, lantern-jawed, mustachioed and an alcoholic, took over command of all Confederate forces in the region. Friction developed between Baylor and Sibley immediately. Sibley complained that Baylor's men had consumed all the supplies and monies that Simeon Hart had put aside for the invasion of not only the entire New Mexico Territory, but Colorado and California as well. Nonetheless, Sibley confirmed Colonel Baylor as military governor, and proceeded to embark on a Confederate dream of empire. On January 27, Sibley sent a detachment to secure Tucson, which would serve as an advance base for the eventual linkup with the secessionist minority in California. This small force was also to protect western Arizona citizens from the Apache terror now raging throughout the new Confederate Territory. Sibley and his army marched north from Mesilla during the first week in February. Within four months, Sibley would return with half his army lost. His expedition could be marked off as a tragic failure.

On January 18, 1862, the Congress of the Confederate States of America passed the Arizona Territory Organic Act, which in effect recognized the territory created by John Baylor. The metes and bounds he assigned were the same as provided by the act. A month later Jefferson Davis, the Confederate States President, approved the act, and on March 13, he submitted to the Congress the name of John R. Baylor for confirmation in the post of territorial governor of Arizona. Baylor further received his commission as brigadier-general in the Confederate States Army.[21]

Full recognition had now been accorded John Baylor. What he had achieved and how he achieved it indicates much of his personality and character—a man of action, without fear, thoroughly proficient as a military leader and frontiersman, a gentleman with high moral values. The forty-year-old Texan not only possessed these many worthy facets, he reflected them in his physical appearance. At this, the peak of his career, old tintypes show finely chiseled features, firm mouth, intense glance, all reflecting the physical embodiment of fortitude and determination.

With Sibley's departure in February, Governor Baylor found himself no better off than when he had appealed for reinforcements the previous fall. He had been stripped of most of his military. His command mustered only a few companies, and these were composed of convalescent troops. The Apache scourge continued unabated. Baylor's infrequent supply trains from Texas were attacked by Lipan and Mescalero Apaches. Mail couriers and travellers were not safe even under escort. The Mimbre Apache allied with the fearsome Chiricahuas were even more troublesome. On September 27, two hundred warriors of these tribes struck at the Pinos Altos mining town. Only a small company of Confederate troops staved off disaster at that place.

Baylor, annoyed to the point of desperation, wrote a letter to Capt. Thomas Helm, Commander of the force at Pinos Altos:

> The Congress of the Confederate [Confederacy] has passed a law declaring extermination of all hostile Indians. You will therefore use all means to persuade Apaches or any other tribe to come in for the purpose of making peace, and when you get them together, kill all the grown Indians and take the children prisoners and sell them to defray the cost of killing Indians. Say nothing about your orders until the time comes and be cautious how you let the Mexicans know it. If you can't trust them, send to Captain Aycock at this place, and he will send 30 men from his company, but use the Mexicans if they can be trusted, as bringing troops from here might excite suspicion with the Indians. To your judgment I intrust this important matter and look to you for success against these cursed pests who have murdered over a hundred men in this territory.[22]

In addition to this extermination order, it was asserted that Baylor caused a sack of flour to be larded with a massive dose of poison. The sack was allowed to fall into Apache hands, and over three score Indians died from this singular dosage for Indian troubles.[23]

Just before Sibley's expedition reached the El Paso region, the governor made the long journey to Richmond. His purpose was to promote another expedition to redeem the Confederate territory. On May 29, 1862, Baylor received authority from Secretary of War George W. Randolph to raise five battalions of partisan rangers for the reinvasion of Arizona. He hastened to San Antonio, and began recruiting.

Suddenly Baylor's extermination order was brought to the attention of the Confederate authorities at Richmond. The reaction of Richmond is graphically shown by this entry in the diary of John B. Jones, a clerk in the Confederate War Department.

> Here is a most startling matter. Gov. Baylor, appointed Governor of Arizona, sent an order some time since to a

> military commander to assemble the Apaches under the pretense of a treaty—*and when they came, to kill every man of them, and sell their children to pay for the whiskey.* This order was sent to the Secretary who referred it to Gen. [Henry] Sibley, of that territory, to ascertain if it were genuine. Today it came back from Gen. S. indorsed *a true bill.* Now it will go to the President—and we shall see what will follow. He cannot sanction such a perfidious crime.[24]

The order raised a storm of criticism, and Secretary Randolph rescinded Baylor's authority to raise troops for the Arizona reconquest. On December 29, 1862, John Baylor composed a lengthy letter to Major-General John Bankhead Magruder, then commanding the military district of Texas. He indicated that his order had been prompted by an article in "either the Charleston Courier or Mercury," which stated the Confederate Congress had declared a war of extermination on the Indians. He told of his experiences with the Indians since his childhood, and of the terrible atrocities committed by them. Baylor argued his order had never been intended for publication; that he did not expect it to be paraded before the country by people who bore him malice. He refused, however, to disavow or retract a word of the order:

> While I sincerely regret that it has been viewed in such an unfavorable light by His Excellency the President, as to induce him to deprive me of the command of the brave men, most of whom are my old frontier comrades whom I was prepared to lead to battle against both abolition and savage foe, yet I cannot alter the convictions and feelings of a life time. I can still do my country some service should my State be invaded and in that hour Texans, I know, will not refuse me a place in their ranks to meet and exterminate a foe hardly less cruel and remorseless than the Comanche or the Apache.[25]

On the first day of 1863, Magruder launched an amphibious assault on the Federal naval squadron and army detachment which had occupied Galveston. The attack was a complete success. John Baylor served in this fiercely contested engagement. Magruder forwarded a copy of Baylor's letter with the following commentary to the Confederate war department:

> Without expressing any opinion as to the policy or propriety of Governor Baylor's letter, I testify with pleasure to his devoted gallantry at the recapture of Galveston, where he served as a private of artillery in the most exposed and dangerous position and rendered most important services, and I respectfully but earnestly recommend him as the most suitable officer for the command of the troops raised by him for Arizona and known as the Arizona Brigade.
>
> I beg leave to ask a perusal by the Secretary of War of the within statement. Colonel O'Bannon informed me that he gave the information to Governor Baylor that our Congress had passed laws for the extermination of these Indians, whom I happen to know well as being not better than wild beasts and totally unworthy of sympathy.[26]

It reached the desk of Jefferson Davis who rejected it with the curt comment, "It is an avowal of an infamous crime and the assertion of what should not be true in relation to troops in Texans.[27] Others rose to Baylor's defense, but those far removed from the Indian depredations scorned these protests with sanctimonious disdain. Texans were outraged, especially the men and officers of Baylor's regiment, at what they considered to be the unjust treatment of a brave and competent officer.

Although deeply disappointed, Baylor remained active in state military affairs. He raised a hundred-man company which he employed on the northern frontier of Texas against Kansas "Jayhawkers" operating south from the Indian territory. In the spring of 1863, the citizens of Parker County urged Baylor to become a candidate for representative to the Confederate Confederate Congress. The election was held in August, and Baylor won handily. Since Texas was isolated by the fall of Vicksburg, the congressman had to pass through the Federal lines amidst considerable hazard and hardship.

During his term in Congress, Baylor was able to explain his motives to the Confederate chief executive, and thus the situation was eased. He was exonerated and reinstated in his military rank.

In December 1864, Federal might moved in close to Richmond, and daily thereafter the plight of Confederacy grew worse. John Baylor tenaciously urged another attempt to retake Arizona and form a linkage with the California secessionists. He wrote to Secretary of War James A. Seddon, setting forth his invasion plan in great detail. Jefferson Davis personally approved, but a realistic Seddon deemed it impractical and visionary.

When the war ended, a broken-hearted John Baylor returned to Texas. For a while, he lived at San Antonio, where he was active in local politics. In 1879, he moved to Uvalde. Here he added to his reputation by winning several encounters with notorious outlaws. On February 8, 1894, the old warrior passed away on his ranch. His grave is at the little town of Montell, and his tombstone bears this epitaph: "As sleep the brave who sink to rest, by all their country wishes blest."[28]

NOTES

[1]J. Marvin Hunter (ed.), "John Robert Baylor—1822-1894," **Frontier Times,** September, 1929, Vol. 6, No. 12, p. 482. The facts for this editorial were furnished to Hunter by W. K. Baylor and H. W. Baylor, sons of John R. Baylor.

[2]Caroline Baldwin Darrow, "Recollections of the Twiggs Surrender," **Battles and Leaders of the Civil War,** ed. Ray F. Nichols (new ed., 4 Vols.; Philadelphia: Thomas Yoseloff, 1956), I, p. 34. This invaluable work was originally edited by Robert Underwood Johnson and Clarence Clough Buel and published in **Century** magazine in 1887. Hereafter cited as **B. & L.**

[3]General Order No. 8, Van Dorn to Ford. **The War of the Rebellion: A Compilation of the Official Records of the Union and Confederate Armies** (128 Vols.; Washington: Government Printing Office, 1880-1900), Series I, Vol. I, p. 574. Hereafter cited as **O.R.**

[4]Franklin was the official name of the community now called El Paso. In 1873, the latter name was formally adopted.

[5]Ernest W. Winkler (ed.), **Journal of the Secession Convention of Texas, 1861** (Austin: Austin Printing Co., 1912), pp. 45-68.

[6]**Mesilla Times,** February 23, 1861, p. 1.

[7]**Mesilla Times,** March 30, 1861, p. 1.

[8]Baylor to Magruder, December 29, 1862, **O.R.,** Series I, Vol. V, p. 914.

[9]Captain James Cooper McKee, **Narrative of the Surrender of a Command of U. S. Forces at Fort Fillmore in July, 1861** (Boston: John A. Lowell Co., 1866), pp. 12-13.

[10]Statement of Captain C. H. McNally, dated August 16, 1861, **O.R.,** Series I, Vol. IV, p. 13.

[11]McKee, p. 15.

[12]Report of Colonel J. R. Baylor, dated August 8, 1861, **O.R.**, Series I, Vol. IV, pp. 16-17.

[13]Horace Greeley, **The American Conflict: A History of the Great Rebellion in the United States of America, 1860-1865** (2 Vols.; Hartford: O. D. Case and Co., Vol. I, 1864; Vol. II, 1886), II, p. 20.

[14]Statement of Captain Alfred Gibbs, **O.R.**, Series I, Vol. IV, p. 11.

[15]United States Army General Order No. 102, dated November 25, 1861, issued by Adjutant-General Lorenzo Thomas, **O.R.**, Series I, Vol. IV, p. 16.

[16]George Wythe Baylor rivaled his brother in many respects. He is reputed to be the first person to raise the Confederate flag in Austin. He served on Johnston's staff until Johnston's death at Shiloh. He commanded the First Arizona Cavalry in the Red River Campaign of 1864. The acrimonies that followed this campaign caused him to kill Major-General John A. Wharton in a duel. As a Texas Ranger captain, he assisted in the defeat of the notorious Apache leader Victorio in 1880.

[17]Baylor Proclamation, dated August 1, 1861, **O.R.**, Series I, Vol. IV, p. 21.

[18]Baylor Proclamation, pp. 20-21.

[19]Baylor Report, **O.R.**, Series I, Vol. IV, p. 23.

[20]Various reports of John R. Baylor, Lieutenant John R. Pulliam, Lieutenant William P. White, and Sergeant W. S. Barrett, for the period August 15 to September 24, 1861, **O.R.**, Series I, Vol. IV, pp. 23-26, 109-110.

[21]**Journal of the Congress of the Confederate States of America, 1861-1865** (7 Vols., Washington: U. S. Government Printing Office, 1904-1905), I, pp. 612-620.

[22]Baylor to Helm, dated March 20, 1862, **O.R.** Series I, Vol. L, p. 492.

[23]Richmond E. Sloan and Ward R. Adams, **History of Arizona**, (Phoenix: Record Publishing Co., 1930), p. 250.

[24]John B. Jones, **A Rebel War Clerk's Diary**, ed. Earl Schenk Miers (New York: Sagamore Press, Inc., 1958), p. 109.

[25]Baylor to Magruder, dated December 29, 1862. **O.R.**, Series I, Vol. XV, pp. 914-918.

[26]Magruder to Adjutant and Inspector Generals Office, dated February 6, 1863. **O.R.**, Series I, Vol. XV, p. 918.

[27]Jefferson Davis to Secretary of War. **O.R.**, Series I, Vol. XV, p. 919.

[28]**Dallas Morning News**, February 9, 1894; **Austin Daily Statesman**, February 9, 1894.

Edward Clark

by

TINSIE LARISON

Edward Clark, although the governor of Texas for nine tense and turbulent months, stands rather obscurely in the annals of Texas history. He was overshadowed by his predecessor on the one hand and his successor on the other. Clark followed the decisive Sam Houston into the governor's chair and then relinquished the same seat to the dynamic Francis R. Lubbock. However, Clark's brief tenure of office, from March 16, 1861, until November 7, 1861, came at one of the most dramatic periods in Texas—when the Lone Star State transferred its allegiance from the Federal Union to the Southern Confederacy.[1]

Edward Clark had run as an independent on the ticket with Sam Houston in 1859, on the platform announced by Houston as "the Constitution and Union."[2] As in the election of 1857, Houston and Clark again were competing against the regular Democratic Party nominees, H. R. Runnels and Frank (or Francis) R. Lubbock.

The campaign of 1859 centered around two major issues. The first, the secession movement, which at the time was considered irrelevant by many Texas citizens, and the second, the reopening of the African slave trade, which was very unpopular with the rank and file of Texas voters. Runnels and Lubbock for the most part disregarded the question of the African slave trade as trivial, but it did have an influence on the outcome of the election.[3]

The Democrats attempted to associate Clark with the discredited Know-Nothings whose political beliefs had earlier been endorsed by Sam Houston. It is true that Clark and Houston were supported by the remnants of the Know-Nothing Party, however, the party had lost much of its strength in Texas and had practically ceased to exist as a political entity by 1859.[4]

Clark vigorously denied his membership in the Know-Nothing party during the 1850's. As early as August, 1855, he had publicly stated that he did not support the American (or Know-

Nothing) party, and that he regarded its political beliefs as "anti-American, dangerous, illegal and unconstitutional."[5] Regardless of such public denials, Lubbock made much of Clark's association with the Know-Nothing party during the 1859 campaign while they canvassed the state together.[6]

Sam Houston's great personal popularity and the unsatisfactory protection of the frontier from Indian depredations during Runnels' administration were the major factors in winning the election for the "Hero of San Jacinto." Houston defeated Runnels by some eight thousand votes, but Clark won over Lubbock by a much narrower margin.[7]

Sam Houston and Edward Clark were inaugurated on the 21st of December, 1859. This event ushered in a new administration in which the views of the chief executive on the questions of secession and the nature of the Federal Union were completely opposite to those of Edward Clark, the lieutenant-governor, and to the majority of the members of the state legislature. Clark was an ardent believer in the doctrine of state's rights and a staunch secessionist whose family had held slaves since the early days of the century. Houston was faced with several serious problems, a radical and extremist element in the legislature, the ever-present threat of Indian raids along the frontier and a growing sectional problem in the nation which grew more foreboding with every passing month.[8]

By the autumn of 1860, the Democratic party was completely disrupted over the question of popular sovereignty, that is, the right of the people to decide for themselves the question of slavery in the territories.[9] The party was so divided that it was impossible to name a candidate at the convention held at Charleston, South Carolina, in April, 1860. The convention adjourned without taking any action. Later, at separate conventions, the northern Democrats named Stephen A. Douglas of Illinois, and the southern faction nominated John C. Breckenridge of Kentucky. A third ticket was put forward by the combined remnants of the Whig and the Know-Nothing parties who claimed to be exclusively "preserve the Union" men. They met in Baltimore in May, gave their party a new name, the Constitutional Union party, and dedicated themselves to the principle that secession would be ruinous to the South and that her only hope lay in fighting for her rights within the Federal Union.

The Republican party, strictly a sectional party that opposed the extension of slavery into the territories, nominated Abraham Lincoln for president.[10] In Texas, only two choices were offered the voters, Breckenridge, representing the Southern Democratic party and Bell, the Constitutional Unionist party.

During the year 1860, the tension and anxiety became more intense as the political situation in the nation deteriorated. In Texas, the abolitionists were charged with frequent fires and of inciting slave uprisings. Vigilante committees were formed in various parts of the state. At Dallas three Negroes were hanged, and at nearby Fort Worth three white men, alleged abolitionists, were hanged because they had been "tampering" with the slaves.[11]

The Knights of the Golden Circle, a small but well-organized group of secessionists, made their sentiments felt in the Lone Star State during the summer of 1860. The objectives of the Knights seemed to have been to stabilize and to entrench the institution of slavery even more firmly in the South and to extend the institution, if possible, into Mexico. The active work of this secret order is credited with inciting a great deal of emotional fervor in favor of secession during these troubled times.[12]

When the news of Lincoln's victory was announced, many Texans were convinced that the election of a "Black Republican administration" would mean the destruction of slavery and spell economic ruin for the South. During the winter of 1860-61, six states seceded and Texas was convinced that her self-preservation lay with her "erring sisters." Leaving the Federal Union was a risk worth taking, for few Texans believed that Lincoln and the North would try to maintain the Union by force of arms. Edward Clark, a native Georgian, the son of a Georgia governor, a Southerner by precept and teaching, was outspoken in his support for secession. Among Clark's close friends and associates were some of the most powerful radicals in Texas including Louis T. Wigfall, William B. Ochiltree, John H. Reagan, and others. These leading statesmen were much in favor of immediately parting company with the North, believing that Texas should not lag behind for she had as much at stake as any of the other Southern states.[13]

The secession of Texas was accomplished smoothly despite the fact that Governor Houston fought valiantly to stop the action of the radicals. He refused to listen to their demands for a special convention. By early December, the secessionists were ready to take matters into their own hands. A group met in Austin urging that the people of Texas elect delegates to a state secession convention to study the matter. Listed among the names of the radicals who suggested the special convention was the name of Edward Clark.[14]

Before the convention was scheduled to meet on January 28, 1861, Houston called a special session of the legislature and urged the representatives not to give formal recognition to the state secession convention. However, the legislature approved the convention, and asked only that the convention's final decision be submitted to the voters for their approval.[15]

On February 1, in the presence of Governor Houston, Lieutenant-Governor Clark, and judges of the supreme and district courts, the convention approved the secession ordinance by a vote of one hundred and fifty-two to six. The members of the convention, after drawing up a number of grievances which had "forced" Texas to take this action, took two other important steps. First, they selected seven delegates to represent Texas at the Montgomery convention, and second, they appointed a Committee on Public Safety, a select group to act while the convention was not in session.

Houston refused to take the oath of allegiance to the Confederacy which the convention required of all state officers. The convention then declared the office vacant, and Edward Clark became the constitutional successor to the office.[16]

Thus the occasion of the ascendancy of Edward Clark to office of chief executive of the state was one wrought with tension and ill-will at one of the most crucial times in the history of Texas. The transfer of office was described by Amelia Barr, an American novelist, who lived in Texas from 1857 to 1867.[17] Amelia Barr wrote:

> With my two friends I went to the capital to witness the ceremony and, as we had seats in front of the gallery, we looked down directly upon a desk just below us, on which the Ordinance of Secession was spread out. One of my companions was a most passionate Unionist, and she pointed out the document with an unspeakable scorn and contempt. The House was crowded; it was really electrified

> with the fiery radiations of men tingling with passion, and glowing and burning with the anticipation of revengeful battle. And the air was full of the stirring clamor of a multitude of voices—angry, triumphant, scornful, with an occasional oath or epithet of contempt.
>
> But when Houston appeared there was a sudden silence. It was the homage involuntarily paid to the man himself, not to his office. Firmly and clearly, he refused to take the oath of allegiance to the Confederate States; but the Lieutenant-Governor, a certain Edward Clark, was eager to do so. He was an insignificant creature, whose airy conceit was a direct insult to Houston's sad countenance and dignified manner; and I remember well how contemptible he appeared as spry and pert, he stepped up to the bar of the House to take the oath.[18]

What kind of man was Edward Clark? James Deshield, historian and writer, said in discussing the merits of Edward Clark and other governors of Texas:

> Not all were great, but few were of a mediocre type, most of them were capable, all were patriotic. Perhaps it has been said of some, "They were first-class second-class men."[19]

Certainly Amelia Barr's prejudiced description of Edward Clark as "an insignificant creature" is wholly unjustified. In physical appearance, he was a handsome man for he was six feet tall, with flashing blue eyes which contrasted with his extremely black hair and full beard. Clark was described as being friendly, courteous, and well-informed in law, politics, and government. Those who knew Clark related that he was a forceful speaker, a logical reasoner, and of able, clear-headed behavior.[20]

Clark was born April 1, 1815, in Georgia where his father, John Clark, was governor of the state from 1819 to 1823. His father died when Edward Clark was seventeen years old, and he and his mother moved to Montgomery, Alabama. While he lived in Alabama, he studied law and was admitted to the bar in that state. He married in Alabama, but his young bride died within a few months after their marriage. In 1842, he moved to Texas and established his law practice at Marshall. In July of 1849, he married Martha Evans of Marshall; they had three boys and one girl.

EDWARD CLARK

Certainly Edward Clark was no stranger to the duties of public office. He had served as a delegate to the Constitutional Convention of 1845 and many of the important provisions written into the State Constitution were either introduced by him or were adopted because of Clark's persuasive urging.[21] He was elected as a member of the first House of Representatives and later served in the State Senate where he made an excellent record as the presiding officer. Clark served as Secretary of State under Governor E. M. Pease from 1853 to 1857.[22]

During the war with Mexico, Clark served on the staff of General James Pinckney Henderson. First assigned to Henderson's staff as a major, he later was promoted to colonel.[23] Colonel Clark received a citation from his superiors for bravery in the battle of Monterrey where he was reported to have been the first man to scale the walls.[24]

When Edward Clark became the eighth governor of Texas, the attitude of General Houston created a delicate situation. For a time the old hero refused to vacate the office to his successor. A graphic scene of the occasion of the transfer of office has been recorded by Norman Kittrell in his book, *Governors Who Have Been and Other Public Men of Texas.* General Houston is quoted as saying:

> I went over to the governor's office after breakfast expecting to proceed with public business, but found little Eddie Clark in possession. I verily believe he camped all night at the woodpile so as to be on hand at an early hour in the morning.[25]

It is easy to understand the hurt and the humiliation that Houston must have been experiencing at this moment. But the term "Little Eddie" was most unjust, for Clark was a tall mannerly gentleman of the old Southern tradition and he conducted himself with dignity, respect, and patriotism during these anxious days. Clark was willing and able to take the oath which Houston was unwilling to accept. It was reported that Houston expressed to Clark the conviction that, as in the past, Texas would call him from his retirement, and that he hoped Governor Clark would be able to give as good an account of his stewardship as he could now render.[26]

There was a sense of uneasiness about the plans that Houston might have for re-capturing the governor's seat. It was rumored that upon his retirement to his home in Huntsville that he waited and plotted either to aid the Union cause or to re-establish the Republic of Texas. Houston was accused of assisting the Union by opposing martial law, conscription, and making derogatory remarks about President Jefferson Davis.[27] On April 4, 1861, Governor Clark wrote to President Davis urging the Confederate government to take effective measures to protect the Texas frontier. He also stated that it was more than probable that Sam Houston would lead a movement in Texas to re-establish the Republic.[28] There are other references in the correspondence of the time to indicate this fear. However, there is no evidence that Houston ever had any such plans, and there is no indication that he ever took any positive action in that direction. As a matter of fact, Houston refused President Lincoln's offer to send Federal troops into Texas to aid the General in regaining the governorship.

History was to reveal that Governor Clark could, indeed, give as good an account of his stewardship of the state as did Houston. During the nine months of Houston's unexpired term that Clark fulfilled, he devoted all of his leadership ability, time, and energies in mobilizing Texas for the Southern cause. There were at this time about twenty-seven hundred Federal troops stationed in Texas, most of them along the frontier. Major General David E. Twiggs, with headquarters in San Antonio, was the commander of the Department of Texas. The Secession Convention had appointed a party of commissioners to confer with General Twiggs about the transfer of United States arms, munitions, and stores to the State of Texas. Twiggs, a native Georgian, was known to be a Southern sympathizer who mixed frequently with known secessionists, "some of them ladies."[29] General Twiggs, realizing his awkward situation, had asked his superiors in Washington repeatedly for operational instructions, but no orders were forthcoming.[30] Twiggs then asked to be relieved of his command, stating, "I will never fire on an American citizen."[31] The commander of the United States army took Twiggs at his word and appointed Colonel C. A. Waite to succeed him. On February 16, 1861, three days before Colonel Waite's arrival to relieve him, Twiggs surrendered to Ben McCulloch, the military commander appointed by the Committee on Public Safey. It was agreed that the Federal troops could leave San Antonio unmolested, but that all Federal property would be turned over to the state. It was further agreed that the Federal troops could keep their side arms, clothing, camp and garrison equipment, hospital stores, and transportation necessary to move them to the coast of Texas.[32] All frontier posts in Texas were surrendered by Twiggs under similar terms. This surrender by Twiggs of all the Federal forts and property came about five days before the people of Texas voted for the secession of Texas from the Union. The effect of the surrender was instantaneous and ecstatic. It was a brilliant maneuver for Texas and was a momentous send-off for Clark's secession administration, for it meant a tremendous gain for the Confederacy in supplies and money (estimated at three million dollars) on the eve of the outbreak of the war.

In accordance with the agreement between Twiggs and the members of the Committee on Public Safety, the United States troops were to march to Green Lake near Indianola where the United States steamer, *The Star of the West,* would take them North. However, after Fort Sumter was fired upon, officials took the position that the war had started and they were not bound by the earlier evacuation terms. Governor Clark directed Colonel Earl Van Dorn, who had previously resigned his commission in the United States Army, to hold the Federal soldiers as prisoners of war and to capture the *Star of the West,* A few days later, the troops from the posts on the upper Rio Grande were captured by Colonel Van Dorn a few miles west of San Antonio, Texas. The officers were at once paroled, and the private soldiers were given the choice of either enlisting in the Confederate Army, becoming citizens of the State of Texas, or remaining prisoners of war. Only a few of the Federal troops joined the Confederate Army.[33]

With the removal of the Federal troops, Colonel W. C. Young was called by Clark to raise a cavalry regiment for the purpose of protecting the Texas frontier from Indian depredations and from an invasion of the state by Federal troops.[34] The problem of the defense of the frontier was a critical one. With the removal of the Federal troops, the northern frontier lay open to an attack by marauding Indians. To make matters worse, there were rumors that in Red River and Grayson Counties runaway Negroes were drilling, preparatory to joining with a Federal invasion force from the Indian Territory.[35] About the first of May, Colonel W. C. Young crossed the Red River and captured Forts Arbuckle, Washita, and Cobb, forcing the Federal troops to withdraw into Kansas.

On April 8, 1861, the Confederate War Department called upon Texas for three thousand volunteers, and on the following day requested of the Governor that all the three thousand volunteers be infantry. Lincoln's call for 75,000 troops on April 15 was followed by another Confederate requisition on Texas for five thousand men to be held ready for movement at a moment's notice.[36]

The *State Gazette* of Austin, Texas, announced on July 6, 1861, that Governor Clark had received a request for twenty companies of infantry to report to Colonel Van Dorn. The *Gazette* was most complimentary of Edward Clark's zeal in assisting Van Dorn in mustering the twenty companies and supplying them with guns, ammunition, and camp equipment. These troops were to be promptly sent to Richmond. Upon their arrival in Virginia, the twenty Texas companies became part of an organization that was to win fame in the war as Hood's Texas Brigade.[37]

In July, 1861, Clark was notified that the "Black Republican Army" had been successful in several encounters in Missouri and was now advancing into Arkansas. Clark issued a proclamation on July 16, 1861, warning the people of Texas on the seriousness of the threat and asking them to take immediate steps to defend themselves. Clark urged the people to put all arms in private use in order and keep them ready for service. He implored all the able-bodied men of Texas to arm themselves as well as possible and to join some military unit.[38]

Governor Clark, aware of the imminent danger and the lack of guns and munitions in the state, requested the merchants of Texas to turn over to the state all ammunition they held in private stock, but this secured only a limited amount. Governor Clark also asked the county judges throughout the state to make an inventory of the number of guns available in their respective counties. The inquiry revealed that forty thousand guns of every type and description were held by private citizens in the state.[39] However, because of the ominous situation, and the constant dread of Indian attacks, many people were reluctant to surrender their firearms to the government. The need for firearms was so critical that several Texas newspapers carried special appeals to the people. The *Texas Republican* of Marshall stated:

> Men who volunteer for the defense of the country ought not to be kept idle for the want of arms, and the man who stays home and is unwilling to surrender his gun for such a cause is, to say the least of it, a poor patriot.[40]

Clark announced in an executive proclamation in August, 1861, that another two thousand men were needed for the Confederate cause. These men were to be organized into companies composed of a captain, one first lieutenant, two second lieutenants, four sergeants, four corporals, two musicians, and from sixty-four to one hundred privates. These individual companies were to be organized, drilled, and prepared for active duty as quickly as possible. Governor Clark also urged that ten companies be raised to be sent to defend the lower Rio Grande and for companies of heavy artillery to be raised and sent to man the coastal fortifications. These troops were to receive equipment and clothing at San Antonio and were to be used primarily for the defense of the state in the event of an invasion.[41]

Not only was Texas expected to provide men for the Confederate cause, the state was also expected to be a source of food and supplies. Governor Clark, realizing that the rigors of a winter campaign would find many Texas soldiers without adequate clothing and equipment, urged his fellow Texans to contribute blankets and warm clothing for the troops fighting in Northern Arkansas, Kentucky, and Northern Virginia. He further urged the people to manufacture all the woolen clothing that they could. The manufactured cloth was to be paid for in Confederate bonds and would serve not only to help the service men, but would help to alleviate the problem of unemployment at home.[42]

On September 4, 1861, William Byrd, the Adjutant-General, issued a plea on behalf of Governor Clark for the people of Texas to supply clothing for the Army. Each county was to form "aid societies" to collect clothing, blankets, comforts, and other articles which the army desperately needed. Depots for receiving the goods were established at Jefferson, Henderson, Dallas, Sherman, Waco, Austin, San Antonio, and other major points in Texas. The contributions from the various points were to be forwarded to the most convenient railroad depot, either at Jefferson, Houston, or Beaumont. Clark received assurances from the managers of the various railroads and express firms that the goods would be transported to these points free of charge.[43]

A military board was created by Governor Clark for the purpose of coordinating the manufacturing of war materials.[44] Clark immediately ordered the warden at the penitentiary at Huntsville to use all of the penitentiary's equipment for the production of woolen cloth. Clark estimated that the inmates at Huntsville could produce as much as one thousand yards of woolen cloth per day.[45] The ladies' aid societies, formed at Clark's request, worked diligently to provide the troops with coats, pants, flannel shirts, heavy underwear, woolen socks, blankets, comforts, etc.[46]

Because of the war, there was no formal nominating convention of the Democratic party in 1861. Governor Clark issued a call for state elections to be held in August, 1861. An attempt was made to hold a state convention at Dallas in May, 1861, but so few counties sent delegates that no nominations were made. Three men announced their candidacy for governor. They were Edward Clark, Frank R. Lubbock, former lieutenant-governor, and General T. J. Chambers, chairman of the committee that drew up the Ordinance of Secession. All three of the men were Democrats and secessionists. Thus, the logical issue of the campaign—the war—was largely ignored and the race concerned itself with the personalities of the candidates. During the war, there was a suspension of party politics. No one could even hope to be elected to public office if he did not favor an active participation in the war effort. Even the private citizens who sympathized with the Union or who desired peace had to be very careful in their speech and actions or else suffer abuse at the hands of their neighbors.[47]

Edward Clark announced his candidacy for the office of governor by issuing a circular to the newspapers in which he stated that the urgent demands of the prosecution of the war would prevent him from actively canvassing the state. The *State Gazette* of Austin was complimentary of Clark's conduct during his brief tenure of office. The editorial praised the governor for his efforts in raising and outfitting men for military service. He was praised for his work in the reorganization of the office of Adjutant-General, and for his introduction of efficiency and order in a department which had previously been most ineffective.[48] In an article written in July, 1861, a reporter of the *State Gazette* said that the race, as he saw it, was between good men each striving to serve the state and each directed by the desire to do what was best for Texas and the Confederacy.[49]

Although several well-known newspapermen in the state campaigned vigorously for Clark, most of the leading newspapers, including the Houston *Telegraph* and the Clarksville *Standard*, came out actively for Frank R. Lubbock. In a scathing denunciation of Clark, the *Standard* made much ado of his alleged membership in the Know-Nothing party during the fifties. The paper accused Clark of riding Houston's coat-tails to victory in the election of 1859 only to forsake Houston and "push the Old Chieftain out of his chair" when the opportunity came for Clark to gain the governorship. The *Standard* deplored Clark's lack of political cohesiveness and called him a "time-server with a pleasant voice and insinuating manner." The writer ended his tirade by saying Clark belonged to that "uncertain tribe who recognize no guide, or light, or tie, except self-promotion."[50]

In the final days of the campaign, it appeared that Lubbock with his tremendous support would be an easy winner, but the final tabulation of votes revealed one of the closest elections in Texas history. The margin of victory by which Frank R. Lubbock won the election was a mere one hundred and twenty-four votes.[51] The election returns of August 5, 1861, showed that of the 57,428 votes cast, Lubbock received 21,854, Clark 21,730, and Chambers 13,759. Clark's running mate, John M. Crockett, won easily over his opponent, F. F. Foscue who received only 12,160 votes.[52]

This bare majority of 124 votes would certainly warrant a

recount of the election returns, yet there is no indication that Clark asked for a recount or an investigation in any way whatsoever.

Thus Clark's brief but important career as governor of Texas was ended. The political star of Texas' eighth governor sank almost before it had arisen on the horizon. Yet the popularity of Clark is shown by the narrow margin by which he was defeated, and while his gubernatorial career may be said to be relatively undistinguished, he was to serve Texas and the Confederacy with valor on the field of battle.

With his defeat in the election of 1861, Clark joined the Confederate Army and raised a regiment of infantry which he led until he was severely wounded. He received his temporary appointment on November 26, 1861, as colonel in command of the Fourteenth Regiment Texas Infantry, Confederate States' Army.[53] Clark's regiment was a part of Walker's Texas (Greyhound) Division.[54] After the death of General Horace Randal late in the war, Colonel Clark commanded Randal's brigade.

After being officially commissioned a colonel by the Confederate Congress in April, 1862,[55] Clark immediately asked for permission to move his regiment by way of Red River to Little Rock and from there to any point in the direction of the theatre of the war. Clark described his regiment as one of the finest in the state, and he reported that his men were anxious to see active duty. He was concerned with the shortage of arms, ammunition, and transportation for his troops. The need for horses and mules had placed a burden on the people, as they could not relinquish all their farm animals to further the war effort.[56]

Clark's Fourteenth Texas Infantry Regiment saw action with Walker's Division in Louisiana in 1863 and 1864, and in the spring of the latter year fought in two of the bloodiest engagements west of the Mississippi. These were the battles of Mansfield and Pleasant Hill. Early in 1864, General N. P. Banks was ordered by General Henry Halleck to begin implementing the Federal plan to invade Texas via the Red River by way of Shreveport to Marshall and thus into the rich farmland of Northeast Texas. This Federal movement, known as the Red River campaign, was launched in March, 1864, and was to be supported by extensive naval forces. It was the most dangerous threat yet directed at the state of Texas. The Confederate troops, under command of General E. Kirby Smith, were aware of the threat and soon every available unit in the state was on the way to Louisiana. General Richard Taylor, field commander for the Confederate Army, was forced to withdraw before the much larger invasion force. Using delaying tactics, Taylor begrudgingly gave ground as he waited for reinforcements.[57] By the end of March, he felt his army was strong enough to make a stand. Among the reinforcements that Taylor received was Walker's Texas division.[58] Falling back to Mansfield, General Taylor formed his battle line consisting of Walker's, Moulton's, and Green's Divisions to await the assault of the Federal troops marching from Grand Ecore. The two forces met at Mansfield on April 8, 1864. After desperate fighting, the Federals were forced to fall back, thus ending their effort to take Shreveport and stifling all hope of occupying East Texas.[59] During the battle of Mansfield, Edward Clark was wounded while leading his regiment in a charge on the Federal position in "the peach orchard." The wound caused Clark little pain, however, and he did not leave the field until the close of the battle.[60]

After retreating from Mansfield, General Banks ordered his troops to re-form during the night a few miles outside of Pleasant Hill. It was during this battle on April 9, one of the bloodiest minor engagements of the Civil War, that Edward Clark was to prove his mettle. One of Clark's fellow officers described the ex-governor's conduct during the battle:

> We had driven the enemy lines back, but one Federal Division had thrown up some logs on a high hill, and it was impossible for lines to pass without dislodging them. General Walker had sent two detachments to attack the position, but they were repulsed. He rode up to General Randal and asked him if he had a regiment that could take the position. Colonel Clark was sitting on his horse near by, and Randal asked him if he could take it. He curtly replied, "I have seven hundred men in line, and can take the place if anyone can." Walker gave him instructions about the position. Colonel Clark saluted and said, "I move forward at once, Sir." He dismounted, went to the center of his regiment, made some remarks to his men, then gave the command, "Right shoulder, shift arms, forward, double quick, march." Colonel Clark was in full uniform, about six feet in advance. When in thirty yards of the enemy the Federals opened fire and Colonel Clark fell shot through

> the leg, just under the knee. His men raised the "rebel yell," rushed the logs, and fired one volley into the retreating mass, killing eight hundred. . . .[61]

When Hamilton P. Bee, a brigadier general, made his official report of the battle of Pleasant Hill, he was highly complimentary of the action of Colonel Clark and Colonel Randal. Colonel Horace Randal was promoted in April to the rank of brigadier general as a result of his gallant conduct in the battle of Pleasant Hill, however, he was killed at the battle of Jenkins Ferry on April 30, 1864, before he received the news of his promotion. After Randal's death Clark commanded the brigade.[62]

The wound which Clark received in the battle of Pleasant Hill failed to respond to treatment and completely disabled him for active duty. He received special orders dated February 25, 1865, from Shreveport, Louisiana, giving him a sixty-day furlough on a surgeon's certificate.[63]

Realizing that he would probably never fully recover complete use of the injured leg again, Clark made formal application for discharge from the Confederate Army with the rank of brigadier general which he had achieved in May, 1864.[64] However, as in the case of numerous other officers promoted to general rank in the Trans-Mississippi Department, Clark's promotion to brigadier general was never confirmed by the Richmond authorities.

During March, 1865, the Texas newspapers carried Edward Clark's name as a candidate for governor. However, fearing the consequences of reconstruction, in June 1865, Edward Clark along with such distinguished figures as Governor Pendleton Murrah, Governors Henry Allen and Thomas Moore of Louisiana, Governor Thomas C. Reynolds of Missouri, Generals E. Kirby Smith, John B. Magruder, and other illustrious Southerners fled to Mexico.[65] This caravan of Confederate military and civilian "brass" was escorted to Mexico by General Jo Shelby who fortified his column with several pieces of artillery and forty wagons of Enfield rifles.[66] Clark's voluntary exile below the Rio Grande did not last long. Within a few months he was in Washington, D. C., seeking to take advantage of the liberal pardon offered to Confederate officers by President Andrew Johnson.[67] Clark returned to his home in Marshall, Texas, to pick up the threads of his private life, disrupted by war and public service to his beloved state. During the trying days of reconstruction, he engaged in several mercantile pursuits with little apparent success. Clark later resumed the practice of law at Marshall. He died on May 4, 1880, and was buried in the city cemetery at Marshall, Texas. An outstanding statesman, a patriotic Southerner, a gallant soldier, Edward Clark earned the right to be remembered as one of the best of the fighting governors of Texas.

NOTES

[1]Paul Bolton, **Governors of Texas** (Corpus Christi: The Corpus Christi **Caller Times**, 1947), p. 36.

[2]Clement A. Evans, **Confederate Military History**, 12 vols. (Atlanta, n.p., 1899), XI, pp. 10-11.

[3]Frank R. Lubbock, **Six Decades in Texas or Memoirs of Francis Richard Lubbock** (Austin: Ben C. Jones Printers, 1900), p. 251.

[4]Ralph A. Wooster, "An Analysis of the Texas Know-Nothings," **Southwestern Historical Quarterly**, LXX (January, 1967), pp. 414-423.

[5]**Texas Republican** (Marshall), August 1, 1855.

[6]Lubbock, **op. cit.**, p. 251.

[7]**Dallas Herald**, November 23, 1859.

[8]John Henry Brown, **History of Texas** (2 vols.; St. Louis: Becktold and Company, 1893), II, pp. 380-381.

[9]John D. Hicks, **The Federal Union** (2nd ed.; Cambridge: Riverside Press, 1952), pp. 528-529.

[10]**Ibid.**, pp. 544-546.

[11]Rupert Richardson, **Texas the Lone Star State** (2nd ed.; Englewood Cliffs, New Jersey: Prentice-Hall, Inc., 1960), p. 183.

[12]Harold B. Simpson, **Gaines Mill to Appomattox** (Waco, Texas: Texian Press, 1963), p. 25.

[13]Anna Irene Sandbo, "First Session of the Secession Convention in Texas," **Southwestern Historical Quarterly**, XVIII (October, 1914), p. 169.

[14]**State Gazette** (Austin, Texas), December 8, 1860.

[15]Ernest W. Winkler (ed.), **Journal of the Secession Convention** (Austin, Texas: Austin Printing Company, 1912), p. 13.

[16]Ralph A. Wooster, **The Secession Conventions of the South** (Princeton, New Jersey: Princeton University Press, 1962), p. 135.

[17]Philip Graham (ed.), "Texas Memoirs of Amelia Barr," **Southwestern Historical Quarterly,** LXIX (April, 1966), p. 473.

[18]Amelia E. Barr, **All the Days of My Life, An Autobiography** (New York: D. Appleton and Company, 1913), pp. 226-227.

[19]James T. DeShield, **They Sat in High Places, the Presidents and Governors of Texas** (San Antonio, Texas: The Naylor Company, 1940), p. 223.

[20]Frank W. Johnson, **A History of Texas and Texans** (5 vols.; Chicago: The American Historical Society, 1914), II, pp. 1081-1082.

[21]L. E. Daniel, **Personnel of the Texas State Government With Sketches of Representative Men of Texas** (San Antonio: Maverick Printing House, 1892), p. 38.

[22]Walter Prescott Webb and H. Bailey Carroll (eds.), **The Handbook of Texas** (2 vols.: Austin, Texas: Texas Historical Association, 1952), I, p. 354.

[23]Marjorie Clark (ed.), "A Mexican War Letter," **Southwestern Historical Quarterly,** XLVII (January, 1944), pp. 326-327.

[24]Letter from W. J. Evans to J. E. Clark, dated July 22, 1907. Clark Papers, Marshall Historical Museum, Marshall, Texas.

[25]Norman H. Kittrell, **Governors Who Have Been and Other Public Men of Texas** (Houston: Dealy-Adey Elgin Company, 1921), p. 31.

[26]Alfred Mason Williams, **Sam Houston and the War of Independence in Texas** (Boston: Houghton Mifflin Company, 1893), pp. 358-359.

[27]Claude Elliott, "Union Sentiment in Texas, 1861-1865," **Southwestern Historical Quarterly,** L (April, 1947), p. 452.

[28]**Official Records** (Armies), Ser. I, Vol. 4, p. 621.

[29]Robert Johnson and Clarence C. Buel (eds.), **Battles and Leaders of the Civil War,** Vol. I (New York: Thomas Yoseloff, Inc., 1956), p. 33.

[30]**Official Records** (Armies), Ser. 1, Vol. 1, pp. 580-581.

[31]**Ibid.**

[32]Johnson and Buel, **op. cit.,** p. 39.

[33]Homer S. Thrall, **A Pictorial History of Texas** (revised ed.; New York: N. D. Thompson Publishing Company, 1885), pp. 388-391.

[34]James M. Day (ed.), **House Journal of the Ninth Legislature Regular Session of the State of Texas** (Austin): Texas State Library, 1964), p. 24.

[35]**Official Records** (Armies), Ser. 1, Vol. 4, pp. 144-145.

[36]Day, **op. cit.,** p. 25.

[37]**State Gazette** (Austin), July 6, 1861.

[38]**Dallas Herald,** July 31, 1861.

[39]Johnson, **op. cit.,** p. 542.

[40]**Texas Republican** (Marshall, Texas), June 8, 1861.

[41]"Proclamation to the People of Texas," August 26, 1861. Clark Papers, Marshall Historical Museum, Marshall, Texas.

[42]**Official Records** (Armies), Ser. 1, Vol. 1, p. 102.

[43]**Ibid.**, p. 103.

[44]Charles W. Ramsdell, "The Texas State Military Board, 1862-1865," **Southwestern Historical Quarterly**, XXVII (April, 1924), p. 253.

[45]**Official Records** (Armies), Ser. 1, Vol. 1, p. 101.

[46]**Dallas Herald**, November 20, 1861.

[47]T. R. Felgar, "Texas In the War for Southern Independence" (unpublished Ph.D. dissertation, University of Texas, Austin, Texas, 1935), p. 454.

[48]**State Gazette**, Austin, Texas, June 22, 1861.

[49]**Ibid.**, July 6, 1861.

[50]Clarksville **Standard**, Clarksville, Texas, July 20, 1861.

[51]Walter B. Moore, **Governors of Texas** (Dallas, Texas: **The Dallas Morning News**, 1947), p. 8.

[52]Brown, **op. cit.**, p. 406.

[53]William E. Bergen, Department of the Army, Office of Adjutant General, Records Division, dated August 27, 1953. Clark's Papers, Marshall Historical Museum, Marshall, Texas.

[54]Joseph Blessington, **The Campaigns of Walker's Texas Division** (New York: Lange, Little and Company, 1875), p. 53.

[55]**Official Records** (Armies), Ser. IV, Vol. I, Part 1, p. 1043.

[56]Letter from Clark to P. O. Herbert, dated April 12, 1862, Clark Papers, Marshall Historical Museum, Marshall, Texas.

[57]Ludwell H. Johnson, **Red River Campaign, Politics and Cotton in the Civil War** (Baltimore: The John Hopkins Press, 1958), pp. 120-122.

[58]Jefferson Davis, **The Rise and Fall of the Confederate Government** (2 vols.; Richmond: Garret and Massie, Inc., 1938), II, p. 455.

[59]Texas Historical Foundation, Centennial Commemoration, **Red River Campaign** (April 4, 1964), pp. 11-12.

[60]**State Gazette**, April 12, 1865.

[61]Letter from C. Cannon to J. E. Clark, dated April 17, 1910, Clark Papers, Marshall Historical Museum, Marshall, Texas.

[62]**Official Records** (Armies), Ser. 1, Vol. XXXIV, Part 1, p. 609.

[63]William E. Bergin, Department of the Army, Office of Adjutant General, Record Division, dated August 27, 1953, Clark Papers, Marshall Historical Museum, Marshall, Texas.

[64]Letter from Clark to J. J. Flenn, dated April 28, 1865, Clark Papers, Marshall Historical Museum, Marshall, Texas.

[65]W. C. Nunn, **Escape from Reconstruction** (Fort Worth: Leo Potishman Foundation, Texas Christian University, 1956), pp. 32-38.

[66]**Official Records** (Armies), Ser. 1, Vol. XLVIII, Part 2, p. 1077.

[67]**Dallas Herald**, January 13, 1866.

Richard W. "Dick" Dowling

by

JAMES R. WARD

A battle of approximately one hour's duration between Union and Confederate forces near the mouth of the Sabine River in September, 1863, catapulted a little-known Confederate lieutenant to lasting fame for his actions. The battle was Sabine Pass, Texas, a brilliant victory for the South, and the officer was twenty-five-year-old Richard William "Dick" Dowling. Although he participated in several actions during the course of the Civil War, Dowling is most remembered for his September victory against tremendous opposition at Sabine Pass. And yet, one of the state's most famous Confederate heroes was neither a native Texan nor an American.[1]

Dick Dowling, the second child and eldest son of William and Mary Dowling, was born in Tuam, Galway County, Ireland in 1838.[2] Little is recorded of the activities of the family in Ireland, but they undoubtedly suffered from the numerous economic reverses that occurred in that country in the 1840's. As a result of such calamities as the potato famine, which saw the failure of large amounts of that staple crop, the Dowlings migrated to the United States after 1846. Here, they settled in New Orleans, a site chosen by many of their fellow countrymen. In the early 1850's after the death of his parents, Dick Dowling and at least one brother and one sister worked their way to Texas through the port of Galveston. Eventually young Dick settled in Houston.[3]

The likeable, red-headed Irishman quickly made a reputation as an enterprising businessman in pre-Civil War Houston. With financial backing which he probably obtained from Benjamin Digby Odlum, his future father-in-law, Dowling purchased, remodeled, and opened in October, 1857, the first of his successful Houston Saloons, *The Shades,* a two-story building at the corner of Main and Prairie. By 1860, however, he had sold his interest in *The Shades* and purchased his most successful saloon, the popular *Bank of Bacchus,* near the Harris County courthouse. In addition, Dowling later operated still another similar franchise, the *Hudgpeth Bathing Saloon,* as well as a liquor importing firm in Galveston.[4]

Dowling's opening of the *Bank of Bacchus* guaranteed his reputation as a businessman extraordinary at the comparatively young age of twenty-two. This particular institution, in addition to serving the finest beverages and "spirits," functioned in the dual capacity of a check-cashing and money-lending agency.[5] Because of its location, it also became a favorite meeting spot of many area newspapermen, including Edward Hopkins Cushing, owner of the influential Houston *Telegraph* and a personal friend of Dick Dowling. The special of the establishment, a concoction conceived by Dowling and entitled "Kiss Me Quick and Go," was reportedly a great favorite with the customers. The *Bank of Bacchus* was Dowling's most lucrative single business investment when the outbreak of the Civil War forced him to interrupt his civilian pursuits.[6]

Evidently Dowling's active business career did not interfere with an equally active domestic life during the period. He married on November 30, 1857, Elizabeth Anne Odlum, daughter of the previously mentioned Houston financier, Benjamin Digby Odlum. Dowling first met his future bride when she was a student at the Ursuline Convent in Galveston. After their marriage, the Dowlings built a large home on the outskirts of Houston. At the outbreak of the Civil War, they had one son, Benjamin Richard, who was born on March 25, 1859.[7]

In addition to his numerous responsibilities as a businessman, husband, and father, Dowling accepted still more responsibility in 1859 when he became an active member of the Houston Light Artillery Company. After this unit virtually disbanded in 1860, he joined a similar organization, the Jefferson Davis Guards. This company, comprised largely of Irish dockworkers and common laborers from the Houston and Galveston areas, was first organized as an infantry unit but was eventually given artillery training and duties. Dick Dowling served as the first lieutenant and treasurer of the company; Captain Frederick H. Odlum, his wife's uncle, commanded the company; and Patrick Hennessy, his brother-in-law, was a second lieutenant. Dowling's younger brother, Pat, also saw some service with this particular unit.[8] "They were a brawling, wike-reveling, clay-pipe-smoking, Irish-jigging lot."[9] One contemporary observer later wrote that the Davis Guards "were men of brawn and muscle; quiet in manner if you treated them right, but woe to you if you offended one . . . you would hear from him in true Irish style."[10]

At the outbreak of the Civil War, Dowling and the Davis Guards were temporarily assigned to the command of Colonel John Salmon "Rip" Ford who would command an amphibious expedition against United States Army outposts on the Mexican border. Acting under orders from the Texas Committee on Public Safety, Colonel Ford was to lead a force to the lower Rio Grande where he was to demand the surrender of the Federal troops and supplies at Fort Brown and other Union outposts in the area. These objectives were accomplished with little resistance by May, 1861. The Davis Guards, however, did very little to demonstrate either their military skills or their ability to take and follow orders.[11]

The most outstanding achievement of the Guards during the Rio Grande Expedition was their repeated arguments with Colonel Ford and several of their senior officers. The immediate cause of the first feelings of bitterness between the men and their commanders occurred over the bad conditions of their quarters aboard the *General Rusk* during the trip to Brownsville.[12] Another reason for the ill feelings between the Guards and Colonel Ford developed when Odlum's company was forced to occupy unsatisfactory housing after they reached Brownsville. This lack of communication between the Guards and the expedition commander resulted in an order for the Irishmen to disband. Fortunately for the career of Dick Dowling and other members of the company, Colonel Ford eventually revoked the order.[13]

Captain Odlum, Lieutenant Dowling, and the Davis Guards returned to the Houston area in the spring of 1861. Here, they remained in a virtual dormant state until the fall of that year.[14] During October, 1861, the company received orders to defend the area around Houston and Galveston as Company F of the Third Texas Artillery Battalion.[15] Dowling's artillery training with this battalion proved to be a great asset in his later successes. Major Joseph J. Cook commanded the Third Texas Artillery, which was to play a major role in the defense of the

Texas coast. When the Federal blockading fleet stepped up activities off the Texas coast, the battalion was augmented to a full regiment, the First Texas Heavy Artillery, and Cook was promoted to colonel.[16] All effective preparations failed, however, for in October, 1862, Federal forces under Commander William B. Renshaw succeeded in breaching the Confederate defenses and in forcing the withdrawal of Cook's forces from Galveston. Thus, that important port fell to the Union.[17]

Although the Federals captured Galveston in the fall of 1862, they lacked sufficient forces to occupy it completely. Consequently, the South began almost immediately to make plans for recapturing the key city. When Major General John B. Magruder, District Commander for Texas, arrived in the state in late 1862, he faced the problem of driving the Federals from Galveston. A carefully planned and executed Confederate assault on January 1, 1863, resulted in the recapture of the Texas port, the death of Commander Renshaw, the destruction of several Union vessels, and the capture of a large number of Union troops.[18] More important, as far as Dick Dowling and the Davis Guards were concerned, the battle afforded them their first actual combat with the enemy. Colonel Cook's artillerists, including the Guards, were most important segments of the attack force, for they occupied several strategic positions in the town, and they took part in the assault on Kuhn's Wharf, where the Federal infantry was barricaded.[19] Following the battle of Galveston, the Houston *Telegraph* said of the Davis Guards: "The artillery boys acted nobly and have covered themselves with glory. . . . The Irish boys surpassed the expectations of their Friends."[20]

Although the Galveston battle effectively introduced Dick Dowling to combat, it remained for a subsequent episode to fully demonstrate his military abilities. That demonstration was not long in coming. In January, 1863, General Magruder transferred Company F of Cook's Regiment to Sabine Pass with orders to take up the defense of that position. Acting under orders from Major Oscar M. Watkins, commander of Confederate land and naval forces on the Sabine River, the Davis Guards moved from Beaumont to Sabine Pass on January 20. The Guards served as crew and artillerymen aboard the steamboat *Josiah A. Bell,* with Lieutenant Dowling commanding the vessel's one serviceable cannon, an eight-inch Columbiad which had been bored as a six-inch rifled gun to give it more accuracy and range.[21] The Guards named the cannon "Annie" in honor of the lieutenant's wife.[22]

Major Watkins' force discovered two Union blockading vessels, the sloop, *Morning Light,* and the schooner, *Velocity,* lying off the entrance to Sabine Pass on January 21. At 10 a.m. on that date, Lieutenant Dowling opened fire on the Federal vessels from a range of over two miles. Despite at least one jam in the artillery piece, Dowling effectively directed its fire and scored repeated hits on the *Morning Light* when the Confederates closed the range. His success, coupled with the eventual precise fire of the sharpshooters aboard the *Josiah A. Bell,* resulted in the quick surrender of the Federal sloop. Subsequent maneuvers and artillery excellence by a second Southern vessel, the *Uncle Ben,* brought about the surrender of the *Velocity.* Thus, in a period of approximately two hours, the Confederate ships captured two vessels, twelve guns, medical supplies, ammunition, and 109 prisoners. Despite the fact that circumstances eventually necessitated the burning of the sloop after many of her supplies had been removed, the Confederate victory was a definite rebuttal to Union efforts to blockade Sabine Pass.[23]

Dick Dowling received special praise for his actions during the engagement off Sabine Pass. Major Watkins singled the young lieutenant out not only because of his excellent artillery achievements but also because of certain of his actions which saved the ship's magazine from becoming flooded.[24] A dispatch by Junius in the Houston *Telegraph* cited both Dowling and the Guards as it stated that they "occupied the most dangerous position during the entire engagement, but not a man flinched, and the enemy gave him credit for making the prettiest shots they ever saw."[25]

Odlum's Davis Guards, fresh from a relatively easy victory over the Federals, now returned to manning the defense positions of Sabine Pass, located thirty miles southeast of Beaumont and the controlling access to the Sabine River. The Irishmen worked on fortifications throughout the late spring and most of the summer of 1863. Fort Griffin, the major Confederate post near the entrance to Sabine Pass and close to Sabine City, Texas, was most certainly not an imposing or impregnable fortress.[26] In fact, its appearance gave little inkling of its future importance to the Confederacy and to the State of Texas. One observer maintained that the fort "was an unfinished earthwork on the Texas side of the Pass, destitute of any outer defenses, presenting three bastioned sides on the east, south, and west, the north and rear enclosed by a redoubt about four feet above the level."[27] Despite its lack of glamor, the fort did, nevertheless, command the Texas and Louisiana channels, both of which were very shallow with approximately five-foot soundings. In addition, a road ran from the fort to Beaumont, a valuable city because of its rail connections with Houston. The defenders of Fort Griffin also benefited from the presence of a sandbar which partially blocked the entrance to Sabine Pass.[28]

The defense capabilities of Fort Griffin were sufficiently strengthened by September 1, 1863 to present a more formidable challenge to any ensuing Federal attack. Particular attention was given to improving the walls and to the construction of several shelters for the cannons, ammunition, and gun crews.[29] Careful consideration was also given to the armament for the fort. This artillery eventually included two thirty-two-pounder smooth bores, two twenty-four-pounder smooth bores, and two thirty-two-pounder howitzers.[30] Furthermore, Lieutenant Dowling and the other gunners resorted to target practice on stakes which were located in the channels at various intervals. By relying on the location of these stakes, the Davis Guards established an operative range-finding device.[31] "This system of targeting, plus the extraordinary gunnery skill of the Guards was to prove an effective barrier to any force attempting to move through the Pass."[32]

While construction took place on Fort Griffin, the men under Captain Odlum's command were garrisoned in Sabine City. Because of a lack of adequate food and housing, they relied on their own abilities to find these necessities. Fortunately, they often received gifts of foodstuffs from the inhabitants of the town. By August, 1863, several of the Guards, including Dowling, secured lodging in a two-story frame house owned by James Stewart, a bar pilot. Most probably this home, located near Fort Griffin, served to store some of the ammunition later used in defense of the fort. During the latter part of August, several of the Davis Guards, including Patrick Dowling, were away on furlough, and, thus, the garrison was somewhat reduced from its assigned strength. Also, by late August, Colonel W. H. Griffin, commander of all troops at Sabine City, had moved north with some of his forces. In the absence of Colonel Griffin, Captain Odlum was placed in temporary command of Sabine City, and Lieutenant Dowling commanded the Guards at Fort Griffin.[33]

Unknown to the Confederate defenders of Fort Griffin and Sabine City, Union plans were already in motion by September, 1863, for an attempted invasion of Texas through Sabine Pass. General H. W. Halleck, General-in-Chief of the United States Army, decided in the summer of 1863 that a foothold in Texas should be secured with the least possible delay. He assigned the task of planning an expedition and choosing an invasion site to General Nathaniel P. Banks, commanding the Federal Department of the Gulf, with headquarters in New Orleans.[34] Banks, accordingly, devised a plan involving both naval and ground forces in an assault on the Confederate fort near Sabine City, Texas. Once Fort Griffin was neutralized, the Federal Army would be free to move into other areas in western Louisiana and eastern Texas. Major General William B. Franklin was assigned tactical command of the Sabine Pass Expedition, and Lieutenant Frederick Crocker was designated as commander of the naval forces.[35]

When the expeditionary force assembled in New Orleans in early September, 1863, it consisted of approximately five thousand troops, most of them infantrymen supported by three field and two heavy Parrott batteries.[36] Lieutenant Crocker's convoy fleet included several transports and four light-draft gunboats, the *Clifton*, the *Sachem*, the *Arizona*, and the *Granite City*, all capable of clearing the sandbar at the entrance to Sabine Pass. The gunboats had a double mission, to support the landing of the ground echelon, most of whom were members of the First Division, Nineteenth Army Corps under the command of Brigadier General Godfrey Weitzel, and to silence the batteries of the fort.[37]

The fleet sailed from New Orleans on September 5 with orders to rendezvous off Sabine Pass with the *Granite City*, the advance scouting vessel for the expedition.[38] Unfortunately for the Federal plans, the *Granite City* saw what was thought to be the dreaded Confederate raider, *Alabama,* and withdrew from its designated position, thus failing to make contact with Franklin's forces off Sabine Pass on September 6. Consequently, the expedition lost the prime element of surprise.[39] Once this advantage was lost, it remained for Franklin to devise a new plan for defeating the forces at Fort Griffin and for landing the infantry troops. Franklin's revised plan, finalized September 8, stated:

> Three of the gunboats were to move up the channel to the point of separation; here two of them, the *Sachem* and the *Arizona,* were to take the channel to the right [Louisiana channel], and were to pass the fort by that channel, drawing its fire. The *Clifton* was to take the left-hand channel [Texas channel], moving slowly up, and, when, about half a mile distant, was to go at full speed, within grape and canister range, and engage the fort at close quarters. General Weitzel was to keep near the *Clifton* with a boat [which was the *General Banks*] containing 500 infantry, who were to land as soon as the *Clifton* began to go at full speed at the old fort; from there they were to advance upon the fort as skirmishers, endeavoring to drive the enemy from his guns, while the *Clifton* engaged the fort at close quarters. The fourth gunboat, the *Granite City,* was to support this movement.[40]

General Magruder's warning on September 4 of a possible Federal attack alerted Captain Odlum to the danger of the existing situation. Odlum, occupied with his duties in Sabine City, ordered Lieutenant Dowling, commanding at Fort Griffin, to maintain a careful vigilance for the supposed attackers. The presence of an enemy fleet was soon detected for Dowling's sentinels spotted numerous signals from vessels off Sabine Pass in the early morning hours of September 7. As a result, the young lieutenant ordered all guns manned and readied against possible attack.[41]

All remained relatively quiet until 6:30 a.m. on September 8, when the *Clifton* moved near the fort and fired twenty-six shells at Lieutenant Dowling's forty-seven-man force. None of the shells did any significant damage, however, and the *Clifton* withdrew about 7:30 a.m., without drawing the fort's fire. Later that morning, the Confederate gunboat, *Uncle Ben,* which had been dispatched from Beaumont by Colonel Leon Smith, steamed near Fort Griffin and drew the fire of the *Sachem.* Again the Federals failed to cause any great damage, and again Dowling refused to give the order to return the fire. Afterwards, the Union forces withdrew from gun range.[42]

By this time, Captain Odlum, Lieutenant Dowling, and the Davis Guards at Fort Griffin were aware of General John Magruder's statement that additional supplies and men could not reach Sabine Pass in time to be of help in the event of an invasion at that point. Odlum considered abandoning the fort and falling back to a better defensive position at Sabine City, but Dowling and the Guards persuaded him that they could hold their position. Consequently, he ordered Lieutenant Dowling and his men to stand fast in their defense of the fort. For the next several hours, the handful of Confederate defenders nervously awaited developments.[43]

At 3:40 p.m. on September 8, the Federal attack began when the lead ship, *Clifton,* moved up the Texas channel and proceeded to shell the fort. At the same time, the *Sachem* and the *Arizona* moved up the Louisiana channel and began to fire on the Southern garrison. During a portion of this early action, Colonel Leon Smith, Captain Odlum, and several other officers arrived at the fort despite the Federal bombardment. They encouraged the men to hold their positions until reinforcements could arrive from Beaumont.[44]

Encouraged by the arrival of his superior officers, Dowling commanded his men to wait for the right moment for returning the Federals' fire. Thus, the garrison withheld its fire until the *Sachem* and the *Arizona* were within twelve hundred yards of the fort. Lieutenant Dowling then ordered all six of his guns into action. At his signal, the six cannons in the fort concentrated on the *Sachem,* which was at that time the nearest Federal vessel to Fort Griffin. After a moment's hesitation, the ships returned the fire. For several minutes, the battle between ship and fort raged. Soon, however, Confederate gunner, Michael McKernan, scored a hit in the *Sachem's* steam drum, and the vessel stopped motionless in the water enveloped in steam.[45] Commander Amos Johnson of the *Sachem* soon realized his precarious position and ordered the thirty-pound Parrott gun spiked and the magazine flooded. Although his vessel was helpless, he did not surrender immediately, but awaited help from the other Federal vessels.[46]

With the *Sachem* rendered harmless and enveloped in steam, Dowling switched his fire to the *Clifton,* which was engaged in a daring zig-zag maneuver up the Texas channel and bearing directly at the fort. The *Clifton* followed orders despite the fact that the *Granite City,* the *Arizona,* and the *General Banks* had apparently abandoned the plan of attack.[47] Eventually the steady Confederate fire shot away the tiller rope of the *Clifton,* and she grounded about five hundred yards from Fort Griffin. The gunboat ran aground in such a position that only three of her guns could be brought to bear on the fort. After a period of extremely heavy fire from the Confederate batteries, a shot smashed the *Clifton's* boiler and doomed the Federal vessel. Following the death of his executive officer, Acting Master Robert Rhodes, and the destruction of one of his three serviceable guns, Lieutenant Frederick Crocker, commanding the *Clifton,* surrendered. Crocker's surrender was soon followed by that of Commander Johnson and the *Sachem.*[48] The remaining Federal vessels, including the gunboats, *Arizona* and *Granite City,* retreated out of range of the Confederate guns, crossed back over the bar, and steamed out to the open sea. The carefully planned Federal attack ended in a fiasco.[49] During the exchange of fire between the gunboats and Fort Griffin, Dowling's gun crews "fired 107 times, or better than once every two minutes; an almost unheard-of speed for heavy artillery."[50]

When the *Clifton* and the *Sachem* showed the white flag, the three Confederate gun sections commanded by Lieutenant Dowling, Lieutenant Niles H. Smith, and Dr. George H. Bailey ceased fire. Then, Dowling made preparations to receive the defeated Federals. He led a small group of the Davis Guards to the beach below the fort where they met Lieutenant Crocker and some of the Union survivors. Reportedly, the Guards, in patched and torn uniforms, formed a distinct contrast to the well-attired Federals. Dowling and Crocker then concluded the formalities of an official surrender. Afterwards, the victorious Irish lieutenant boarded the *Clifton* and found the gunboat to contain many needed supplies. Lacking small boats which were necessary to board the *Sachem,* he instructed the Confederate gunboat, *Uncle Ben,* to tow the motionless vessel to the wharf. After this task was accomplished, a close examination showed that the crew of the *Sachem* had spiked her main battery and had flooded her magazine.[51]

Following Crocker's formal surrender, which ended the battle of Sabine Pass after approximately forty-five minutes of actual fighting, a wave of panic and bewilderment seized the remaining Federal vessels. Although in numbers the force was far superior to that of the Confederates, this fact was completely ignored. Instead, the Federal commanders organized a complete retreat, giving little thought to their captive comrades. For example, the *Arizona* attempted to leave Sabine Pass in such haste that the vessel momentarily grounded on the sandbar at the mouth of the pass. The *Arizona* finally worked free during the night of September 8. General Franklin transferred those infantry forces that had been placed on the gunboats to the transports in preparation for the trip back to New Orleans.[52]

Although Franklin had made no plans for a second assault and was only interested in abandoning the project as soon as possible, Dowling and his men remained alert, expecting a counter-attack at any time. Consequently, the Davis Guards maintained battle stations throughout the night of September 8. The next morning, however, they observed that the entire Federal force had departed. It was not until this time that Dowling and his men realized that the victory was theirs.[53]

Lieutenant Dowling's official battle report was most complimentary to several individuals and to the Guards as a unit. He applauded Lieutenant N. H. Smith and Assistant Surgeon George H. Bailey for their leadership; he praised Private Michael McKernan for his precise marksmanship against the *Sachem,* and he singled out Colonel Leon Smith for his activities.[54] About the Davis Guards, he wrote: "All my men behaved like heroes; not a man flinched from his post. Our motto was 'victory or death'."[55] As a reflection of his own modesty, the young lieutenant failed to mention that a shell fired from the *Clifton's* guns barely missed him during an early portion of the battle.[56]

The results of the Sabine Pass engagement were very lucrative to the South. In addition to the heavy guns taken from the two gunboats, large quantities of small arms, rations, ammunition, medicine, and other naval stores were captured. Of course, the gunboats themselves were very important prizes. Although the garrison at Fort Griffin underwent heavy bombardment from the Federal vessels, very little damage occurred inside the fort, and not a member of the Guards was killed or wounded.[57] The Federal forces, in their unsuccessful attempt to secure a foothold at Sabine Pass, suffered losses totaling approximately four hundred men.[58]

Despite the unusual circumstances associated with the battle, the repulse of the Federal forces by Dick Dowling's small group was most certainly an important victory for Texas and the Confederacy. General Magruder termed the Sabine Pass achievement as probably "the most extraordinary feat of the war."[59] He wrote: "I beg that the Department [Trans-Mississippi] will notice the conduct of Captain Odlum, Lieutenant Dowling, commanding, and the men of the Davis Guards."[60] The Confederate Congress, in a resolution of February 8, 1864, maintained that Dowling's success was "one of the most brilliant and heroic achievements in the history of the war."[61] Jefferson Davis later wrote: "The success of the single company which garrisoned the earthwork was without parallel in ancient or modern war."[62]

Area newspapers responded quickly to the news of the victorious stand by Dick Dowling and the Davis Guards. For several weeks after the battle, stories of the gallant stand at Fort Griffin crowded out the other news. In fact, the publicity in the Houston newspapers resulted in several fund-raising projects for the benefit of the Guards.[63]

The failure which the Federal forces of the Department of the Gulf experienced at Sabine Pass resulted in a change in Union strategy. The Gulf forces were content to try and control the state by seizing and holding certain Texas coastal towns and the lower Rio Grande instead of securing a military foothold by full-scale invasion.[64] Dowling's victory was a major factor in causing this change in Federal plans. One historian of Texas and the Southwest later stated:

> Dick Dowling's defense of Sabine Pass was one of the brilliant exploits of the war, not only because of its entire success against such overwhelming odds, but because it undoubtedly saved Texas from a formidable invasion which

might have made the state the scene of an extended campaign.[65]

Although the Davis Guards remained on active duty at Sabine Pass and Galveston for the final years of the Civil War, Dick Dowling saw no action after his dramatic September victory. In the fall of 1863, General Magruder assigned Dowling to recruiting duties within Texas, particularly in the Houston area, in an effort to take advantage of the lieutenant's newly-won reputation. Dowling was not adverse to his new assignment, for it allowed him time to visit his family in Houston. He served as a recruiting officer until he was eventually discharged and paroled with the rank of major on June 21, 1865.[66]

After the Civil War, Dowling once more turned his full-time attention to the operation of his several businesses in Houston. Once again his previously successful *Bank of Bacchus* thrived as did his liquor importation firm in Galveston.[67] His brother, Pat, assisted him in operating the former establishment.[68] Not content with these investments, Dowling branched out in 1866 and 1867 by purchasing sizable amounts of property within the city limits of Houston.[69] At the same time, Dowling and several Irish business associates bought oil and gas leases in Harris, Jefferson, Clay, Tyler, and Bexar counties.[70] He also became associated with the Houston Gas Light Company as a director, and he obtained interests in a steamboat operating on the Trinity River.[71]

Dowlings' post-war financial successes appeared to insure a bright future for the Ireland-born hero of Sabine Pass. Fate, however, intervened in the form of a yellow fever epidemic which swept the Texas Gulf coast during 1867. The disease struck down Dowling in early September, and, after a partial recovery, he succumbed on September 23, 1867, survived by his wife, a daughter, Mary Annie, and a son, Felix Sabine.[72] The *Telegraph* stated: "The far-off echoes of the guns of Fort Griffin have served as funeral salvos for the warm-hearted hero, Dick Dowling."[73] "He was a highly respected citizen, a friend of the poor, a Christian gentleman, a devoted husband and father, generous to a fault."[74]

Dick Dowling's untimely death ended the career of one of the most unusual of the state's Confederate heroes. His claim to fame rested almost entirely on his accomplishments associated with Sabine Pass. Dowling's brilliant victory on September 8, 1863, achieved largely as a result of his leadership coupled with Federal ineptitude, was probably the Confederacy's greatest military success in Texas during the Civil War. It was more than enough to insure his position in Texas history.[75]

NOTES

[1]The Battle of Sabine Pass and aspects of the career of Dick Dowling are covered in a number of publications. Among these are the following: Frank X. Tolbert, **Dick Dowling at Sabine Pass** (New York: McGraw-Hill Book Company, Inc., 1962); Frances Robertson Sackett, **Dick Dowling** (Houston, Texas: Gulf Publishing Company, 1937); Mrs. R. F. Pray, **Dick Dowling's Battle: An Account of the War Between the States in the Eastern Gulf Coast Region of Texas** (San Antonio, Texas: The Naylor Company, 1936); Alwyn Barr, "Sabine Pass, September, 1863," **Texas Military History,** II (February, 1962), 17-22; Andrew Forest Muir, "Dick Dowling and the Battle of Sabine Pass," **Civil War History,** IV, 394-428; and Jo Young, "The Battle of Sabine Pass," **The Southwestern Historical Quarterly,** LII (April, 1949), 398-409. For the most recent treatment of Dowling and Sabine Pass, see Colonel Harold B. Simpson's article, "The Battle of Sabine Pass," in Seymour V. Connor, **et al., Battles of Texas** (Waco, Texas: Texian Press, 1967). Cited hereafter as Simpson, **Battles of Texas.**

[2]Conflicting months are listed as Dick Dowling's date of birth. The months of May, 1838 and July, 1838 are the two most frequently suggested dates. The name Dowling is often listed as O'Dowling in Irish records.

[3]Tolbert, **Dick Dowling at Sabine Pass,** pp. 16-21; Simpson, **Battles of Texas,** p. 137; Sackett, **Dick Dowling,** pp. 1-5; Pray, **Dick Dowling's Battle,** pp. 129-131. Because of a lack of authentic records, little is known of Dick Dowling's activities prior to 1857. Most probably, at some time during this period, he received some type of formal or informal education.

[4]Tolbert **Dick Dowling at Sabine Pass,** pp. 21-24; Simpson, **Battles of Texas,** pp. 137-138. See also the Houston **Telegraph** for December 30, 1857 and October 23, 1860.

[5]Houston **Telegraph,** February 8, 1860.

[6]Tolbert, **Dick Dowling at Sabine Pass,** pp. 24-25; Simpson, **Battles of Texas,** pp. 138-139.

[7]Sackett, **Dick Dowling,** pp. 6-15. Frances Sackett cites several records of St. Vincent de Paul's Church in Houston, Texas which pertain to the marriage of Richard William Dowling and Elizabeth Anne Odlum. She also quotes records that refer to the births and deaths of the Dowling children.

[8]Simpson, **Battles of Texas,** p. 139; Tolbert, **Dick Dowling at Sabine Pass,** pp. 25-26; Marcus J. Wright, comp., **Texas in the War 1861-1865,** ed. by Colonel Harold B. Simpson (Hillsboro, Texas: The Hill Junior College Press, 1965), pp. 48, 131.

[9]Ernest Jones, **Port Arthur News,** August 26, 1963. This is one in a series of articles.

[10]Margaret L. Watson, quoted in Tolbert, **Dick Dowling at Sabine Pass,** p. 27.

[11]John Salmon Ford, **Rip Ford's Texas,** ed. by Stephen B. Oates (Austin, Texas: University of Texas Press, 1963), pp. 318-330; Colonel Earl Van Dorn to Colonel John S. Ford, May 27, 1861, **The War of the Rebellion: A Compilation of the Official Records of the Union and Confederate Armies** (128 vols.; Washington, D.C.: Government Printing Office, 1880-1901), Series I, Vol. I, pp. 577-578. Cited hereafter as **Official Records, Armies.**

[12]Houston **Telegraph,** quoted in Tolbert, **Dick Dowling at Sabine Pass,** p. 30. The Guards may have been discriminated against because they were Irish Catholics.

[13]Simpson, **Battles of Texas,** pp. 140-141; Tolbert, **Dick Dowling at Sabine Pass,** pp. 30-32.

[14]Simpson, **Battles of Texas,** p. 141.

[15]Wright, comp., **Texas in the War 1861-1865,** p. 131; **Sackett, Dick Dowling,** p. 16.

[16]Alwyn Barr, "Texas Coastal Defense, 1861-1865," **The Southwestern Historical Quarterly,** LXV (July, 1961), pp. 5, 10. This article contains an excellent account of activities on the Texas coast between 1861 and 1865. See also Simpson, **Battles of Texas,** pp. 140-141.

[17]Commander W. B. Renshaw to Admiral Farragut, October 8, 1862, **Official Records of the Union and Confederate Navies in the War of the Rebellion** (31 vols.; Washington, D.C.: Government Printing Office, 1894-1927), Series I, Vol. XIX, pp. 254-260. Cited hereafter as **Official Records, Navies.** Report of Colonel Joseph J. Cook, October 9, 1862. **Official Records, Armies,** Series I, Vol. XV, pp. 151-153.

[18]Report of General J. Bankhead Magruder, February 26, 1863, **ibid.,** Series I, Vol. XV, pp. 211-220.

[19]Tolbert, **Dick Dowling at Sabine Pass,** pp. 35-48; Simpson, **Battles of Texas,** pp. 142-144.

[20]Houston **Telegraph,** quoted in Tolbert, **Dick Dowling at Sabine Pass,** p. 46.

[21]Detailed Report of Major Oscar M. Watkins, January 23, 1863, **Official Records, Navies,** Series I, Vol. XIX, pp. 564-566.

[22]"The Naval Fight off Sabine," Special by Junius to the Houston **Telegraph,** January 25 [21], 1863, **ibid.,** Series I, Vol. XIX, p. 570.

[23]Reports of Major Oscar M. Watkins, January 21, 1863, January 23, 1863, March 14, 1863, **ibid.,** Series I, Vol. XIX, pp. 564-570; Report of acting Master John Dillingham, U.S. Navy, April 1, 1863, **ibid.,** Series I, Vol. XIX pp. 556-558; Detailed Report of Acting Assistant Surgeon J. W. Sherfy, U.S. Navy, **ibid.,** Series I, Vol. XIX, pp. 558-563; "The Naval Fight of Sabine," Special by Junius to the Houston **Telegraph,** January 25 [21], 1863, **ibid.,** Series I, Vol. XIX, pp. 570-573. See also the Houston **Telegraph.**

[24]Detailed Report of Major Oscar M. Watkins, January 23, 1863, **ibid.,** Series I, Vol. XIX, pp. 565-566.

[25]"The Naval Fight off Sabine," Special by Junius to the Houston **Telegraph,** January 25 [21], 1863, **ibid.,** Series I, Vol. XIX, pp. 570-571.

[26]Fort Griffin (sometimes referred to as Fort Grigsby, an earlier fortress) was built in 1863 after information was obtained concerning an impending Federal attack in East Texas. It was named for Colonel W. H. Griffin, commander of troops at Sabine City during a portion of the war. It was approximately one hundred yards wide and was located about four thousand yards from the mouth of Sabine Pass near Fort Sabine, a garrison which had been abandoned in 1862. It lay opposite the upper end of a wide oyster reef which separated the Sabine River into the Texas and Louisiana channels. Construction of Fort Griffin was largely the responsibility of Colonel Valery Sulakowski, chief of Magruder's engineers, Major Getulius Kellersberger, and Lieutenant Nicholas Smith. The Guards assisted this project. The fort was adjacent to the Texas channel and about one thousand yards from the upper end of the Louisiana channel.

[27]E. P. Alsbury, quoted in John Thomas Scharf, **History of the Confederate States Navy: From Its Organization to the Surrender of Its Last Vessel** (New York: Rogers and Sherwood, 1887), pp. 524-525. Cited hereafter as **Confederate Navy.**

[28]Getulius Kellersberger, **Memoirs of an Engineer in the Confederate Army in Texas,** trans. by Helen S. Sundstrom (Austin, Texas: Privately Published, University of Texas Library, 1957), pp. 29-30; P. S. Hagy, "Military Operations of the Lower Trans-Mississippi Deparmtent, 1863-64," **Confederate Veteran,** XXIV (December, 1916), p. 545. Scharf, **Confederate Navy,** pp. 524-526.

[29]Tolbert, **Dick Dowling at Sabine Pass,** pp. 81-91.

[30]Report of Lieutenant R. W. Dowling, September 9, 1863, **Official Records, Armies,** Series I, Vol. XXVI, Part I, p. 311.

[31]Tolbert, **Dick Dowling at Sabine Pass,** p. 86; Francis R. Lubbock, **Six Decades in Texas; or, Memoirs of Francis Richard Lubbock, Governor of Texas in War Time, 1861-1863,** ed. by C. W. Raines (Austin, Texas: B. C. Jones and Co., 1900), p. 507. Kellersberger, **Memoirs of an Engineer in the Confederate Army in Texas,** pp. 30-31.

[32]Simpson, **Battles of Texas,** p. 147.

[33]Tolbert, **Dick Dowling at Sabine Pass,** pp. 85-88. This contains a good description of Sabine Pass and Sabine City.

[34]General H. W. Halleck to General N. P. Banks, August 6, 1863, **Official Records, Armies,** Series I, Vol. XXVI, Part I, p. 672.

[35]Major General N. P. Banks to Major General William B. Franklin, August 31, 1863, **ibid.,** Series I, Vol. XXVI, Part I, pp. 287-288; Itinerary of First Division, Nineteenth Army Corps, for 1863, **ibid.,** Series I, Vol. XXVI, Part I, p. 299.

[36]Report of Major General Nathaniel P. Banks, September 5, 1863, **ibid.,** Series I, Vol. XXVI, Part I, p. 286.

[37]Commodore H. H. Bell to Secretary of the Navy, Gideon Welles, September 4, 1863, **Official Records, Navies,** Series I, Vol. XX, pp. 515-516; Itinerary of First Division, Nineteenth Army Corps, for 1863, **Official Records, Armies,** Series I, Vol. XXVI, Part I, p. 299.

[38]For an account of activities in New Orleans before the expedition sailed, see Clement A. Evans, ed., **Confederate Military History** (Atlanta, Georgia: Confederate Publishing Company, 1899), Vol. XI, p. 106.

[39]Second Report of Acting Volunteer Lieutenant Frederick Crocker, April 21, 1865, **Official Records, Navies,** Series I, Vol. XX, pp. 544-548.

[40]Report of General Franklin, September 11, 1863, **Official Records, Armies,** Series I, Vol. XXVI, Part I, p. 295.

[41]Report of Lieutenant R. W. Dowling, September 9, 1863, **ibid.,** Series I, Vol. XXVI, Part I, p. 311; Order of Major General Magruder to Colonel V. Sulakowski to fortify Sabine Pass, September 4, 1863, **Official Records, Navies,** Series I, Vol. XX, p. 555; John A. Drummond, "The Battle of Sabine Pass," **Confederate Veteran,** XXV (Aug. 1917), p. 364. This is an account written by a Confederate participant in the battle. See also the **Dallas Morning News,** April 23, 1902, for a study written from articles by Southern war correspondent W. P. Doran.

[42]Report of Captain F. H. Odlum, September 9, 1863, **Official Records, Armies,** Series I, Vol. XXVI, Part I, pp. 309-310; Report of Lieutenant R. W. Dowling, September 9, 1863, **ibid.,** Series I, Vol. XXVI, Part I, p. 311. Discrepancies have occurred concerning the number of Davis Guards at Fort Griffin during the Battle of Sabine Pass. Dowling's report maintains that forty-seven men were present. **Ibid.,** p. 312.

[43]Drummond, **Confederate Veteran,** Vol. XXV (August, 1917), p. 364. See also Letter from Colonel Leon Smith to Brigadier General Luckett, September 8, 1863, **Official Records, Navies,** Series I, Vol. XX, p. 555.

[44]Report of Lieutenant R. W. Dowling, September 9, 1863, **Official Records, Armies,** Series I, Vol. XXVI, Part I, p. 311; Report of Colonel Leon Smith, September 8, 1863, **ibid.,** Series I, Vol. XXVI, Part I, pp. 307-308; Tolbert, **Dick Dowling at Sabine Pass,** pp. 95-119; Simpson, **Battles of Texas,** pp. 148-166. These last two entries refer to the entire battle. James B. Simpson, "The Battle of Sabine Pass," **Frontier Times,** XXI (August, 1944), p. 419; Houston **Tri-Weekly Telegraph,** Sept. 16, 1863. The reinforcements arrived after the battle.

[45]Report of Lieutenant R. W. Dowling, September 9, 1863, **Official Records, Armies,** Series I, Vol. XXVI, Part I, pp. 311-312; Report of Captain F. H. Odlum, September 9, 1863, **ibid.,** Series I, Vol. XXVI, Part I, pp. 309-310.

[46]Report of Acting Master Amos Johnson, March 4, 1865, **Official Records, Navies,** Series I, Vol. XX, p. 553.

[47]Report of General Franklin, September 11, 1863, **Official Records, Armies,** Series I, Vol. XXVI, Part I, p. 296; Report of Lieutenant R. W. Dowling, September 9, 1863, **ibid.,** Series I, Vol. XXVI, Part I, p. 311.

[48]Report of Acting Lieutenant Frederick Crocker, September 12, 1863, **ibid.,** Series I, Vol. XXVI, Part I, pp. 301-302; Report of Acting Master Amos Johnson, March 4, 1865, **Official Records, Navies,** Series I, Vol. XX, p. 553.

[49]Report of Captain F. H. Odlum, September 9, 1863, **Official Records, Armies,** Series I, Vol. XXVI, Part I, p. 310; Houston **Tri-Weekly Telegraph,** September 16, 1863; Scharf, **Confederate Navy,** pp. 523-526.

[50]Barr, **Texas Military History,** Vol. II, p. 21.

[51]Report of Lieutenant R. W. Dowling, September 9, 1863, **Official Records, Armies,** Series I, Vol. XXVI, Part I, pp. 311-312; Report of Acting Lieutenant Frederick Crocker, September 12, 1863, **ibid.,** Series I, Vol. XXVI, Part I, p. 302; Scharf, **Confederate Navy,** p. 526; Drummond, **Con-**

federate **Veteran,** Vol. XXV (August, 1917), p. 365; Houston **Tri-Weekly Telegraph,** September 16, 1863.

[52]Report of General Franklin, September 11, 1863, **Official Records, Armies,** Series I, Vol. XXVI, Part I, p. 297; Report of Acting Lieutenant Crocker, September 12, 1863, **ibid.,** Series I, Vol. XXVI, Part I, p. 302.

[53]Report of Colonel Leon Smith, September 8, 1863, **ibid.,** Series I, Vol. XXVI, Part I, p.. 309.

[54]Report of Lieutenant R. W. Dowling, September 9, 1863, **ibid.,** Series I, I, Vol. XXVI, Part I, pp. 311-312.

[55]**Ibid.,** p. 312.

[56]Scharf, **Confederate Navy,** p. 525.

[57]Report of Colonel Leon Smith, September 8, 1863, **Official Records, Armies,** Series I, Vol. XXVI, Part I, pp. 308-309; Report of Captain F. H. Odlum, September 9, 1863, **ibid.,** Series I, Vol. XXVI, Part I, p. 310.

[58]Federal Losses Report of Acting Lieutenant Frederick Crocker, November 9, 1863, **Official Records, Navies,** Series I, Vol. XX, pp. 542-543; Alfred T. Mahan, **The Navy in the Civil War: The Gulf and Inland Waters** (Subscription edition; New York: Charles Scribner's Sons, 1885), Vol. III, pp. 186-187.

[59]Report of General J. B. Magruder, September 27, 1863, **Official Records, Armies,** Series I, Vol. XXVI, Part I, p. 305.

[60]**Ibid.**

[61]Joint Resolution of thanks to Captain Odlum, Lieutenant Dowling, and the men under their command, February 8, 1864, **Official Records,** Armies, Series I, Vol. XXVI, Part I, p. 312.

[62]Jefferson Davis, **The Rise and Fall of the Confederate Government** (New York: D. Appleton and Co., 1881), Vol. II, p. 239.

[63]See various articles in the Houston **Telegraph,** the Houston **Tri-Weekly Telegraph,** the Dallas **Herald,** and the Galveston **News** for September and October, 1863.

[64]Lester N. Fitzhugh, "Saluria, Fort Esperanza, and Military Operations on the Texas Coast, 1861-1864," **The Southwestern Historical Quarterly,** LXI (July, 1957) pp. 66-100.

[65]Louis J. Wortham, **A History of Texas: From Wilderness to Commonwealth** (Fort Worth, Texas: Wortham-Molyneaux Company, 1924), Vol. IV, p. 359.

[66]Tolbert, **Dick Dowling at Sabine Pass,** pp. 136-139; Simpson, **Battles of Texas,** p. 168; Sackett, **Dick Dowling,** p. 65; Dispatch from the Adjutant General's Office to Mrs. R. F. Pray, May 25, 1932, in Pray, **Dick Dowling's Battle,** pp. 133-134. See also the Houston **Telegraph** for this period.

[67]Houston **Telegraph,** June 26, 1865.

[68]Sackett, **Dick Dowling,** pp. 65-66.

[69]This property included: Block 239 in the City of Houston; lots six, seven, and twelve in block 238; a brick building on lot five in block 33; and six acres of land on the south side of Buffalo Bayou within Houston's city limits. **Pray, Dick Dowling's Battle,** p. 137.

[70]C. A. Warner, "Texas and the Oil Industry," **The Southwestern Historical Quarterly,** L (July, 1946), p. 6; see also a statement from Flake's **Daily Galveston Bulletin,** quoted in Tolbert, **Dick Dowling at Sabine Pass,** pp. 140-141.

[71]Simpson, **Battles of Texas,** p. 169; Tolbert, **Dick Dowling at Sabine Pass,** p. 140.

[72]Funeral notice for Richard W. Dowling, dated September 23, 1867, Probate Records, in County Clerk's Office, Houston, Texas; Tolbert, **Dick Dowling at Sabine Pass,** p. 142; Simpson, **Battles of Texas,** p. 169; Pray, **Dick Dowling's Battle,** pp. 137-138; Sackett, **Dick Dowling,** pp. 67-69.

[73]See the obituary notice in the Houston **Telegraph,** September 25, 1867, quoted in Tolbert, **Dick Dowling at Sabine Pass,** p. 143.

[74]Galveston **News,** September 26, 1867.

[75]Dick Dowling is buried in St. Vincent's Cemetery, Houston, Texas. A statue of Dowling now stands in Houston's Hermann Park; another statue, made by Herring Coe for the Texas Centennial Commission in 1936, stands at the Dick Dowling State Park at Sabine Pass, Texas. The inscription on it reads as follows: "In Memory of Lt. Richard W. Dowling And His Men: Texas Remembers The Faithfulness And Valor Of Her Sons And Commends Their Heroic Example To Future Generations." In addition, the statue lists the names of the Davis Guards who fought at Sabine Pass.

John Bell Hood

by

Harold B. Simpson

July the fifth, eighteen fifty-seven, dawned dry, hot, and cloudless at Fort Mason, Texas, duty station for Companies F and G of the elite U. S. 2nd Cavalry Regiment.[1] As the sun nudged over the rolling hills, a column of troopers filed from the fort, riding west on a routine search for savages. Leading the scouting party was John Bell Hood, a young, tawny-bearded lieutenant, just four years out of West Point and an officer destined to reach the coveted rank of full general in the Confederate Army. With an Indian guide and twenty-four horse soldiers carrying supplies for thirty days jogging along behind him, Lieutenant Hood pressed westward beyond the headwaters of the Llano.[2]

Ten days out the detachment struck a fresh Indian trail and veered southward in pursuit of the war party. With parched throats and jaded horses, the sweaty troopers and their tenacious commander relentlessly pursued their elusive quarry toward the Mexican border. Brought to bay on the afternoon of July 20 near the headwaters of the Devil's River, the hostiles—a mixed force of some one hundred Lipan-Apaches and Comanches—turned with vengeance on their pursuers.

Lieutenant Hood, with remarkable coolness and complete disregard for his own personal safety, led his men into the midst of the howling horde. Time and again he rallied his troopers to stem the rushes of the half-naked, painted savages that swarmed in and around his small detachment. Sustaining a loss of nineteen warriors killed and probably as many or more wounded, the surviving savages, splitting into small groups to frustrate pursuit, fled the field. Included among the Indian dead were two minor chiefs. Hood, himself, had accounted for a couple of the marauders early in the fight. Successive blasts from his double-barreled shotgun had defaced two warriors attempting to pull him from the saddle. The troopers could count six casualties of their own, one being their aggressive commander

Lieutenant Hood, who had suffered a painful wound late in the battle when a Comanche arrow pinned his hand to the reins.[3]

Its mission accomplished, the cavalry detachment limped back to Fort Mason on August 8. Hood and his men had been absent almost five weeks, had ridden five hundred gruelling miles through desolate, dry country, and had fought a major Indian engagement.[4]

The remarkable feat of Lieutenant Hood and his men did not go unnoticed. Hood's report of the battle, which was forwarded through channels to Secretary of War John B. Floyd, was endorsed by both Major General David E. Twiggs (commander of the Department of Texas) and Lieutenant General Winfield Scott (commanding general of the United States Army). Both Scott and Twiggs regarded Hood's Devil's River fight as a "most gallant one."[5] Thus, while most of the Confederacy's ranking generals received their initiation to battle in the Mexican War, Hood had won his spurs against the Apaches and Comanches on the Texas frontier.

John Bell Hood's heritage had its taproot in Virginia and its surface roots in Kentucky. He was born on June 29, 1831, at Owingsville in Bath County, Kentucky. His forebears were hardy Virginia frontiersmen who had fought against both the Redcoats and the Redskins. Two of his grandfathers, Luke Hood and Richard Callaway, were well-known Indian fighters. The former fought against Little Turtle and his Miamis in the Ohio Territory under Generals Josiah Harmar and Mad Anthony Wayne, and the latter fought alongside Daniel Boone in the "dark and bloody hunting grounds" of early Kentucky.[6]

Although Luke Hood had three sons, not one of them followed a military career or appeared to have inherited the adventurous spirit of his father. By coincidence, all three of Fighting Luke's boys became frontier physicians. It would be his grandson, John Bell Hood, who would carry on the Indian fighting tradition, but on a frontier far removed from the Ohio Valley.

John Bell Hood was the youngest of four children born to Dr. John W. Hood and Theodosia French. When John B. was a few years old, his family moved to Montgomery County, Kentucky, settling near Mt. Sterling. Here Dr. Hood established a small medical school, acquired considerable farm land (and a few slaves), and engaged in a lucrative frontier practice.[7] Thus the future Confederate general was brought up in good circumstances and early in life acquired a taste for good living that never deserted him.

Hood was physically attractive. This, plus the fact that his family had money, tended to make him a sort of frontier Lochinvar. He stood six feet, two inches in height and had broad shoulders, a small waist, light blue eyes, and blondish auburn hair.[8] These physical characteristics, combined with a shy, deferential manner, made him most attractive to the opposite sex. The ladies found him fascinating, and he apparently returned the compliment, considering the number of women that were linked with him romantically during his long bachelorhood. Hood was not adverse to drinking, smoking, and gambling (all in moderation); and, while his mother reared brothers William and James and sister Olivia as good Baptists, John was a non-conformist.[9] His non-conformity ended, however, when he was baptized into the Episcopalian faith by the "Fighting Bishop," General Leonidas Polk, during the Atlanta campaign in June, 1864.

Although Dr. Hood desired that his youngest son follow in his footsteps, even offering him the benefits of a European medical school education, Young John preferred the excitement and romance of a military career.[10] All of his life he had heard stories about the exploits of his grandfathers in the Revolutionary War and in fighting Indians along the frontier. This, coupled with the stories of the great American victories during the recently concluded Mexican War, fired young Hood's imagination. And, despite his father's objection, he determined to be a soldier. Fortunately for Hood, his mother's uncle, Judge Richard French, was the United States Congressman from the 9th District of Kentucky.[11] Thus, an appointment to the United States Military Academy at West Point was relatively easy to secure. Hood applied and was accepted. The appointment was made on January 27, 1849, to be effective the following July 1, the reporting date for the Class of 1853. Dr. Hood, still not reconciled to the fact that his youngest boy preferred the saber to the scalpel, was reported to have said as his son made ready to depart for West Point, "If you can't behave, don't come home. Go to the nearest gatepost and butt your brains out."[12]

Cadet John B. Hood's record at the Military Academy was not impressive, but certainly not bad enough to cause him to "butt his brains out." He ranked number forty-four out of fifty-two graduates in the Class of 1853,[13] a class that was presented its diplomas by Lieutenant-Colonel Robert E. Lee, Superintendent of the Military Academy. The cadet from Kentucky made his best grades in drawing and mathematics, but he stood close to the bottom of his class in English, French, and Ethics.[14] His deportment became progressively worse as time passed; he drew 18 demerits his first year, 66 his second, 94 his third, and a resounding 196 demerits his last year at the Academy.[15] As great as the number of demerits may seem, Cadet Hood's total of 374 was about average for a West Point graduate of the day.[16]

Upon his graduation from the United States Military Academy, Hood was promoted to brevet second lieutenant and assigned to the 4th U. S. Infantry Regiment stationed on the West Coast. Lieutenant Hood served with the 4th Infantry only about a year and a half, but during that time he, no doubt, made the acquaintance of the regimental quartermaster, a rather small, carelessly dressed captain by the name of Ulysses S. Grant.

On March 3, 1855, infantry officer Hood was assigned to the famous 2nd U. S. Cavalry, a new mounted regiment authorized by Congress to protect the Indian-ravaged frontier of Texas.[17] The officers of the 2nd Cavalry were hand picked by Secretary of War Jefferson Davis. The non-commissioned officers were selected by the officers of the regiment who were permitted to request personnel from the existing mounted regiments, the 1st and 2nd Dragoons and the Mounted Rifles. The horses for the 2nd Cavalry were purchased by a special procurement team operating in Ohio, Indiana, and Kentucky. Each company of the regiment was to ride horses of one color. The 2nd Cavalry was armed with the latest type weapons and carried the best accoutrements.[18] Because of Jeff Davis' great interest in the regiment, it was sometimes known as "Jeff Davis' Own."

No regiment has spawned so many general officers over so short a span of time as has the original 2nd U. S. Cavalry. It was studded with future stars. Of approximately forty officers assigned to the regiment during its short life,[19] fifteen were promoted to general officer rank. Four became full generals in the

Confederate Army: Albert Sidney Johnston, Robert E. Lee, Edmund Kirby Smith, and John Bell Hood. Thus, this one regiment contributed half of the full generals in the Confederate service. Seven other officers in the regiment became Confederate lieutenant generals, major generals, or brigadier generals, and four were promoted to general rank in the Federal service. The remaining officers in the regiment who fought in the Civil War were promoted to high field grade rank, the majority of them to full colonel.[20]

Hood joined the 2nd Cavalry at Jefferson Barracks, Missouri, where it was being formed in the fall of 1855.[21] After an uneventful ride from Missouri, the 2nd Cavalry reached Texas in mid-December, 1855. In crossing the Red River with his company, Company G, on December 15,[22] John Bell Hood first became associated with the Lone Star State—an association that would grow closer with the years and would bring glory to both himself and his adopted state.

While in Texas, Hood served at various military posts. He was stationed at Fort Mason (Mason County) for over two years, serving with Company G there until he was promoted to first lieutenant on August 18, 1858.[23] Soon after his promotion he was transferred to Company K with duty station at Camp Cooper (Throckmorton County). Late in the same year (1858), Company K was transferred to Camp Colorado on Jim Ned Creek in present-day Coleman County. In mid-1859, a detachment from Company K, commanded by Lieutenant Hood, re-established Camp Wood (Real County). Hood remained in command of Camp Wood (except for a leave of absence back East during November and December, 1860)[24] until Texas secessionists forced its abandonment on March 15, 1861.[25]

The only serious battle in which Hood participated while serving with the 2nd Cavalry on the frontier was the previously mentioned Devil's River fight. However, he did have several brushes with the Indians while conducting scouting expeditions into West and Southwest Texas.

Service in Texas enabled the young lieutenant to renew his acquaintance with Robert E. Lee, who commanded the 2nd Cavalry at various times during its tenure in the Lone Star State. Hood and Lee traveled together several times while they were stationed on the frontier, and the two became well acquainted with each other. Hood idolized Lee, and the great Virginian regarded his former cadet with much affection.

Hood returned to Camp Wood early in 1861,[26] and although technically still on leave, accompanied his regiment in mid-March to Indianola, where it awaited transportation to the North. After bidding a "reluctant farewell" to his comrades, Hood journeyed to Kentucky to determine first-hand the secession sentiment in his native state. Disappointed at Kentucky's reluctance to leave the Union, in late April, 1861, Hood went to Montgomery, Alabama, where the provisional Confederate government was sitting, and offered his services to the Confederacy.[27] Lieutenant Hood had resigned his commission in the United States Army on April 16, 1861,[28] presumably while he was still in Kentucky.

When tendering his service to the Southern government, the cavalry lieutenant listed himself as a Texan. Although some historians are reluctant to consider the Confederate general a Texan, Hood was explicit in proclaiming his affiliation to the Lone Star State. On page 16 of his memoirs he wrote:

> During my long service in Texas I had had the occasion to visit almost every portion of that extensive and beautiful territory, and was able to form an idea of the future prosperity of that state. So deeply impressed had I become with its vast and undeveloped resources that I had, just prior to the war, determined to resign and make it my home for life. Therefore when Kentucky failed to act, I entered the Confederate service from the State of Texas, which thence forth became my adopted land.

General Hood's Civil War career falls into two distinct periods; the period when he was assigned to the Army of Northern Virginia during the years 1861 through 1863 and the period that he served with the Army of Tennessee during 1864 and the first few days of 1865. During the years that Hood fought under Lee in Virginia he was eminently successful, a soldier of great promise, a battlefield leader without a peer, and the toast of Richmond society. The other side of the coin—his service with the Army of Tennessee—was as disappointing as his service in the East was promising. With the Western Army in 1864 Hood never fought a successful battle; bad luck, fatigue, and poor judgment combined to tarnish his glittering reputation. In the end, disappointed and despondent, bitter and frustrated, he would ask to be relieved as commander of the Army of Tennessee.[29]

Hood had a meteoric rise in the Confederate Army. While most of the officers who were destined to gain high rank in the Confederacy commenced their Civil War careers as colonels or brigadier-generals, Hood started close to the bottom as a first lieutenant. He was mustered into the Southern Army at Montgomery, Alabama at this rank in late April, 1861.[30] In May, Hood was ordered to Richmond, to report to General Robert E. Lee, commander of the military forces of Virginia, for further orders. Apparently the Kentuckian-turned-Texan was promoted to captain enroute from Montgomery to Richmond, for when Lee assigned him to Colonel "Prince John" B. Magruder's command on May 27, 1861, he was assigned as a captain.[31] Hood did yoeman work as Magruder's chief of cavalry and for his aggressiveness was promoted to major and then to lieutenant-colonel.[32]

In late September, 1861, Lieutenant-Colonel Hood was assigned as commander of the 4th Texas Infantry Regiment—one of two Texas regiments that had recently arrived from the Lone Star State. Concurrent with Hood's assignment to the 4th Texas Infantry was his promotion to full colonel. His commission to this rank was dated September 30, 1861.[33] The assignment to the Texas regiment was probably the "big break" of John Bell Hood's Civil War career.

When General Louis T. Wigfall resigned as commander of the Texas Brigade on February 20, 1862,[34] he was succeeded in command by Colonel Hood. Wigfall, a hard-drinking South Carolinian who had migrated to Texas in 1846, had organized the 1st Texas Infantry Regiment in Virginia in the early summer of 1861.[35] After the 4th and 5th Texas Infantry Regiments arrived from Texas in late September, 1861,[36] they were consolidated with Wigfall's 1st Texas Infantry on October 22[37] to form the famous Texas Brigade with Wigfall in command as a brigadier-general. The 18th Georgia Infantry was added to the three Texas regiments during the winter of 1861-62[38] to bring the brigade up to full strength. This was the organization that Hood officially assumed command of on March 12, 1862, after being promoted to brigadier-general on March 3.[39]

By showing great battlefield leadership in command of the Texas Brigade at Eltham's Landing (May 7, 1862) and Gaines' Mill (June 27, 1862) and in command of a demi-division of two brigades at Second Manassas (August 29-30, 1862) and Antietam (September 17, 1862), John Bell Hood earned his second star. Both Generals Stonewall Jackson and James "Pete" Longstreet praised Hood's conduct during the bloody summer battles of 1862. Jackson, who was not prone to praising his subordinates, wrote to Adjutant-General Samuel Cooper shortly after Antietam that he regarded Hood "as one of the most promising officers of the army" and urged his promotion. Longstreet's praise was just as profuse. Lee, well aware of Hood's brilliant service, recommended to President Davis on October 27, 1862, that John Bell Hood be promoted to major-general.[40] Hood received his second star on November 6, 1862,[41] and his small division was increased to four brigades.[42] Hood was but thirty-one at the time of his promotion; only Jeb Stuart of the Confederate major-generals was younger than the tall Texan.

Evaluating Hood at this stage of his career, Douglas Southall Freeman wrote: "There was something about him—some of the effulgence of the true captain of men. Anyone, who had followed the operations of the Army after Gaines' Mill would have said that of all the officers under Longstreet, the most likely to be a great soldier was Hood."[43]

Major-General Hood led his division at Fredericksburg (December 13, 1862), at the Siege of Suffolk (April, 1863), and at the greatest battle of the war—Gettysburg. Gettysburg, fought the first three days of July in 1863, has been called the turning point of the war and the high tide of the Confederacy. Although military historians will argue over the "high tide" and the "turning point" concept, Gettysburg has been regarded as the greatest battle ever fought in the Western Hemisphere. The divisions of Hood and Lafayette McLaws, of Longstreet's Corps, spearheaded the Confederate attack on the Federal left during the crucial second day of battle. Hood, unfortunately, was painfully wounded early in the battle; consequently, he had very little influence on its outcome—a Confederate defeat.

In early September, 1863, Longstreet's Corps (minus Pickett's Division)[44] was sent to northern Georgia to bolster the Army of Tennessee under General Braxton Bragg. At bloody Chickamauga, fought in the tangled brush along the Georgia-Tennessee border on September 18-20, General Hood, still somewhat incapacitated from his Gettysburg wound, temporarily commanded Longstreet's Corps.[45] During the last day of this sanguinary engagement, Hood was dangerously wounded and remained incapacitated for almost four months. During his long period of convalescence in Richmond, the maimed hero was lionized and feted and in time became most friendly with the Confederate President, whom he accompanied on canters about the capital.

In their official reports both Braxton Bragg and James Longstreet had praised the conduct of Hood at Chickamauga. Bragg referred to him as "the model soldier and inspiring leader,"[46] and Longstreet mentioned him "as distinguished for conduct and ability" during the engagement.[47] Later, Longstreet, on September 24, wrote to Adjutant-General Samuel Cooper requesting that Hood be promoted to lieutenant-general "for distinguished conduct and ability in the battle of the 20th instant." The commander of Lee's 1st Corps added: "General Hood handled his troops with the coolness and ability that I have rarely known by any officer on the field."[48] However, neither President Davis nor the Confederate Congress was to take action on Longstreet's recommendation until the following year. Hood's promotion was not confirmed until February 4, 1864, but his date of rank went back to September 20, 1863—the day of his wound at Chickamauga,[49]

His wound healed, Lieutenant-General Hood reported to General Joseph E. Johnston, commander of the Army of Tennessee, on February 4, 1864,[50] and was assigned a corps consisting of the divisions of T. C. Hindman, C. L. Stevenson, and A. P. Stewart.[51] Hood commanded his corps during the Confederate retreat from Dalton to Atlanta in the spring of 1864. Johnston's Fabian policy so alarmed President Davis that he sent his military adviser, General Braxton Bragg, to the Atlanta front to determine the situation. Finally convinced that Johnston would not fight to hold Atlanta, Davis replaced him with the aggressive Hood on July 17, 1864.[52] At the same time that Hood succeeded Johnston as commander of the Army of Tennessee he was promoted to the temporary rank of full general in the Provisional Army of the Confederate States.[53] John Bell Hood was the eighth and last full general to be appointed in the Confederate Army. At the age of thirty-four he was also the youngest of the Confederate four-star generals. Hood had risen in rank from first lieutenant to full general in a little over three years. No other officer in the Civil War could boast such rapid promotion.

Jefferson Davis gave Hood the Atlanta command because he wanted the Confederate Army to take the offensive. The President did not have long to wait. The fighting Texan struck savagely at Sherman's forces pressing on the Georgia city. In quick succession he fought the battles of Peachtree Creek (July 20), Atlanta (July 22), and Ezra Church (July 28). Repulsed in these three actions, Hood withdrew his shattered army into the inner defenses of Atlanta. On September 1, 1864, with all rail lines into Atlanta cut, he abandoned the city to the Federals.

The Tennessee Campaign of November and December, 1864, marked Hood's last fighting during the war. It proved to be one of the most disastrous Confederate campaigns of the entire conflict. Following a segment of Sherman's Army north into Tennessee (while the main Federal Army under Sherman was marching to Savannah), Hood was stopped at Franklin (November 30) by West Point classmate John Schofield in one of the bitterest fought battles of the war. Still determined to win a victory regardless of the cost, Hood pursued the Federals to Nashville and entrenched his army on the frozen hills south of the Tennesse capital. The barefoot, ragged, half-starved Army of Tennessee was no match for the Federals when they struck the Southern lines on Decembr 15 and 16, 1864. The result was a complete rout of Hood's forces, the first and only time during the war that a major Confederate army fled the field. As the remnant of the once-powerful Army of Tennessee staggered south toward Tupelo, Mississippi—its rendezvous point—some wag composed the following parody of the popular "Yellow Rose of Texas" to emphasize the army's forlorn condition.

And now I'm going southward,
For my heart is full of woe,
I'm going back to Georgia,
To find my Uncle Joe,
You may talk about your dearest maid
And sing of Rosalie,
But the gallant Hood of Texas
Played hell in Tennessee.[54]

Following the disastrous Tennessee Campaign, Hood, bitter and disillusioned, asked to be relieved from the command of the Army of Tennessee. His request was granted, and the crippled commander bade farewell to his army on January 23, 1865, at Tupelo, Mississippi.[55] Returning to Richmond, Hood received the blessings of Jefferson Davis to go to Texas for the purpose of raising an army to help the Confederate cause in Virginia. As Hood was progressing on this mission, the Confederacy collapsed—he surrendered to Major General John W. Davidson at Natchez, Mississippi, on May 31, 1865.[56] Thus ended the military career of one of the most amazing soldiers to ride across the pages of American history.

John Bell Hood had started his career in the Army of the Confederacy, appropriately enough, as an outpost commander of cavalry for Colonel (later General) Magruder. He performed well as Magruder's cavalry commander and saw much outpost and scouting action in the area between Yorktown and Fort Monroe in the late spring and summer of 1861.[57] From this initial assignment Hood was promoted to regimental command—the 4th Texas Infantry. He moved on to brigade command after six months and then on to division command in five months. Hood commanded his own division for a little over a year (August, 1862-September, 1863), but during this period he temporarily commanded a corps at Chickamauga. The Texan served as a *bona fide* corps commander for four months and then finally, in mid-1864, reached the pinnacle of his career, a full general in command of one of the two major Confederate field armies—the Army of Tennessee.[58]

General Hood had three narrow escapes from death during the war. Considering the fact that he personally led his men into battle on many occasions and occupied a position just behind the front lines on other instances, it is surprising that he was not brushed by the grim reaper more often. Hood's first scrape with death came early in the war, as a matter of fact, at the first battle in which he commanded the Texas Brigade, Eltham's Landing (May 7, 1862). As the Brigade was feeling its way forward (with Hood in the lead) toward the Federals advancing from their landing on the Pamunkey River, it was suddenly confronted by a strong body of the enemy's skirmishers. One of the Federals, a corporal, who was only a few paces from Hood, leveled his Springfield point blank at the Confederate commander. However, before he could get a shot away, he fell victim to the accurate fire of Private John Deal, Company A of the 4th Texas. Believing that he was still well within his own picket lines, Hood had ordered the guns not to be loaded. Deal, fortunately, had disobeyed this order and in doing so had saved the life of the young general.[59] There is no record of Private Deal being punished for disobeying Hood's order.

General Hood's next close call came at Gettysburg, where he suffered a painful wound in his left arm. The general was leading his division across the Emmitsburg Road toward the Peach Orchard when he was struck by a shell fragment that ranged through his hand, forearm, elbow, and biceps.[60] The wound occurred early in the battle and the command of Hood's Division devolved upon Evander Law.[61] Perhaps it was best that the Texan did not witness the costly and futile attempts of his division to drive the Federals from their impregnable position on Little Round Top. As the Confederate Army retreated from the bloody field of Gettysburg, Hood and General Wade Hampton shared the same ambulance. Hampton was so badly wounded that he was unable to sit up; and Hood, because of his wound, could not lie down. In this condition the two generals rode the two hundred miles back to Staunton, Virginia.[62]

Hood's arm was saved by the skill of John T. Darby, Chief Surgeon of his Division,[63] and after a short period of recuperation in the Shenandoah Valley, Hood returned with Dr. Darby to Richmond. Here the wounded hero was idolized by the citizens, particularly the women. He was the hero of the hour and the "matinee idol" of the younger set. Hood caught the eye of at least two young Richmond belles, Sally "Buck" Preston and Louise "Louly" Wigfall, daughter of his old commander. Miss Wigfall, although not quite eighteen, left for posterity a romantic picture of her thirty-three-year-old knight in shining armor:

> A braver man, a purer patriot, a more gallant soldier never breathed than General Hood. . . . He was a man of singular simplicity of character and charm of manner—boyish in his enthusiasm—superbly handsome, with beautiful blue eyes, golden hair and flowing beard—broad shouldered, tall and erect—a noble man of undaunted courage and blameless life.[64]

Sally Preston would be linked romantically with Hood for the duration of the war.[65] While the Texan gave considerable attention to Sally, he had boasted that he was courting four girls at the same time.[66]

At Chickamauga, Hood came closest to being killed. On the second day of the battle (September 20, 1863) he was hit by a minie ball in the upper thigh of the right leg. By coincidence when the general was struck he happened to be riding in front of his old brigade, and as he slipped from the saddle he fell into the arms of his Texans.[67] There was some question of where the fire came from that wounded Hood. Stonewall Jackson had been killed accidentally by firing from his own men; some thought that Hood was also the victim of Confederate fire.[68] Inasmuch as the ball had shattered the bone in Hood's leg, there was no question but that the limb would have to be amputated. Dr. John T. Darby, who had done such a fine repair job on Hood's arm at Gettysburg, had not yet joined the division from Richmond,[69] so the amputation was performed by Dr. T. G. Richardson, Chief Medical Officer of the Army of Tennessee. The leg was taken off just a few inches below the hip and left barely stump enough to accommodate an artificial limb.[70] Learning of their old commander's condition, the members of the Texas Brigade raised almost five thousand dollars to buy him an artificial leg.[71]

Apparently Hood had tremendous recuperative power. The day following the amputation he was carried by litter to a residence in Armuchee Valley (some fifteen miles away). He moved to Atlanta the last of October, and then on to Richmond a few days later. By the middle of January, 1864, he was able to mount his horse and ride. Hood rode strapped in the saddle during the remainder of the war and never required a vehicle for transportation day or night.[72] Under the serious handicaps of a useless left arm and a missing right leg, disabilities that would completely incapacitate most soldiers and cause them to leave the fighting scene, Hood continued to fight in the field until near the end of the war.

While in Richmond recuperating from his second wound, the battle-scarred hero was again the toast of the Confederate capital. Doting matrons, starry-eyed maidens, a thankful Congress, and an appreciative President—all paid homage to the crippled general. Wherever Hood went he was the center of attention as he shuffled along on crutches. A never-ending retinue of admirers, including Jefferson Davis, were at hand to assist and comfort him.[73] Linked romantically with several eligible young women of Richmond, Hood seemed to have eyes for only Sally "Buck" Preston, but she shrugged off his attentions and only half-heartedly agreed to an engagement before Hood left for the Atlanta front in late February, 1864.[74]

No biography of John Bell Hood, regardless of how short, would be complete without at least a short reference to the Texas Brigade, the command with which his name and, to a certain extent, his fame, have been linked. The Texas Brigade, known as Hood's Texas Brigade after he took command of the organization in March, 1862, was composed basically of three Texas infantry regiments—the 1st, 4th, and 5th. The 18th Georgia Infantry and the eight infantry companies of Hampton's South Carolina Legion were members of the Brigade during most of 1862. However, the Georgia and South Carolina regiments were transferred elsewhere in November, 1862, and replaced by the 3rd Arkansas Infantry. The 3rd Arkansas served with the Brigade until the end of the war. The three Texas regiments, the backbone of the Brigade, were composed of thirty-two companies raised in twenty-six Texas counties. The 1st, 4th, and 5th Texas Infantry were the only soldiers from the Lone Star State to fight in Lee's Army of Northern Virginia.

The war record of this famous fighting brigade was an able one. It was a record written in blood, battle-smoke, and bandages from the swamps of the Chickahominy in Virginia to the scrub oak and rocks of Little Round Top in Pennsylvania. Hood's Texas Brigade played a prominent part in six of the great battles of the war—Gaines' Mill, Second Manassas, Antietam, Gettysburg, Chickamauga and The Wilderness. On September 17, 1862, at the battle of Antietam, the 1st Texas Infantry suffered the highest casualty rate of any regiment, North or South, for a single day's action during the war—82.3 per cent.[75] In all six of these battles, the Brigade, as a whole, suffered a casualty rate in excess of 33 per cent. Besides these six major battles, the Brigade participated in twenty-two other engagements. Of the some six thousand men who fought under the shredded battle flags of Hood's Texas Brigade, but 617,[76] or a little over 10 per cent, were left to surrender at Appomattox. Bullets and disease had killed hundreds, and hundreds more had been invalided home from crippling wounds and prolonged sieges of sickness. For sustained battle action and combat losses Hood's Brigade stood first in the Army of Northern Virginia.

Although Hood commanded the Texas Brigade for less than six months, his aggressiveness, pride, and tenacity were indelibly etched upon the unit. The Texans were so attached to Hood that the Brigade carried his name throughout the war (regardless of subsequent commanders) and even after the war when it organized as a veterans' association. The Hood-Texas team was one of the best combat combinations that the Confederacy fielded.

In his memoirs Hood duly recorded his appreciation and esteem for his old Brigade.

> In almost every battle in Virginia it [the Texas Brigade] bore a conspicuous part. It acted as the advanced guard of Jackson when he moved upon McClellan, around Richmond; and almost without an exceptional instance, it was among the foremost of Longstreet's Corps in an attack or pursuit of the enemy. It was also, as a rule, with the rear guard of the rear guard of this corps, whenever falling back before the adversary. If a ditch was to be leaped, or fortified position to be carried, General Lee knew no better troops upon which to rely. In truth, its signal achievements in the War of Secession have never been surpassed in the history of nations.[77]

John Bell Hood's relatively short post-war career closely paralleled his Civil War successes and failures. His early business success and marital happiness was ultimately crowned by failure and tragedy. At thirty-five, a bachelor, penniless and crippled, the gallant Hood made his way back to Texas after surrendering on May 30 in Mississippi. He was received with enthusiasm in the Lone Star State. The press praised him and his old soldiers vied with one another to entertain their old commander.[78] Hood left Texas suddenly in October, 1865, ostensibly to visit Jefferson Davis (then languishing in prison at Fort Monroe) and to visit his mother in Kentucky. Hood did not get to see the ex-President, who was held incommunicado, but he did spend some time with his mother and relatives in and around Mt. Sterling. During this time Hood probably decided that New Orleans offered better business opportunities than Texas. Too, a half dozen high-ranking ex-Confederate generals had made their home in the Crescent City, most of them friends of Hood.[79]

With some $10,000 in capital (put up by forty Kentucky friends) Hood went into business in New Orleans as a cotton broker and commission merchant.[80] New Orleans had recovered rapidly after the war; wharves were crowded with vessels; and business was booming.[81] In 1869 Hood expanded his operations by taking over General Longstreet's insurance business. Hood assumed the presidency of the insurance company at a salary of five thousand dollars per year[82]—more money than he made as a full general in the Confederacy.

The general had other things on his mind besides business while establishing himself in New Orleans. Soon after taking up residence in the bustling river town he had met and fallen in love with Anna Maria Hennan, the daughter of a prominent New Orleans attorney. Anna Maria, a woman of beauty and culture, had been educated abroad, and while not rich her family was "comfortable." John Bell Hood and Anna Maria Hennan were married on April 30, 1868, with General Simon Bolivar Buckner as the best man.[83] The Hoods, together with Anna's widowed mother, moved to a large home in the Garden District of New Orleans, a home that in time came to be called "The Hood Mansion." Here the general was to spend the most peaceful and satisfying ten years of his life. Business was good; old war cronies visited often; and his family grew by leaps and bounds. Hood appeared to be as aggressive on the home front as he had been on the battlefield: eleven children were born to the general and Anna in ten years—three sets of twins and five singles. According to family sources, when the Hoods journeyed north for the summer accompanied by several retainers and Mrs. Hennan, hotel employes would joke about the invasion of "Hood's Brigade."[84]

In the summer of 1878, the wonderful world of General Hood started to fall apart. The severe yellow fever epidemic of that year caused a serious business depression in New Orleans.[85] The cotton exchange was closed; the wharves were empty; and the city was virtually isolated. By the winter of 1878-79, Hood was practically broke; his insurance company as well as his mercantile business had collapsed; and he had lost heavily on the cotton market.[86]

The summer of 1879 found Hood and his family in dire straits. In the summers before, the general was able to take his family north away from the humid heat of the Mississippi port and away from the dreaded yellow fever epidemics. In 1879, however, because of financial circumstances, Hood and his family were forced to remain in New Orleans. The epidemic of 1879, although mild, struck the Hood household three times with mortal effects. Mrs. Hood was the first to die. After an illness of only a few days, she passed away on August 24. At the time of Mrs. Hoods death, the youngest Hood child, Anna, was only six months old. The eldest child, ten-year-old Lydia, took sick on the twenty-sixth (she died August 29), followed by the general on the 27th.[87]

Hood lived but three days after the first symptoms of the fatal disease had appeared. Dr. S. M. Bemiss was called to the Hood home at 3:00 a.m. on the twenty-seventh and immediately diagnosed the general's illness as a virulent case of yellow fever. Hood was delirious most of the twenty-seventh and twenty-eighth. Once on the twenty-eighth his mind returned to the war days, and in a commanding tone he called, "I want those stores taken from my commissary." On the twenty-ninth abdominal pains became worse and twice he had black vomit—the sign that death was close. By that evening his breathing was heavy, and he became stuporous. At 3:35 a.m., Saturday morning August 30, 1879, the gallant Hood crossed over the river to his last bivouac.[88]

There was no military funeral with the pomp and ceremony that befits a great field commander. The fear of fever prevented the gathering of crowds, and but a few mourners followed the hearse through the hushed streets of New Orleans to Metaire Cemetery. Here, the idol of the Texas Brigade was committed to the Hennan vault. Etched on the door of the tomb was the simple inscription: John Bell Hood, 1831-1879.

As a fighting general and battlefield leader, John Bell Hood had few peers in American history. Had his wound at Chickamauga been fatal (like Jackson's at Chancellorsville) he probably would have gone down in history as one of America's greatest generals.

NOTES

[1]**Post Returns, Fort Mason,** Texas, July, 1857. National Archives, Washington, D. C.

[2]John Bell Hood, **Advance and Retreat** (New Orleans: G. P. T. Beauregard, 1880), p. 8.

[3]**Ibid.,** pp. 10-14.

[4]Harold B. Simpson, "Fort Mason," **Frontier Forts of Texas** (Waco: Texian Press, 1966), p. 144.

[5]Headquarters 8th Army, **General Order No. 14,** November 13, 1857. United States Secretary of War, **Annual Report,** 1857, 35th Congress, 1st Session, House Executive Documents 2, p. 56.

[6]John P. Dyer, **The Gallant Hood** (Indianapolis: Bobbs-Merrill, 1950), pp. 17-20.

[7]**Ibid.,** pp. 21-22.

[8]**Ibid.,** p. 23.

[9]**Ibid.,** pp. 22-23.

[10]**Hood, op. cit.,** p. 5.

[11]Dyer, **op. cit.,** p. 26; **Biographical Dictionary of the American Congress, 1774-1961** (Washington: USGPO, 1961), pp. 916-17.

[12]Dyer, **op. cit.,** p. 26.

[13]**Register of Graduates, United States Military Academy, 1802-1946** (The West Point Alumni Foundation, 1946), p. 145.

[14]Letter to the writer from Kenneth W. Rapp, Assistant Archivist, USMA, dated July 2, 1965.

[15]**Ibid.**

[16]Demerits were easy to accumulate and were awarded for the slightest

infraction of the strict rules. Demerits were given for such things as the smell of tobacco smoke in the quarters, swearing, failure to attend church, whistling during study hours and lack of neatness. (Harold B. Simpson, "West Pointers in the Texas Confederate Army," **Texas Military History,** Vol. 6, No. 1 (Spring, 1967), p. 61; Letters to the writer from Kenneth W. Rapp, Assistant Archivist, USMA, dated July 2, 23 and September 13, 1965; September 20, 1966).

[17]George F. Price, **Across the Continent With the Fifth Cavalry** (New York: Antiquarian Press, 1959) p. 11. (Reprint.)

[18]**Ibid.** pp. 29-31.

[19]The 2nd Cavalry was authorized on March 3, 1855, and retained this designation until August 3, 1861, when an Act of Congress changed it to the 5th U. S. Cavalry. (Price, **op. cit.,** p. 11.)

[20]Simpson, "Fort Mason," **op. cit.,** pp. 152-53.

[21]Hood, **op. cit.,** p. 7.

[22]Price, **op. cit.,** p. 34.

[23]George W. Cullum, **Biographical Register of the Officers and Graduates of the U. S. Military Academy, West Point, New York,** 3 vols. (New York, 1907), Vol. 1, p. 587.

[24]While Hood was at Indianola (Texas) awaiting a ship to take him East on leave he received an order directing him to report to duty as Chief of Cavalry at West Point. He astonished the Adjutant-General, Colonel Samuel Cooper, by refusing the assignment. (Hood, **op. cit.,** p. 15.)

[25]Hood, **op. cit.,** p. 15; Walter P. Webb (ed.), **The Handbook of Texas,** 2 vols. (Austin: The Texas State Historical Association, 1952), Vol. 1, p. 285.

[26]**Post Returns, Camp Wood** (Texas), January, 1861. National Archives, Washington, D. C.

[27]Hood, **op. cit.,** p. 16.

[28]Cullum, **op. cit.,** Vol. 1, p. 567; Charles B. Hall, **Military Records of the General Officers of the Confederate States of America** (New York, 1898), p. 8.

[29]Hood, **op. cit.,** p. 310.

[30]Hood, **op. cit.,** p. 16.

[31]United States War Department, **The War of the Rebellion: Official Records of the Union and Confederate Armies,** 128 vols. (Washington: GPO, 1880-1901), Series I, Vol. 2, p. 883. Hereafter referred to as **Official Records.**

[32]**Ibid.,** pp. 576, 957.

[33]Hall, **op. cit.,** p. 8.

[34]Ezra J. Warner, **Generals in Gray** (Baton Rouge: Louisiana State University Press, 1959), p. 337.

[35]**Official Records,** Series I, Vol. 5, pp. 215, 529, 1030.

[36]Harold B. Simpson, **Gaines' Mill to Appomattox** (Waco: Texian Press, 1963), p. 50.

[37]**Official Records,** Series I, Vol. 5, pp. 914, 938.

[38]**Ibid.,** p. 1030.

[39]Hall, **op. cit.,** p. 8.

[40]**Official Records,** Series I, Vol. 19, p. 683.

[41]**Ibid.,** p. 699.

[42]In late November, G. T. "Tige" Anderson's and Henry L. "Rock" Benning's brigades were assigned to Hood's Division.

[43]Douglas Southall Freeman, **Lee's Lieutenants,** 3 vols. (New York: Charles Scribner & Sons, 1944), Vol. 2, p. 273.

[44]James Longstreet's 1st Corps was composed of the divisions of John B. Hood, Lafayette McLaws and George Pickett.

[45]Hood's command at Chickamauga consisted of his own division and the divisions of J. B. Kershaw, A. P. Stewart, Bushrod Johnson and Thomas Hindman.

[46]**Official Records,** Series I, Vol. 30, Part 2, p. 35.

[47]**Ibid.,** p. 290.

[48]Hood, **op. cit.,** pp. 65-66.

[49]Dyer, **op. cit.,** Note 56, p. 352; Hall, **op. cit.,** p. 8.

[50]Hood, **op. cit.,** p. 68.

[51]Robert Underwood Johnson, and Clarence Clough Buel (eds.), **Battles and Leaders of the Civil War,** 10 vols. (New York: The Century Co., 1884-87), Vol. 4, p. 291.

[52]**Official Records,** Series I, Vol. 38, Part 5, p. 885.

[53]**Ibid.** Hood's promotion to full general was made by Jefferson Davis, but was never confirmed by the Confederate Congress.

[54]Richard Barksdale Harwell, **Songs of the Confederacy** (New York: Broadcast Music, Inc., 1951), p. 62.

[55]Hood, **op. cit.,** p. 311.

[56]**Ibid.**

[57]**Official Records,** Series I, Vol. 2, pp. 132, 297-98, 576, 957, 991, 1003-04. 1003-04.

[58]Previous commanders of the Army of Tennessee included such well-known Confederate generals as Braxton Bragg, William J. Hardee, Leonidas Polk and Joseph E. Johnston.

[59]Hood, **op. cit.,** p. 21; Nicholas A. Davis, **Campaign From Texas to Maryland** (Richmond: Presbyterian Committee of Publication of the Confederate States, 1863), p. 32; Mrs. A. V. Winkler, **Confederate Capitol and Hood's Brigade** (Austin: Von Boeckmann, 1894), p. 59.

[60]Dyer, **op. cit.,** p. 198.

[61]Hood, **op. cit.,** p. 59.

[62]**Ibid.,** p. 80.

[63]Although Hood's arm was not amputated, it was of little use to him the rest of his life. After the war he often wore a glove on his left hand. (Dyer, **op. cit.**, p. 310.)

[64]Mrs. Giraud Wright, **A Southern Girl in '61** (New York: Doubleday, Page & Co., 1905), p. 230.

[65]Dyer, **op. cit.**, pp. 199, 212-216, 219-224.

[66]**Ibid.**, p. 216.

[67]Hood, **op. cit.**, p. 64.

[68]Simpson, **Gaines' Mill, op. cit.**, p. 162.

[69]Dyer, **op. cit.**, p. 211.

[70]**Ibid.**, note 3, p. 350; Hood, **op. cit.**, p. 64.

[71]Freeman, **op. cit.**, Vol. III, pp. 231-32.

[72]Hood, **op. cit.**, p. 67.

[73]Dyer, **op. cit.**, pp. 212-226.

[74]**Ibid.**, pp. 223-26. As Hood left for his assignment as a corps commander with Johnston's command he presented Miss Preston with the diamond-studded silver Texas star that he had worn on his hat.

[75]Francis Trevelyan Miller. **The Photographic History of the Civil War,** 10 vols. (New York: The Review of Reviews Co., 1911), Vol. 10, p. 158.

[76]Harold B. Simpson. "Hood's Texas Brigade at Appomattox," **Texana,** Vol. 3, No. 1 (Spring, 1965), pp. 11-19.

[77]Hood, **op. cit.**, p. 64.

[78]Dallas **Herald,** June 24, July 22, 1865.

[79]Dyer, **op. cit.**, pp. 307-312.

[80]**Ibid.**, p. 311.

[81]Guilio Adamoli, "New Orleans in 1867." **Louisiana Historical Quarterly,** Vol. 6 (April, 1923), p. 272.

[82]Dyer, **op. cit.**, p. 314.

[83]New Orleans **Times,** April 30, 1868.

[84]Dyer, **op. cit.**, p. 315.

[85]The yellow fever epidemic in New Orleans in 1878 claimed some 3,000 lives.

[86]Dyer, **op. cit.**, p. 317.

[87]**Ibid.**

[88]H. T. Englehardt. "A Note on the Death of John Bell Hood," **The Southwestern Historical Quarterly,** Vol. LVII, No. 1 (July, 1953), pp. 91-93; New Orleans **Times,** August 31, 1879.

Francis Richard Lubbock

by

LEANN COX ADAMS

Through the chilly mist of an early May morning, a slow drizzle was falling over the Georgia countryside. In the dim light of daybreak, a small party of fleeing Confederates was camped beside a stream a few miles from Irwinsville. Suddenly awakened by the sharp crack of rifle fire, they jumped to their feet. There was the sound of hoof beats, a flash of blue uniforms, the curt demand for surrender, and it was over. Jefferson Davis, a man who only a few days before had headed a government, was now in the hands of his captors. It was May 10, 1865, and all had ended. This brief episode in central Georgia had brought to a close a long, sad chapter in the history of a nation. Among those few heartbroken followers who witnessed this scene, stood Francis Richard Lubbock, aide-de-camp to President Davis, Confederate patriot, and ex-governor of Texas,[1] having served as state executive from 1861 to 1863.

Born October 16, 1815, in Beaufort, South Carolina, Francis R. Lubbock, was the son of a Palmetto State physician, Dr. Henry Thomas Willis Lubbock. The second of seven children, young Frank was educated in private schools and obtained his first business experience at the age of twelve, as a bookkeeper in the family's steamship business. After the death of his father in 1828, he found employment as a clerk in a Charleston hardware store.[2] In 1832, Lubbock declined an appointment to West Point and accepted instead a managerial position at a cotton warehouse in Hamburg, South Carolina. Moving to New Orleans in 1834, he opened a drug store,[3] and February 5, 1835, Francis Lubbock married Adele Baron, daughter of N. A. Baron Jr., a prominent cotton and sugar dealer in the Crescent City.[4]

In 1835, Frank was joined in New Orleans by his brother Thomas, who was the first volunteer to join the New Orleans Grays, an elite military company organized for the sole purpose of aiding Texas in her struggle for independence from Mexico. It was Tom's departure and a failure to hear from him after several months leave, that prompted Lubbock to set out for Texas in search of his brother. Boarding the schooner *Colonel Fannin,* he landed at Velasco, Texas, in October, 1836. Finding his brother well and being favorably impressed with the opportunities offered by this new land, Frank returned to New Orleans and made preparations to move to Texas. Shortly after Christmas, 1836, the Lubbocks embarked on the schooner *Corolla* bound for the Lone Star Republic. Velasco, located on the left bank of the Brazos at its mouth, was at this time the chief port of the Republic, while Quintana on the opposite side, was the center of an extensive foreign trade. Galveston had not been established.[5]

Lubbock, a shrewd businessman, knowing that the new republic was short of many things, took with him a large cargo of guns and ammunition as well as one hundred barrels of flour and other foodstuffs.[6] After arriving at Quintana, Lubbock proceeded up to Houston on the first steamer to dock at that city.[7] Here, he opened up a small business and proceeded to dispose of his New Orleans stockpile at respectable prices.[8]

Arriving in Texas too late for the battle of San Jacinto, a fact he always regretted,[9] Lubbock was soon serving the young republic in another capacity. At the first session of the second Congress which convened in September of 1837, he was elected assistant clerk of the House and at the second session on May 6, 1838, he was elected chief clerk.[10] After serving a short time in the latter position, Lubbock was appointed public comptroller for the Republic by President Sam Houston, who had recognized his ability, although Lubbock was only twenty-two at the time.[11]

In the fall of 1838, the Indians stirred up so much trouble along the Brazos that the government was forced to organize a military force to punish them. The port city's military company, known as the Milam Guards, of which Lubbock was a member, volunteered for service with Major George W. Bonnell's Battalion. Lubbock served as adjutant of Bonnell's command. As this was Lubbock's first experience in the field, it proved to be quite a challenge.[12]

Anti-Houston feeling had grown quite strong, and when Lamar was elected president in 1838, Lubbock, who had supported the Houston faction, was asked to resign his position as comptroller. Although Lubbock was a loyal friend and staunch supporter of Houston at this time, he later, in 1857, campaigned vigorously against the old "Hero of San Jacinto" when Houston and H. R. Runnels were running for governor and lieutenant governor.[13]

After Houston was inaugurated to his second term as president of the Republic in 1841, he again appointed Lubbock comptroller of the Republic.[14] Lubbock accepted, but later resigned to fill the district clerk's position in Harris County.[15] After Texas entered the Federal Union, in 1846, Pinckney Henderson was elected governor, and Sam Houston was elected to the United States Senate. Houston and Lubbock remained good friends until 1855, when the split because of Houston's support of the Know-Nothing party.[16] A state meeting of the Democratic party was held in the House of Representatives on January 15, 1856, and Lubbock was appointed secretary of the state Democratic organization.[17] The Democratic convention that was held in Waco on May 4, 1857,[18] nominated H. R. Runnels of Bowie for governor and Frank Lubbock for lieutenant governor.[19] Sam Houston and Jesse Grimes ran on the opposing ticket.[20] Lubbock, accompanied by his wife, canvassed the state in behalf of Runnels and himself. Runnels defeated Houston for governor by a vote of 32,552 to 23,628; for lieutenant-governor, Lubbock received 33,399 votes to Jesse Grimes' 20,318.[21] This was the only major political defeat that Houston suffered in his long political career.

The inauguration of Governor Runnels and Lieutenant-Governor Lubbock took place in the House of Representatives December 21, 1857. In his inaugural address, the governor called attention to the important question of Northern supremacy and what it meant for Texas and the South in general. To Lubbock, it was clear that the North would soon dominate the Union, and with Northern hostility to slavery, it would be impossible for the South to have peace in the Union. Governor Runnels said that unless the threat of abolition be removed, he believed "that the determination of Texas will be taken to assume the guardianship of her own destinies and bid adieu to a connection no longer consistent with the rights, dignity, and honor of an equal and independent State."[22]

The next Democratic state convention was held in Houston in May, 1859, and the Runnels ticket was renominated. Meanwhile, Sam Houston had decided to run on an Independent Democratic ticket with Edward Clark, basing their campaign on opposition to Runnels' frontier policy. The Houston ticket won; Runnels being defeated by a vote of 36,327 to 27,900 and Clark defeating Lubbock 31,458 votes to 30,325.[23]

A State Democratic Convention was held in Galveston in April, 1860 and drew up resolutions proclaiming Texas' right to withdraw from the Union and promising increased frontier protection. Eight delegates were also selected to attend the National Democratic Convention at Charleston, South Carolina. Lubbock was a member of this delegation.[24]

The National Democratic Convention assembled in Charleston on April 23, 1860.[25] Due to the failure of the delegates to come to a firm decision on the question of slavery in the territories, the Alabama delegation withdrew. Alabama was soon followed by the delegates from the states of Florida, Mississippi, South Carolina, Louisiana, Texas, Arkansas, and Georgia.[26] Due to the lack of a quorum the convention adjourned to meet at a later date in Baltimore. The representatives for the Southern states after walking out at Charleston met on June 11 at Richmond, Virginia and formed the Constitutional Democratic Party. Lubbock was elected temporary chairman of this gathering, and it was decided that they would attend the Baltimore convention of the regular Democratic Party and present their demands. If these were not accepted, they would return to Richmond and make nominations. The delegates were not seated at the Baltimore convention, and when they reconvened immediately following the Baltimore convention at noon on June 23, John C. Breckenridge of Kentucky was selected as their candidate for the presidency. Steven A. Douglas was the choice of the Baltimore convention of the Democratic Union Party; the Constitutional Union Party chose John C. Bell of Tennessee; and Abraham Lincoln became the Republican nominee.[27]

Despite the split in the Democratic Party, Lubbock did not feel that Lincoln's election was certain. However, his opinions were quite clear as to the course Texas should take if Lincoln were elected. "I feel no hesitation in saying that our safety and honor forbids our submitting to Black Republican rule, my own opinion is that secession is the proper remedy, as far as I am concerned I am for prompt and energetic action."[28]

After Lincoln's election, one by one the states of the South began their procession of secession. Lubbock, outspoken on the subject of secession, publicly remarked that Texas should not lag behind her sister states in leaving the Union as she had as much at stake as did the other Southern states.[29]

Meanwhile, Governor Houston, determined to prevent the secession of Texas, refused to call an extra session of the legislature to debate the matter, but the overwhelming pressure of public opinion compelled him to do so. This special session convened at Austin, January 21, 1861, and while it took no action on secession it did specify that any such action taken by the upcoming Secession Convention would have to be ratified by the voters to be legal. The Secession Convention called by a group of prominent "Texans for Secession" met January 28, 1861, and after several days of debate passed the secession ordinance by a vote of 167 to 7.[30] After the Texas electorate had sustained the action of the Secession Convention by a three-to-one majority, Texas requested and was accepted into the Southern Confederacy on March 2, 1861. Texas had united with the Confederate States of America. Due to the bitter opposition of Governor Sam Houston and his refusal to take the oath of allegiance to the Confederacy, the convention declared the office of governor vacant, and on March 18 Lieutenant-Governor Edward Clark formally entered upon his duties as governor of Texas.[31]

With the fall of Fort Sumter on April 14, 1861, Virginia, North Carolina, Tennessee and Arkansas linked their fortunes with those of the other Southern states. The Confederacy, as finally composed, had eleven states with a white population of about 5,500,000 and a slave population of about 3,500,000, but the opposing odds were immense—a population of 22,000,000, a regular army and navy, and the prestige of an established government. It was little wonder that Secretary of State William H. Seward boasted that the Confederacy would be knocked to pieces in less than ninety days.[32]

April 18, 1861, Frank Lubbock threw his hat in the ring for governor of the Lone Star State.[33] He wrote:

> I wished to be the executive head of Texas, that I might support the Confederacy and assist in the vigorous prosecution of the war for independence. My experience in canvassing for Lieutenant-Governor gave me an idea of public sentiment towards me, and I thought, as did some of my friends that I could be elected. I believe I could make Texas a passably good Governor. I knew that if elected I would give to the people an honest, faithful administration.[34]

The State Democratic Convention met in Dallas, May 27, 1861. Due to minimum attendance, only twenty-six counties were represented, no nominations were made, and the race was thrown wide open. Lubbock's competitors for governor were General T. J. Chambers and Governor Edward Clark. Both Chambers and Clark were Democrats and secessionists, and were as fully committed on the major issues as was Lubbock. The race devolved into a personality contest, as Lubbock put it, "merely to choose the man to enforce the existing policy." Fortunately, he received the support of a few principal Texas newspapers, such as the *Texas State Gazette* of Austin and the *Clarksville Standard.*[35]

The election of 1861 was a remarkable one in a number of ways. It was the first time in Texas history that the two major candidates for governor had both been lieutenant-governors; and both at one time had been defeated for that office.[36] After the votes were tallied, it was discovered that Lubbock had won by the narrowest margin in the state's history—127 votes. The outcome was so uncertain that even after Lubbock was informed of his victory and had packed and journeyed to Austin with his family, Mrs. Lubbock felt it wise for him to go into the city alone, in order to avoid the embarrassment of making a triumphal entry, only to discover their information had been a bit inaccurate.[37]

The new executive head of Texas was not a big man either physically or intellectually, but he was an absolutely honest man. He possessed what Kittrell called the most "valuable asset to political office, the reputation for incorruptible, personal integrity." He was a bright and amusing speaker, but he was not a reasoner or a deep man mentally. His annoying habit of indulging in various brands of profanity was abandoned a number of years before his death, and he became a devout member of the Presbyterian Church.[38]

Shortly after being elected, Lubbock decided to journey to Richmond to acquaint himself more fully with the activities and plans of the Confederate government. Since Colonel B. F. Terry and Tom Lubbock had recently been authorized to raise a regiment for Virginia, Governor Lubbock decided to accompany his brother and Colonel Terry on their march to New Iberia, Louisiana. Late in August, Terry's command, known as Terry's Texas Rangers, and also as the Eighth Texas Cavalry, departed Houston. The governor-elect was placed in charge of a detail to collect wagons and carts to enable a more rapid movement of the footsore men. Frank Lubbock accompanied Terry's command as far as Chattanooga, where the Rangers were notified of their reassignment to General A. S. Johnston's command in Kentucky. Lubbock bade the Rangers a long farewell. Although he did not know it at the time, this was to be Lubbock's last look at both Colonel Terry and his brother Tom—the former was killed at Woodsonville, Kentucky in December, 1861, and his brother, who succeeded Terry in command, took ill and died the following month.[39]

Upon arriving in Richmond, the Texas governor-elect found the city astir with military preparations. After being cordially welcomed by President Davis, the two men discussed proposed plans of operation. The President acquainted Lubbock with the ways in which the governors of the Southern states could strengthen the power of the Confederacy. Lubbock was favorably impressed by President Davis. He found him to be a man "pre-eminently fitted for the high position to which he had been called by the unanimous voice of the South."

Before leaving Richmond, Lubbock visited with the Texas troops there, primarily the Fourth and Fifth Texas Infantry Regiments, and reported finding them "generally well."[40]

Upon his return to Texas, preparations were made for his inauguration, which took place on November 7, 1861. The tenor of Lubbock's inaugural address can be gleaned from the following:

> I feel deeply conscious of the great responsibilities attaching to the position at this important crisis. Much has already been done by the retiring executive to place Texas

> side by side with her sister states in the present struggle; but, gentlemen, it must be borne in mind that we have as yet but seen the beginning, and I am resolved, with your aid and support, so long as I occupy the position confided to me by the people, that her footsteps in the career of honor and patriotism shall be onward, . . .
>
> The Lincoln government vainly boasted the base and hireling soldiery would overrun and subjugate the South in sixty days. Eight months have passed away, and we find this wicked and boastful government, after warring for that length of time against a power not half their equal in numbers, forced to pursue on every line of military operations a defensive policy; their armies defeated on every battlefield, and their hireling soldiers panic-stricken before our army of citizens.
>
> . . . abundance has been given to us; our granaries are filled; plenty prevails in our midst, and the people feel that the great God who presides over the destinies of nations and 'sits on the throne judging right', is on our side and will bless us in this struggle.
>
> It has been said, gentlemen, that this is a war for slavery. I tell you it is a war for liberty.[41]

He further pointed out the necessity for Texas to pay promptly her portion of the war tax to the Confederacy and called upon the legislature to provide for the soldiers so faithfully serving the nation. He also recommended that the state be placed in an attitude of self-defense and while defending the state from Union forces, he should not overlook the need for frontier protection from the Indian foe.[42]

On November 8, the night after Lubbock's inauguration, Galveston was attacked, and the *Royal Yacht*, a Confederate vessel, was captured and burned. Demoralization spread, and General P. O. Hebert wrote the secretary of war that he felt that Galveston would be almost impossible to defend with the few troops and artillery at his disposal in the area. Yet he realized the necessity of retaining possession of the key Texas city as long as possible, for such an important cotton port was too great a prize to hand over to the enemy.[43]

When the letter reached Lubbock that Galveston Island might have to be evacuated as a military necessity, he offered to share with Hebert the responsibility of burning the city upon its evacuation. Although this suggestion for the total destruction of Galveston was supported by a number of its prominent citizens, it caused a wave of resentment toward Lubbock, which was still evident many years later.[44] General Hebert thanked Lubbock for his support but said nothing of the governor's suggestion regarding the burning of Galveston.[45]

Considering Indian hostilities to be the greatest immediate danger to the state, the governor called for a new frontier policy in his first message to the Ninth Legislature. Immediately after the withdrawal of Federal forces from the state, the Texas frontier had been protected by local minute companies and then later by regiments of mounted men under state control. But as time passed and more and more of these state troops had been conscripted into Confederate service the line of defense was greatly weakened. The governor reminded the legislature that if the state were invaded, they would have to rely almost entirely on the state militia for protection—a militia that was being bled daily for Confederate service outside of the state.

While on the subject of defense Lubbock pointed to the "exposed condition of our gulf coast,"[46] and hoped that heavy guns would be previded to guard the coastal cities. He also called for the establishment of a foundry for the manufacture of arms within the state. A small arsenal was finally established at Austin where arms and light artillery were manufactured. Copper used in the manufacturing was brought from Mexico. A cap and cartridge factory was also established at the state capital using, for the want of a better place, the chambers of the Supreme Court.[47]

Only a short time after his inauguration, Governor Lubbock was faced with one of the major problems of his administration, that of meeting Confederate manpower quotas. This problem was a complex one for Texas, for in addition to supplying the required troops for the Confederate service, enough men had to be retained to provide adequate protection for defense of the frontier, the extensive seacoast, and the Mexican border. When it was learned from Brigadier-General Paul O. Hebert, former Louisiana governor and Confederate military commander of Texas, that only Colonel "Rip" Ford's cavalry regiment was to be assigned to occupy the lower Rio Grande, Lubbock requested that no soldiers from Ford's command be conscripted into the Confederate service, since an invasion was expected daily in that area. This request was honored by the Confederate authorities.[48]

Believing that the storage of cotton along the coast invited attack, Lubbock issued a proclamation on November 30, forbidding the transportation and storage of cotton at any point within striking distance of the enemy's vessels. Also, to prevent enemy launches from landing for the purpose of depredation, Lubbock organized a body of irregular troops called the "coast guards."[49]

From the time of the Secession Convention, Texans were volunteering for service, and regiments were being organized throughout the state. Each Southern state was required to furnish men for the Confederate armies at a ratio of six per cent of the white population.[50] On this basis, Texas' quota was approximately 15,500 men. When Lubbock took office, Texas had nearly 20,000 men in arms, and camps of instruction had been established at various points in the state, where men were mustered in, equipped, and drilled for service.[51] The age requirement for military service was from eighteen to thirty-five years, with aliens liable to military duty only if necessary to aid in repelling invasion. In 1862, two hundred and ninety-eight aliens in Texas claimed exemption from military service and contacted their respective consuls for protection. However, many German and British aliens rendered excellent service in the defense of Galvston Island.[52]

In a message to the legislature in December, 1861, Lubbock called for a more efficient organization of the military force within Texas. In response to the governor's plea, a law was enacted to perfect the organization of the state troops and place them on a war footing. The new state mobilization law was approved on Christmas Day, 1861, and made all white male residents between the ages of eighteen and fifty years with certain exceptions liable for state military duty. The state was to be divided into thirty-three military districts, each to be commanded by a brigadier-general.[53] The companies created to man the districts not only had the duty to defend the frontier, but were to be held in readiness for a possible call into Confederate service. The law further stated that if the response to a call for volunteers to man the district companies was not adequate, it would be necessary to resort to a state draft.[54]

The problem of frontier defense was a frustrating one. Although President Davis had, at an early date authorized the raising of a Confederate regiment of mounted riflemen for frontier protection, the service of the men in this regiment, commanded by Colonel Henry E. McCulloch, was about ready to expire, leaving the frontier settlements open to Indian attack. To meet this emergency, a law was enacted in December, 1861, calling into state service an organization known afterwards as the "Frontier Regiment." The companies of this regiment were to be stationed along the perimeter of advance settlments from the Red River to the Rio Grande at posts approximately twenty-five miles apart. This regiment was not to leave the limits of Texas and was to be disbanded by the governor, whenever their services were no longer necessary. It was to be officered by men of frontier experience. The non-commissioned officers and privates assigned to the regiment were, almost to a man, residents of the counties to be protected. As a matter of fact, all able-bodied men in the frontier counties were expected to serve in the regiment; this kept those who wished to avoid Confederate service from moving into the area.[55]

On January 11, 1862, an act was passed creating a military board, consisting of the governor, the comptroller, and the treasurer. This board was empowered "to provide for the defense of the State by using any United States bonds in the treasury" and was given the authority to substitute the Federal bonds in equal amounts for bonds of the Confederate States. The Confederate bonds were then to be used by the board for the purchase of arms and ammunition and to provide for the manufacture of arms within the state. It was at this time that Lubbock was advised by Judah P. Benjamin, Confederate Secretary of War, that an arrangement had been worked out by the Richmond government regarding the purchase of arms, whereby Texas could exchange United States bonds in her possession which bore only six per cent interest, for the Confederate bonds bearing interest at eight per cent. The bond exchange plan was carried out by Lubbock after receiving recommendations in its favor from such prominent Texas figures in Richmond as General Louis T. Wigfall, Senator John Hemphill, and Postmaster General John H. Reagan.[56]

Throughout his administration, Lubbock endeavored to provide large quantities of clothing and supplies as well as guns and ammunition for the men at the front. One of his first acts was to use state penitentiary personnel and equipment to produce clothing and supplies for the soldiers. Later, after the Union forces occupied the Mississippi and severed the Trans-Mississippi Department from the Confederacy, it became necessary to establish additional factories to supplement the penitentiary workshops.[57]

Due to the blockade of the Gulf ports and war operations to the north and east of Texas, outside trade was seriously curtailed, and the supplies of merchandise on hand gradually diminished with little opportunity to replenish them. Early in 1862, Texans were forced to set about providing themselves with the necessities of life and substitutions were the order of the day. Women had to supply clothing for their families as well as for their sons and husbands in the army. Texas, besides providing for her civilian population scattered throughout an immense area also had to provide cattle and wagonloads of bacon and flour for the Confederate Army operating west of the Mississippi as well as for the state troops. At many of the towns, centers were established for the collection of farm products for the use of the army. These were transported to the fighting front by large freight wagons. Salt being a necessity, salt works were established at various points near the coast. Iron works and foundries were built near Jefferson and Rusk, and jug factories were established in Rusk and Henderson Counties. Harness, shoe and tailor shops were kept busy all over the state.[58] Texas had mobilized her small manufacturing complex for maximum production.

On February 3, 1862, Secretary of War Judah P. Benjamin requisitioned Texas for fifteen regiments. To fulfill the levy, Lubbock issued a proclamation to the people of Texas, asking for 15,000 volunteers. Each soldier was to receive fifty dollars bounty money when his company was mustered into service, and his transportation expenses were to be paid by the Confederate government. Lubbock went on to say that he was confident that the required number would present themselves for service, but if the quota was not filled, the remainder would be obtained by draft.[59]

A misunderstanding soon arose between Lubbock and the

Confederate government over the troop levies. Lubbock, in a letter to Secretary Benjamin, stated that it had been called to his attention that Confederate recruiting agents had been sent to Texas for the purpose of procuring troops. These agents seldom notified state authorities of their presence or actions, therefore it was impossible to determine how much manpower they had drained off and what reserve manpower existed in the state. Lubbock felt that Texas was furnishing more men than her share to the Richmond government. It was reported in the spring of 1862 that Benjamin had given Texas credit for only 6,635 men in the Confederate service, but Lubbock argued that twelve regiments were manned by Texans, not counting some 1,250 men in artillery companies or a total close to double the figure that Benjamin quoted. The men in these twelve regiments Lubbock argued, had been recruited primarily by agents from Richmond. And furthermore, Lubbock wrote, he had just learned of the departure of some 1,500 additional troops to fill the ranks of the three Texas regiments in Virginia. Lubbock continued:

> Now let's see how this places Texas. On February 3, you called on me for fifteen regiments, saying this is our quota for the war. On the same day, somebody is authorized to come into Texas and take five regiments over and above her quota without even informing the state authorities of the fact. Again on February 12, I am asked for about fifteen hundred men to fill these regiments on the Potomac, making 6,500 men by your own calculations we are due to the service. Should these requisitions be filled, we would have some 47,000 men in the field, having over twelve instead of six per cent of our white population. I most respectfully demur and protest against the government taking the men out of the state except by call through state authorities.[60]

By June, 1862, the Mississippi River was largely in the hands of the enemy, and the feeling began to spread that the Confederate authorities were neglecting and abandoning that portion of the Confederacy west of the Mississippi. Although Governor Lubbock refused to entertain such an idea, Governor Henry M. Rector of Arkansas became unduly alarmed and issued a proclamation in which he stated that Arkansas, southern

Missouri, and Texas would withdraw from the Confederacy and carve out their own future, rather than be abandoned before the enemy.[61]

Immediately upon receiving knowledge of Rector's proclamation, Governor Lubbock sent a personal letter to President Davis assuring him of Texas' loyal support of the Southern Confederacy. As a result of both Lubbock's letter and the Arkansas proclamation, President Davis took the initiative of calling a conference of the governors of Arkansas, Louisiana, Missouri, and Texas to meet at Marshall, Texas, on July 20, for the purpose of proposing plans for the defense of the states west of the Mississippi. Three demands by the Trans-Mississippi governors came from the conference. First, they declared that a high-ranking general with territorial jurisdiction over the entire Trans-Mississippi area was urgently needed. Second, they expressed a dire need for arms, ammunition, and money to support the army, and third, they demanded that a branch of the treasury department be established west of the river to assure payment for the troops in the Trans-Mississippi Department. This meeting brought the desired results, buttressed public morale, and restored confidence in the Confederacy.[62]

The governors' conference had hardly adjourned when the Union forces occupied Galveston Island. Upon being notified of this startling bit of news, Lubbock departed immediately for the threatened area. On October 12, 1862, he officially notified the people of Texas that Galveston was "in possession of the enemy" and issued an order prohibiting all communications with that key port during the occupation.[63]

In response to the governor's desire for a change in the military commander of Texas, the Confederate government sent General John B. "Prince John" Magruder of Virginia to replace General Hebert. It was rumored about the time of Magruder's arrival in the Lone Star State that a Federal invasion force was being assembled in New Orleans to invade Texas. Upon learning of the contemplated invasion of Texas, General Magruder requested from the Confederate government permission to retain all Confederate troops in the area for the defense of Texas. Magruder then requested that Lubbock call into service at once all the militia that the state could possibly arm, and call for them to rendezvous without delay at Harrisburg. After speedily massing the troops, Lubbock wrote, "Old Harrisburg presented a more warlike appearance than when the Texan government officials were fleeing before the legions of Santa Anna in 1836."[64] On January 1, 1863, Magruder, with a mixed army of Confederates and state troops and a couple of armed steamers, drove the Federals from the city of Galveston.

Early in war, the Confederates were forced to call for more men, and thus resorted to the first conscription of military manpower in American history. The Confederate Conscription or draft act went into effect on April 16, 1862.[65] Under this law Governor Lubbock was authorized to call into service all white males between the ages of eighteen and thirty-five for a period of three years or for the duration.[56] This was later extended in September, 1862, to include men up to forty-five years of age with certain exemptions for public office holders, workers in key industries, and stockmen.[67]

Opposition to the draft was soon felt in Texas. One of the centers of protest was in Austin County, which had a heavy German population. At one large meeting, the Germans petitioned the governor for permission to delay their induction in order to provide for their families preliminary to their military service.[68] When Lubbock called for a draft in Austin County, the men refused to be sworn into service and assaulted the officer who was to administer the oath of allegiance to the Confederacy. The Germans in Austin County remained in open rebellion to Confederate conscription all during 1862. On the last day of December, 1862, the Teutonic citizens of the county met *en masse* and drew up a resistance program that specified that each precinct in the county was to organize a military company to resist conscription by force of arms if necessary. A few days later eight hundred Germans assembled in open resistance to the draft laws.[69] Lubbock placed the county under martial law and ordered General Magruder to dispatch troops to the area to restore law and order and to enforce the conscription act. With the appearance of Magruder's troops on the scene the Germans quietly submitted to the draft and were enrolled as soldiers.[70]

On January 24, 1863, General Magruder issued the official report of his campaign in Texas, the results of which were indeed awe-inspiring—at least from "Prince John's" viewpoint. The enemy's land and naval forces at Galveston had been defeated, and the re-occupation of the key island effected. Three subsequent enemy naval attacks on Galveston had been repulsed, and the blocking fleet off Sabine Pass had been utterly destroyed by river cotton-clads operating some thirty miles at sea. The Federal blockade on the Texas coast had been raised from the Brazos to the Sabine. According to Governor Lubbock, Magruder's actions had greatly raised the morale of the Texas troops, and a feeling of confidence and hope had been restored to the civilian population. "Texans had at last found a leader worthy of their confidence," continued Lubbock, and "it wasn't hazarding much to say that the campaign was the most brilliant in the annals of Texas."[71]

Because of the issuance of Lincoln's Emancipation Proclamation and the slow response to Lubbock's last call for troops, the governor announced that a special session of the legislature would be held on February 2, 1863. The special session finally convened on February 5, with a notable change in personnel—many of the original members of the legislature had gone to war. Lubbock's message to the lawmakers reaffirmed Texas' support of the Confederacy. The governor called for a renewed effort to sustain the men in the field and the families of the soldiers at home, and reprimanded the actions of some in the state who used the war as a means for personal profit. A higher rate of taxation was also called for, primarily because of an increase or inflation of Confederate money. Lubbock made other important recommendations to the legislators. Among other things, he requested action for the impressment of slave labor for government work, the approval of the recent additions to the conscript law, and the adoption of a new plan for frontier protection. Lubbock's new frontier protection plan called for the twenty-five counties on a line from the Red River to the Rio Grande to each select a captain and twenty men to serve as a county defense force. The captains were to be paid $750 annually and the men $500 out of state funds. Each member of the defense force was to furnish his own horse, arms and subsistence. This practical plan offered by Governor Lubbock was not adopted, for the legislature still hoped the responsibility for the frontier regiment would be transferred to the Confederate government.[72]

Before closing his address, the governor reviewed the great

military contribution that Texas had made to the war effort.

> Texas has furnished to the Confederate States military service thirty-three cavalry and ninety infantry regiments, thirty of which (twenty-one cavalry and nine infantry) have been organized since the requisition of February 3, 1862, for fifteen regiments, being the quota required from Texas to make her quota equal to the quotas from other States; besides thirteen battalions, two squadrons, and six detached companies of cavalry, and one legion of twelve companies of infantry, two batteries, one company unattached, one legion of two battalions, and one light battery, and one regiment of artillery and eleven light batteries, making 62,000 men, which, with the state troops in actual service, namely 6,500 men, form an aggregate of 68,500 Texans in military service constituting an excess of 4,773 over the highest popular vote, which was 63,727.
>
> From the best information within reach of this department upon which to base an estimate of the men now remaining in the State between the ages of 16 and 60 years, it is thought that the number will not exceed 26,000.[73]

On June 4, 1863, Magruder requisitioned Lubbock for 10,000 more troops, for a Federal invasion was anticipated due to a probable opening of the Mississippi to their gunboats. These troops had to be supplied, organized, and trained and important points fortified, for Texas was in greater danger than ever before, especially if the enemy succeeded in opening the Mississippi. Magruder's demands were slowly met, but Texas was near the bottom of the "manpower barrel" and effective firearms were next to impossible to procure. It was not unusual to see Texas militia drilling without weapons of any kind.[74]

The issuance of the governor's call for more troops signaled the renewed opposition to conscription. Male citizens massed once again, armed and equipped to resist the enrolling officers. This time the threat of rebellion was even greater, for now these men were supplemented by hundreds of deserters and draft dodgers that had gathered along the border and the frontier. It once again became necessary for armed forces to assist in the enforcement of the conscript laws.[75] The conscript officer at Brownsville found it necessary, in order to secure the enrollment of those subject to conscription, to guard the avenues of departure from the town with a military force until the enrollment was completed.[76]

With the fall of Vicksburg, demoralization within Texas reached its zenith. In an effort to raise morale, the governor issued a cheering proclamation on July 24, 1863. Texans were once again urged to exert every effort to aid and support the Southern cause. But the cause looked dark indeed; the Federal victory at Vicksburg had split the Confederacy into two parts, and communications with Richmond were severed. Unless this situation was remedied, the results could be disastrous. In recognition of the gravity of the situation, General E. Kirby Smith called another conference of the governors of the states west of the Mississippi to meet at Marshall on August 15, 1863.[77]

The governors assembled as planned and appointed Lubbock their chairman. Nothing of major consequence was accomplished at this meeting, but an effort was made by proclamation to restore the people's confidence in the Confederacy and to check the spread of disloyalty. On the subject of disloyalty, Lubbock ordered strict adherence to the conscript laws and emphasized punishment for deserters.[78]

After Lubbock's return to Texas in late August he received a letter from B. Theron, serving as both the French and Spanish consul at Galveston, suggesting an alliance between Texas and France. This was the only official proposal Lubbock received for an alliance with a foreign power. French assistance was offered, if Texas would resume her status as an independent nation. A copy of the letter was sent to President Davis, who promptly expelled Monsieur Theron from the Confederacy.[79]

Possibly due to the widespread criticism of his strict adherence to the Confederate conscription law, Lubbock did not choose to be a candidate to succeed himself in the election of 1863.[80] Pendleton Murrah polled the majority of the popular vote in the August election, and when the Tenth Legislature convened, Lubbock, on November 5, 1863, issued his valedictory message. He stated that since the time of his address to the special session of the legislature on February 5, 22,000 additional men had been furnished to the Confederate armies, bringing the total to over 90,000 men enrolled in both the Confederate and state military services during his administration.[81] Governor Lubbock claimed no particular honor for accomplishing this feat but did believe that he had fulfilled his duties honestly, faithfully, and impartially. And according to the press, his message breathed the very soul of patriotism.[82]

On the very day, November 5, 1863, that he ceased to be the chief executive of the state, Lubbock entered the army, and at Governor Murrah's inaugural ball, he surprised the guests by appearing in the uniform of a Confederate officer. He had received the appointment of assistant adjutant-general, with the rank of lieutenant-colonel from General E. Kirby Smith. This appointment was approved by President Davis and confirmed by the Confederate Senate, March 16, 1864.[83]

Early in December, Lubbock joined the staff of General Magruder, and was appointed by "Prince John" as inspector of field transportation. After learning of a planned federal invasion of northeast Texas, Magruder ordered Lubbock to arrange for the transportation of the Confederate Army in Texas to Louisiana. After the completion of this staff duty, Lubbock, who desired service in the field, requested and received a transfer to the cavalry command of General Tom Green in Louisiana, an officer whose ability Lubbock greatly respected. However, before Lubbock reached Louisiana, he received word that Green had been killed in action at the battle of Blair's Landing on April 12, 1864. Consequently, Lubbock was reassigned to the headquarters of the Trans-Mississippi Department as an assistant adjutant-general on the staff of General John A. Wharton.[84]

Soon after Lubbock joined Wharton's command he saw action. The Confederate cavalry under Wharton engaged in a running battle with a large Federal force from Alexandria, Louisiana, to Natchitoches where the enemy was finally brought to bay on April 28, 1864, and defeated.[85] This was Lubbock's first experience in battle.[86] On May 13th, Lubbock saw further action when Wharton's command engaged a Union force at Mansure, Louisiana. Although the Confederates were forced to withdraw in the face of superior numbers, they inflicted heavy casualties on the Federals before leaving the field. This ended, for the time being, the fighting of Wharton's men in that part of Louisiana, and Lubbock was ordered back to headquarters.[87]

On August 12, 1864, the ex-governor received a letter from Jefferson Davis, informing him of the President's desire "to have near him someone well qualified by acquaintance with the people and affairs of the Trans-Mississippi Department who could keep him informed as to the requirements of the service there and advise him upon all matters relating to it."[88] The message went on to say that Lubbock had been appointed an aide-de-camp to President Davis with the rank of a colonel of cavalry.[89]

Immediately accepting the appointment, Lubbock departed for Richmond and arrived at the Confederate capital on September 8, 1864. He found the duties assigned him sufficiently agreeable, although Lubbock would have preferred active service in the field. After a short time in Richmond he visited Hood's Texas Brigade and reported finding them well.[90]

Lubbock's associates on the President's staff were Major-General George Washington Custis Lee, son of Robert E. Lee; Colonel William Preston Johnston, son of Albert Sidney Johnston; Colonel John Tyler Wood, grandson of Zachary Taylor; Colonel Ives and Colonel William Browne.[91]

In February, 1865, General Robert E. Lee was made commander of all Confederate armies, and in early spring, the Yankees pressed their siege of Richmond, ever tightening the noose around the beleaguered capital. Attempts to raise the siege were unsuccessful, and on April 2, 1865, Davis received word of Lee's intention to abandon Richmond and retreat to Lynchburg in western Virginia. Davis then directed the evacuation of the Confederate capital and gave orders for all government personnel and records to be transferred to Danville, Virginia. The President and his staff were transported to Danville by train[92]—the last train out of Richmond!

The presidential party had been at Danville scarcely a week when they learned of Lee's surrender at Appomattox Court House. Realizing that they would be the next target for the victorious Federal Army, the remnant of the Confederate government moved farther west to Charlotte, North Carolina and then south to Washington, Georgia. From this point it was expected that they would journey west and join General E. Kirby Smith in Texas, an area still comparatively secure from Federal invasion.[93]

Enroute to Washington, Georgia, the troops escorting the presidential party were given a portion of the gold brought out from Richmond. Judge John H. Reagan remained at Washington awhile, after President Davis and his escort left to close out the Confederate treasury. This he accomplished in short order, causing about $700,000 in Confederate notes to be burned, rejoining the presidential party soon thereafter. At Sandersville, Georgia, they were joined by the acting Secretary of the Treasury, M. H. Clark who provided the members of the President's staff with $1,500 each in gold coin, the property of the Confederacy, for safekeeping and eventual transmission abroad. Lubbock received his share and placed it in his saddlebags.[94]

On May 8, the President and his wife bade each other farewell, for Mrs. Davis and the children, urged by the President, had decided to go where it was hoped they could board a blockade runner for England. Only a short while after his family had departed, Davis was informed of a band of deserters following his wife's party. Risking capture, he decided to wait until Mrs. Davis' party could join them again. The reunion accomplished, the Davis family camped together on the evening of May 9. During the night, the Fourth Michigan Cavalry overtook Davis' rear guard who, overcome with fatigue, had fallen asleep. At daybreak, on May 10, the Federals "surprised the encampment and captured the whole party without firing a gun."[95]

Immediately, the search began for plunder, and in the confusion, Lubbock grabbed his saddlebags and attempted to escape. In the meantime, the Fourth Michigan and an Indiana regiment approaching from opposite directions took each other to be Confederates and began firing. Before the mistake was realized, a number of men in both the Federal regiments were killed or wounded.[96]

Failing in his attempt to escape, Lubbock was returned by his captors to where the other Confederates were under guard. Here he found Davis sitting on a log calmly awaiting events. Lubbock later wrote that Jefferson Davis, "sitting firmly erect, looked in all respects more the ideal hero than in the hours of his greatest prosperity." Lubbock was enraged by the rude treatment of his leader, and threatened to kill a private who approached Davis and said: "Well, Jeffy, how do you feel now?"[97]

The prisoners were taken to Macon, Georgia, and from there were transported by rail to Augusta, thence by river boat to Savannah, and finally by gunboat to Fortress Monroe, the Federal bastion at the mouth of the James.[98]

Upon arrival at Fortress Monroe, Davis did the ex-governor a great honor by requesting that his captors allow Lubbock to share the same prison cell. This, however, was promptly refused. While Davis was to spend the next two years languishing at Fortress Monroe, Lubbock, along with General "Fighting Joe" Wheeler and Colonel Preston Johnston were conveyed to Fort Delaware, on the west side of Delaware Bay. After spending several months in solitary confinement, Lubbock was released finally on November 23, 1865. He arrived back in the Lone Star State on December 16, 1865.

The ex-governor began to draw together remnants of his pre-war existence and settled into the routine of reconstruction. After returning to ranching he tried his hand at the meat-packing business in Houston and Galveston. When this venture proved a total disaster, he returned to politics by entering the mayor's race in Galveston.[99] "But," he related, "the old story of my once having advised the burning of Galveston and that my heart was really in Houston, being revived, I was beaten."[100] In a gesture of good will, his opponent offered to appoint him the city's tax collector, and he accepted.

With the trials of war and reconstruction fading into the past and three years as tax collector behind him, Lubbock turned his attention to state politics. As a delegate, Lubbock appeared at the state Democratic convention which convened in Galveston in 1876. This was the ex-governor's first appearance at the political gathering since 1860.[101] In 1878, the state convention nominated him for state treasurer on the Democratic ticket with Oran M. Roberts for governor and Joseph D. Sayers for lieutenant-governor. The campaign proved to be a success, and Lubbock began his first of six terms as treasurer of the Lone Star State.

Texas finances were in a rather sad condition, and the treasurer's job was far from an easy task. Lubbock had nursed the state through difficult days in the past, and with perseverance, the treasury was returned to a stable position.

While Lubbock was serving as treasurer, it was discovered that there were several million dollars in the coffers, and one legislator suggested that the treasurer's bond be increased. When asked his opinion of such action, Lubbock replied, "I would resign the damned office in fifteen minutes. I'm not going to crawl around on my belly and ask any man to go on my bond."[102]

Elected treasurer for the last time in 1888, Lubbock was succeeded in January of 1891 by W. B. Wortham.[103] During the James Stephen Hogg administration, he served on the state Board of Pardons. In 1895, at the age of eighty, he retired from public service. In 1883, after the death of his first wife, he married Mrs. Sarah E. (Black) Porter, and on August 12, 1903, he married Lue Scott.[104] Settling in Austin, the last years of his life were spent writing his memoirs, *Six Decades in Texas.* Four months short of his ninetieth birthday, the ex-governor passed away on June 22, 1905. Following services at his Austin home, Lubbock, dressed in his suit of Confederate grey, was carried to his final resting place in the state cemetery. His coffin was draped with both Confederate and United States flags.[105]

NOTES

[1]C. W. Raines (ed.), **Six Decades in Texas or Memoirs of Francis Richard Lubbock** (Austin: Ben C. Jones and Company, 1900), pp. 57-72. Hereafter cited as **Lubbock Memoirs**; and John H. Reagan, **Memoirs**, Walter Flavius McCaleb (ed.), (New York: The Neale Publishing Co., 1906), pp. 219-20. Hereafter cited as **Reagan Memoirs.**

[2]J. T. DeShields, **They Sat in High Places** (San Antnoio: The Naylor Company, 1940), p. 235; **Lubbock Memoirs,** p. 1.

[3]Walter Prescott Webb (ed.), **The Handbook of Texas,** Vol. II (Austin: The Texas State Historical Association, 1952), p. 89.

[4]**Lubbock Memoirs,** p. 23.

[5]**Ibid.,** pp. 28-41.

[6]**Ibid.,** p. 42.

[7]**Ibid.,** p. 46.

[8]**Ibid.,** p. 48.

[9]DeShields, p. 235.

[10]**Telegraph and Texas Register** (Houston), November 11, 1837, p. 2; **Lubbock Memoirs,** p. 65.

[11]**Dallas Morning News,** June 23, 1905, p. 6.

[12]**Lubbock Memoirs,** p. 85.

[13]William McCraw, **Professional Politicians** (Washington, D. C.: The Imperial Press, 1940), pp. 95-97.

[14]**Ibid.,** pp. 97-98.

[15]**Lubbock Memoirs,** p. 101.

[16]McCraw, pp. 101-103.

[17]**The Texas State Gazette** (Austin), November 3, 1855, p. 2.

[18]**Lubbock Memoirs,** pp. 199-202.

[19]**The Texas State Gazette** (Austin), May 9, 1857, p. 1.

[20]Ernest W. Winkler (ed.), **Platforms of Political Parties in Texas** (Austin: University of Texas, 1916), pp. 68-71.

[21]**The Clarksville Standard,** November 28, 1858.

[22]**Lubbock Memoirs,** p. 226.

[23]**The Dallas Weekly Herald,** March 7, 1874, p. 1; and **Lubbock Memoirs,** pp. 243-254.

[24]**Lubbock Memoirs,** pp. 260-63.

[25]**Ibid.,** p. 267.

[26]McCraw, p. 114.

[27]**Lubbock Memoirs,** pp. 280-96.

[28]**The Texas State Gazette,** October 6, 1860, p. 3.

[29]**Lubbock Memoirs,** p. 302.

[30]**Ibid.,** pp. 304-305.

[31]**Ibid.,** p. 310.

[32]**Ibid.,** p. 312.

[33]**Ibid.,** pp. 312-13.

[34]**Ibid.,** p. 321.

[35]**The Texas State Gazette,** June 22, 1861, p. 2.

[36]Norman G. Kittrell, **Governors Who Have Been and Other Public Men of Texas** (Houston: Dealy-Adey-Elgin Co., 1921), p. 32.

[37]**Lubbock Memoirs,** p. 328.

[38]Kittrell, p. 32.

[39]**Lubbock Memoirs,** pp. 326-27.

[40]**Ibid.,** pp. 327-28; Donald E. Everett (ed.), **Chaplin Davis and Hood's Texas Brigade** (San Antonio: Principia Press of Trinity University, 1962), p. 5.

[41]James M. Day (ed.), **State Journal of the Ninth Legislature of the State of Texas,** November 4, 1861-January 14, 1862 (Austin: Texas State Library, 1963), pp. 14-15.

[42]**Lubbock Memoirs,** pp. 334-36.

[43]**Ibid.,** p. 346.

[44]McCraw, p. 121.

[45]**Lubbock Memoirs,** pp. 348-49.

[46]**Ibid.,** p. 338.

[47]Clarence R. Wharton, **History of Texas** (Dallas: Turner Company, 1935), pp. 273-74.

[48]**Lubbock Memoirs,** pp. 344-45.

[49]**Ibid.,** p. 347.

[50]"Jefferson Davis to the Confederate Congress," February 28, 1862, in **War of the Rebellion: A Compilation of the Official Records of the Union and Confederate Armies,** 128 vols. Washington: U. S. War Dept. 1880-1901, Series I, Vol. XIV, pp. 429-30. Hereafter cited as **Official Records.**

[51]**Lubbock Memoirs,** p. 355.

[52]"Report of General J. B. Magruder to General S. Cooper," February 26, 1863, **Official Records,** Series I, Vol. XV, pp. 211-220.

[53]**Lubbock Memoirs,** pp. 358-59.

[54]**The Clarksville Standard,** February 15, 1862, p. 1.

[55]**Lubbock Memoirs,** pp. 357-58.

[56]**Ibid.,** pp. 362-65.

[57]**Ibid.,** pp. 478-83.

[58]Frank Johnson, **A History of Texas and Texans,** Eugene C. Barker and W. E. Winkler (eds.), Vol. 1 (Chicago: American Historical Society, 1914), pp. 545-46.

[59]Lubbock, "Proclamation to the People of Texas," **Official Records,** Series IV, Vol. I, p. 980.

[60]"Letter From Lubbock To Benjamin," March 7, 1862, **Official Records,** Series IV, Vol. I, pp. 977-78.

[61]**Lubbock Memoirs,** pp. 388-89.

[62]**Ibid.,** pp. 389-95.

[63]**The Texas State Gazette** (Austin), October 22, 1862, p. 2.

[64]**Lubbock Memoirs,** pp. 424-28.

[65]Mark Mayo Boatner, III, **The Civil War Dictionary** (New York: David McKay Co., 1959), p. 172.

[66]"General Order," April 28, 1862, **Official Records,** Series IV, Vol. I, p. 1,095.

[67]**Ibid.,** Series IV, Vol. II, p. 162.

[68]"A. J. Bell to J. P. Llewellen," November 28, 1862, **Official Records,** Series I, Vol. XV, p. 887.

[69]"Bell to Llewellen," January 3, 1863, **Official Records,** Series I, Vol. XV, pp. 925-26.

[70]"Webb to Captain Turner," January 12, 1863, **Official Records,** Series I, Vol. XV, p. 955.

[71]Reports of Major General J. Bankhead Magruder, October, 1862-February 26, 1863, **Official Records,** Series I, Vol. XV, pp. 210-227.

[72]**Ibid.,** pp. 463-71.

[73]**Ibid.,** p. 471.

[74]**Ibid.,** p. 487.

[75]"Colonel J. S. Ford to Captain Edmund P. Turner," July 22, 1863, **Official Records,** Series I, Vol. XXVI, Part II, p. 119.

[76]"J. T. Dashiel to Captain Edmund P. Turner," August 15, 1863, **Official Records,** Series I, Vol. XXVI, Part II, p. 170.

[77]**Lubbock Memoirs,** p. 493.

[78]**Ibid.,** p. 503.

[79]**Ibid.,** p. 512.

[80]**The Texas State Gazette,** June 24, 1863, p. 1.

[81]**Valedictory of Governor F. R. Lubbock to the Tenth Legislature of the State of Texas,** November 5, 1863 (Austin: State Gazette and Job Office, 1863), p. 6.

[82]**The Tri-Weekly Gazette,** November 6, 1863, p. 2.

[83]**Lubbock Memoirs,** p. 525.

[84]**Ibid.,** pp. 534-37.

[85]Report of General J. P. Banks to Secretary of War E. M. Stanton, April 6, 1865, **Official Records,** Series I, Vol. XXXIV, Part I, pp. 194-218.

[86]**Lubbock Memoirs,** p. 539.

[87]Report of General J. P. Banks to Secretary of War E. M. Stanton, April 6, 1865, **Official Records,** Series I, Vol. XXXVI, Part I, pp. 194-218.

[88]**Lubbock Memoirs,** p. 548.

[89]**Ibid.**

[90]**Ibid.,** p. 551.

[91]**Ibid.,** pp. 552-53.

[92]Alfred Jackson Hanna, **Flight Into Oblivion** (Richmond: Johnson Publishing Company, 1938), p. 11.

[93]**Lubbock Memoirs,** pp. 563-66.

[94]**Ibid.,** pp. 568-69.

[95]**The Clarksville Standard,** June 24, 1865, p. 2.

[96]**Lubbock Memoirs,** p. 572.

[97]**Ibid.**

[98]**Ibid.**

[99]McCraw, p. 125.

[100]**Lubbock Memoirs,** p. 572.

[101]McCraw, p. 126.

[102]Kittrell, p. 34.

[103]L. E. Daniell, **Personnel of the Texas State Government** (San Antonio: Maverick Printing House, 1892), p. 40.

[104]Webb, p. 89.

[105]McCraw, pp. 127-128.

John Bankhead Magruder

by
THOMAS M. SETTLES

When the first shots of the Civil War were fired on Fort Sumter on April 12, 1861, Texas found herself in a particularly vulnerable position. Besides a thousand-mile frontier open to Indian attack, she had over 600 miles of defenseless coastline which lay open to a possible Federal naval attack or invasion. Coast artillery and fortifications were desperately needed, but sandbags and driftwood constituted the only readily available building material, and slaves, borrowed from owners throughout the state provided the only form of labor. There also existed a great scarcity of lead, powder, ammunition and arms.[1] Indeed, other than small arms, the only guns available were a few cannon captured from the Federals at Brownsville and Brazos Santiago. When General Paul O. Hebert assumed command of the District of Texas in mid-September, 1861, he surveyed the coast and immediately reported this critical situation to the Secretary of War:

> I regret to say that I find this coast in almost a defenseless state, and in the almost total want of proper works and armaments; the task of defending successfully any point against an attack of any magnitude amounts to a military impossibility.[2]

After the United States Navy blockaded the Texas coast, General Hebert made extensive preparations for the abandonment of principal ports and military fortifications claiming that in the event of a large-scale naval landing "it would be folly to attempt resistance."[3] Later, in October, 1862, when the Federal blockading fleet moved in to capture Galveston, the leading port and largest city in the state, they entered the harbor in peaceful triumph as Hebert had given advance orders for the complete evacuation of the city.[4] Hebert's surrender of Galveston without a fight so incensed the citizens of Texas that they petitioned for his removal.[5] Finally, he was transferred to Louisiana and

General John B. Magruder was selected by the Confederate War Department to command the District of Texas, New Mexico, and Arizona.[6]

John Bankhead Magruder received his formal education at the United States Military Academy where he was "one of the most soldierly looking men in the Corps."[7] Magruder graduated in the class of 1830, one year behind Robert E. Lee and Joseph E. Johnston, with the brevet rank of second lieutenant in the infantry. The next year he transferred to the artillery and for the following fifteen years, served at scattered garrisons in the occupation of Texas and in the Seminole Indian district. After the outbreak of the Mexican War he was put in charge of the light artillery of Pillow's division. "For gallant and meritorious conduct" he was thrice promoted, finally being appointed, after Chapultepec, lieutenant colonel. While other officers showed no eagerness to serve under the "restless and hot-tempered" Magruder, Thomas J. Jackson exerted a determined effort and got command under him, for Jackson knew that "if any fighting was to be done Magruder would be on hand."[8] After the Mexican War, Magruder commanded the Federal garrisons at Fort McHenry, Maryland, and San Diego, California. Later he was transferred to Newport, Rhode Island, where he devoted a large portion of his time, energy, and money toward social affairs. Magruder was described as being "tall, dark, and handsome, a snappy dresser, a fast man with a buck, and a lover of beautiful women."[9] He had been nicknamed "Prince John" because of his courtly appearance and affinity for extravagant parties.

On the eve of the Civil War, Magruder resigned his commission in the United States Army and offered his services to the Confederacy. He received the rank of colonel in the Confederate Army and was placed in command of troops on the Virginia peninsula. Magruder led his forces to victory in the first land battle of the war at Big Bethel (May 10, 1861) and was promoted to brigadier-general shortly thereafter. During the early weeks of the Peninsula campaign (April-July, 1862) General Magruder, stationed at Yorktown, commanded a small force of 12,000 men. By rapidly erecting defensive works and utilizing "quaker" guns, he completely deceived McClellan (commanding an army of 100,000) as to the size and strength of his force and thus slowed the Union advance upon Richmond until reinforcements could arrive. Magruder was promoted to major-general and played an active role in the Seven Days Battles (June 26-July 1, 1862) around Richmond. He displayed extraordinary courage at Malvern Hill (July 1, 1862) but was transferred to Texas as a result of a misunderstanding with General Lee.[10]

General Magruder arrived in Texas in late November, 1862, and soon realized that he was expected to retrieve the disgraceful loss of Galveston.[11] He immediately began to devise a plan, making several visits to Galveston under cover of darkness where he carefully observed the strength and position of the enemy.[12] Magruder planned to transport a large force to Galveston at night for the purpose of securing strategic positions from which he could fire upon the decks of the enemy vessels in the harbor at a close range. After the battle had started and the Federal ships were actively engaged in repelling the land assault, there was to be a surprise naval attack, thus forcing the Federals to oppose the Confederates on two fronts.[13]

To execute this bold plan, General Magruder commissioned Captain Leon Smith to command the naval part of the expedition which consisted of the river steamers *Bayou City* and *Neptune.*[14] Each vessel carried a force of one hundred and fifty volunteer riflemen as well as a small complement of artillerymen. As the river steamers possessed very little armor, Captain Smith ordered cotton bales to be stacked on the boiler and hurricane decks to protect both the sharpshooters and vital machinery from the shot and shell of the enemy.[15] Hence, these two ships were referred to as "cotton clads."

Magruder's task was a difficult one, as the Federals enjoyed a decided advantage in manpower, firepower, and naval strength. The Federal fleet consisted of the *Harriet Lane,* mounting four heavy guns and two 24-pound howitzers, commanded by Captain Jonathan Wainwright; the flagship *Westfield,* carrying eight heavy guns, commanded by Commodore William Renshaw; the *Owasco,* which also carried eight heavy guns; the *Clifton,* a steam propeller with four heavy guns; the *Sachem,* a similar vessel armed with four guns; two armed transports, two large barks, and an armed schooner. In addition to the naval forces, Colonel Isaac Burrell commanded troops of the 42nd Massachusetts Infantry Regiment which were stationed on a wharf near the *Owasco.* Two lines of barricades impeded the land approaches to the wharf, and communication with the shore was cut off by the removal of large partions of the wharf planking in front of the barricades.[16]

Finally when Magruder and Smith had agreed upon all the details of the battle plan, the Confederate forces began their co-ordinated advance toward Galveston on December 31, 1862. Captain Smith cautiously moved his fleet to a point about ten miles above Galveston to wait for the land forces to begin the battle. At the same time that Smith's cotton-clads were positioning themselves, Magruder silently led his entire army, under the cover of night, across the railroad bridge that connected the mainland with Galveston.[17] When his troops had taken cover and the artillery was positioned where it would be most effective, General Magruder fired the first cannon and, reportedly, triumphantly shouted to his men, "I've done my duty as a private. Now I will attend to my duties as a general."[18]

Magruder's opening shot received prompt response along the entire Confederate line and shortly thereafter the guns of the Union fleet poured forth a similarly devastating volley. In the midst of the artillery duel, Confederate troops led by Colonel Joseph J. Cook plunged into chest-deep water with cumbersome scaling ladders and advanced toward the Federal infantrymen on the end of the wharf. Simultaneously, Confederate sharpshooters deployed on either side of the wharf, opened with a deadly supporting fire. Colonel Cook's forces made a valiant and determined attack but upon reaching the end of the wharf, much to their dismay they found the scaling ladders too short to accomplish their mission and thus were forced to retreat.[19]

The battle for the wharf a failure, the artillery duel at best a standoff, and Captain Smith and his steamers not in sight, at daylight on January 1, 1863, Magruder gave orders to fall back from the wharf area into the city. Just prior to the execution of these orders, however, the *Bayou City* and the *Neptune* arrived and engaged the *Harriet Lane,* the nearest of the Union vessels as well as one of the best prizes in the bay.[20] The *Bayou City* opened fire on the *Lane* and struck her a damaging blow near her wheelhouse.

On the third round, however, the *Bayou City's* 32-pounder

exploded, leaving her void of artillery.[21] Leon Smith, who was on the *Bayou City*, reacted quickly and ordered his pilot, Captain McCormick, to ram the *Harriet Lane* to facilitate boarding by the sharpshooters. McCormick steamed for the *Lane* but due a strong ebb-tide, struck her only a glancing blow in which he lost his port wheelhouse. Meanwhile, the *Neptune*, closing in to attack, struck the *Lane* on the starboard side causing her to leak badly. Immediately after the collision the *Lane* fired a tremendous broadside into the *Neptune* which struck her amidships, causing her to sink. The shallow water did not reach the upper portion of the sunken vessel and the undaunted sharpshooters continued to pour a deadly fire into the crew of the *Lane*. Meanwhile, the partially crippled *Bayou City* returned to the attack and under a full head of steam, struck the *Harriet Lane* aft of the port wheelhouse with such force that her iron prow remained firmly embedded in the Federal vessel and the two ships stuck fast together. Riflemen of both Confederate cotton-clads continued close-range firing while troops led by Captain Smith boarded and succeeded in capturing the Union ship after a desperate struggle.[22]

Immediately after seizing the *Harriet Lane*, Captain Smith dispatched Henry Lubbock,[23] captain of the *Bayou City*, to demand the surrender of the remainder of the Federal fleet. Captain Lubbock and his party rowed, under a flag of truce, to the *Clifton* where they confronted Captain Richard L. Law with the demand.[24] Lubbock explained that all Federal ships except one were to be surrendered and all crews of the surrendered vessels were to be allowed to withdraw on the one remaining ship. The alternative would be an immediate resumption of the battle in which, Captain Lubbock declared, the only possible result would be the complete destruction of the Federal fleet.[25] Captain Law secured a three-hour truce from Lubbock and proceeded immediately to the *Westfield*, which had accidentally run aground and consequently had been kept out of action, to present the terms of the surrender to Commander Renshaw.

During the three-hour truce, Magruder sent Brigadier-General William R. Scurry to demand the surrender of the Federal infantrymen on the wharf. Colonel Burrell asked for a three-hour truce to coincide with that which was granted to Captain

Law, but as he was refused the truce and faced an immediate resumption of action without the support of the fleet, he had no other choice but to surrender.[26]

Meanwhile, Commander Renshaw decided not to surrender but to withdraw his remaining ships from the harbor. He therefore ordered the other vessels to abandon their positions in the bay, with the proviso that their commanders were to destroy their own ships should they be in danger of capture by the Confederates.[27] Since the *Westfield*, was aground, Renshaw hastily evacuated his crew to the transport *Mary Boardman* and made preparations to scuttle her. He poured turpentine over the magazine and set her afire with his own hand. As he prepared to depart his ship, the magazine prematurely exploded with such a tremendous force that it ripped the forward half of the *Westfield* apart and killed Renshaw and the crew that was standing by to row him to the *Mary Boardman.*[28]

As the period of truce drew to a close, General Magruder sent Captain Lubbock under a flag of truce, to ascertain if the demand for surrender was going to be met. Lubbock had boarded Captain Law's ship when, to his utter dismay, the *Owasco, Sachem, Saxon, Mary Boardman,* and the *Clifton* began simultaneously steaming out of the harbor still flying their flags of truce. Lubbock protested the Federal action vigorously, charging Captain Law with breach of faith. Law, however, maintained that he was obligated to follow his commander's directive and therefore stubbornly refused to issue orders to the contrary.[29] Captain Law stopped his vessel only long enough to permit Lubbock to depart in a rowboat, and then resumed full speed as he departed the harbor for New Orleans.

When it was discovered that the Federal fleet had resorted to the ruse of running out of the harbor under a flag of truce, Leon Smith issued an urgent plea for volunteers to board the *John F. Carr.* Instantly, one hundred and fifty men joined Smith and pursued the Federals until the *Carr,* a small tender, came very near being swamped by breakers. Captain Smith was forced to abandon the chase but in returning, he captured the barks *Cavallo* and *Elias Pike* and the pilot schooner *Lecompte.* The barks were laden with seven hundred tons of coal, six hundred barrels of Irish potatoes, and a considerable quantity of military supplies.[30]

Despite the escape of a major portion of the fleet, General Magruder achieved a victory in which the Confederates lost only twenty-six killed and 117 wounded. Magruder proudly recounted the following results of the battle in his report to the adjutant general:

> We thus captured one fine steamship, two barks, and one schooner. We ran ashore the flagship of the Comodore, drove off two war steamers and sunk another . . . and took 300 or 400 prisoners. The number of guns captured was fifteen, and . . . a large quantity of stores, coal, and other material was also taken.[31]

Magruder was the hero of the hour and his victory stimulated a great wave of enthusiasm and patriotism throughout Texas. Few had believed that such favorable results could be obtained by men handicapped by insufficient resources, even when sustained by courage and spirit. General Magruder received warm and deserved commendation for his victory in congratulatory letters from Jefferson Davis, Sam Houston, Governor Lubbock and prominent citizens of the Confederacy. Both the Congress of the Confederate states and the Texas legislature passed resolutions praising Magruder and his men for their heroism and patriotism. Indeed, the victory at Galveston heartened people throughout the Confederacy.

News of the Battle of Galveston, on the contrary, shocked the Federals. Admiral David G. Farragut, commander of the West Gulf Squadron, described the disaster as "not only the most unfortunate thing that has ever happened to the Navy, but the most shameful and pusillanimous."[32] He had no intention of permitting the city to remain in Magruder's hands; and on January 3, 1863, issued orders to Commodore H. H. Bell, commanding the U.S.S. *Brooklyn,* to recapture Galveston.[33] Farragut also expressed hope that Bell could retake the *Harriet Lane* because he feared that if she managed to elude the blockade, "she would be a most formidable cruiser . . . on account of her speed and battery."[34]

Only a week after Magruder's successful battle, Commodore Bell arrived off Galveston, reestablished the blockade,[35] and cautiously prepared to recapture the city. Soon his invasion fleet, larger and more powerful than that commanded by Commodore William Renshaw, consisted of the *Brooklyn, Hatteras, Cayuga, New London, Owasco, Sciota, Itasca* and *Katahadin.* The masts of the captured *Harriet Lane,* clearly visible to Bell's fleet, served only to antagonize the Federal blockaders. "Galveston," reported a correspondent aboard the U.S.S. *New London,* "is a doomed town; the disgrace attending the capture of the *Harriet Lane* must be wiped out, and vengeance upon its butchers and captors will be awful. On Monday [January 12, 1863] we shall attempt to pass the forts at the mouth of the harbor."[36] The day before the proposed attack, however, the Federal lookout sighted a sail on the horizon, and Commodore Bell, suspecting it was a large blockade runner, dispatched the U.S.S. *Hatteras* to intercept the sighted vessel. [37] Unfortunately for the *Hatteras,* the vessel she unsuspectingly pursued turned out to be the Confederate "Grey Ghost," the steam cruiser *Alabama,* commanded by the intrepid Raphael Semmes.

After having been sighted by the blockading fleet, Captain Semmes took advantage of the situation by luring the *Hatteras* into open sea while simultaneously preparing his ship for combat. When the vessels were about twenty miles from the fleet, Semmes wheeled his ship about and engaged the *Hatteras* in a broadside duel.[38] After thirteen minutes of furious battle the *Hatteras* went down and Captain Semmes headed his vessel for Jamaica, never to return to Texas waters.

The *Hatteras* incident had a pronounced psychological effect on Bell's blockading fleet and for more than a year after the sinking, Admiral Farragut received reports that the *Alabama* had been "sighted" in Texas waters.[39] Thus one of Captain Semmes' most significant accomplishments was to weaken and confuse the blockading fleet long enough to enable General Magruder to strengthen Galveston's defenses by placing several heavy guns from the *Westfield* and *Harriet Lane* in key positions near the harbor area. With the city now firmly in Magruder's hands, Commodore Bell was forced to abandon his plans of recapturing Galveston and subsequently devoted his energies toward the business of preventing blockade running.

When the invasion threat passed, General Magruder returned to his headquarters in Houston to concentrate on administrative matters within his department. Although a good artillery officer, he unfortunately lacked both interest and ability in administrative affairs.[40] Furthermore, Magruder surrounded himself with poor assistants, most of whom had been selected because of their fighting or drinking abilities rather than their aptitude for administration.

The most frustrating problem which Magruder faced was an inability to secure adequate supplies. As the war progressed, the Confederates became increasingly dependent upon blockade runners. However, with the establishment of a more strict naval blockade, the Federals captured vessel after vessel resulting in a desperate need for food, clothing, and military supplies. Magruder's troops often went without pay and constantly lacked even basic supplies, particularly food. Their meager diet consisted of meat (usually beef), molasses, and corn meal, the latter which was "sour, dirty, weevil-eaten, and filled with ants and worms."[41] Several of the soldiers became sick because of the wretched food and most of the others complained of military life in general. Morale was low, dissatisfaction high and on August 10, 1863, the Third Regiment of Texas Infantry mutinied when they were ordered to drill.[42] Discontent spread rapidly, and the following day, the miners and sappers refused to work, claiming six months' pay was due them. Then Colonel Joseph J. Cook's heavy artillery regiment refused to leave the batteries. So few men remained loyal that no force could be found to guard the armory.[43]

General Magruder was "deeply mortified" to hear of the mutiny and responded by sending General Philip N. Luckett to make a thorough investigation into the causes of the dissatisfaction. Luckett reported that the complaints were just and that he found that no real disloyalty existed among the troops. He consequently issued an order suspending further drills until better provisions could be obtained. As far as he was concerned the mutiny ceased to exist when the troops were made to realize that they had adopted an improper mode of expressing their grievances and were thoroughly ashamed of their rash actions.[44]

In addition to the decline in military discipline, General Magruder was frustrated in his efforts to maintain firm control of the Texas coast because of the constant reduction of his forces. Desertions were common after Vicksburg fell (July, 1863), and it required the utmost vigilance to prevent men from escaping to the Federals or returning to their homes. And because of the troop shortage, men could not be spared to apprehend the deserters and thus very few were captured. Furthermore, a large portion of Magruder's command was transferred to Arkansas by order of General Edmund Kirby Smith, commander of the Trans-Mississippi Department. Kirby Smith believed the Federals would attempt an invasion of northeast Texas and thus felt justified in ordering Magruder to move a good portion of his command toward the Red River.[45] Magruder had no alternative except to obey Smith's orders, but he dispatched a letter to his commander on September 4, 1863, in which he voiced his disapproval and issued the following words of caution:

> It is my duty to state, for the information of the lieutenant-general commanding, that in taking these troops from the defense of the coast, I am compelled to leave vital points on the coast almost destitute of the means of defense . . . Should the enemy succeed in forcing the Sabine, or Galveston, or the Brazos, he will . . . virtually be master of Texas.[46]

Subsequent events proved Magruder's fears well-founded for when he reached Millican, a short distance south of the present-day Bryan, Texas, and then the northernmost station of the Houston and Texas Central Railroad, he received the dreaded news of a massive Federal landing attempt at Sabine Pass. Magruder immediately halted the movement of his troops toward the Red River and rushed all available forces to Beaumont where he hoped to thwart the progress of the Federals.[47] When he arrived, however, he was astonished to learn that the Federal invasion force which consisted of four gunboats and eighteen transports with over 5,000 troops aboard had been defeated by Lieutenant Richard W. Dowling and his forty-seven man garrison of Fort Griffin.[48]

Dowling captured two gunboats with a full supply of ordnance stores, eighteen heavy guns, and two hundred prisoners. Fifty Union soldiers were also killed and wounded. There were no battle casualties on the Confederate side.[49] Magruder was unrestrained in his praise for Lieutenant Dowling and his men and called their victory "the most extraordinary feat of the War."[50] At the same time, however, he was apprehensive that with so large a force still intact, the Federals would make another invasion attempt on the weakly defended Texas coast.

When the remnants of the Sabine Pass expedition returned to New Orleans, General Nathaniel P. Banks attempted to invade Texas by an overland troop movement across southern Louisiana. This plan, however, proved highly impracticable because of a lack of water and supplies in the area of the attempted attack.[51] Banks withdrew his troops but soon developed plans for another water-borne expedition. He intended to gain a foothold in the Rio Grande region of South Texas and then move northward along the coast until all important passes and ports on the Texas coast were under Federal control. General Banks personally organized the expedition which departed from New Orleans on October 26, 1863, and arrived at Brazos Santiago in early November. The Federals succeeded in capturing Brazos Santiago, Brownsville, Port Isabel, Aransas Pass, and Fort Esperanza until the only important coastal positions remaining in the hands of the Confederates were the works at the mouth of the Brazos River, Galveston, and Fort Griffin.[52]

General Magruder had philosophized that "Texas is virtually the Trans-Mississippi Department, and the railroads of Galveston and Houston are virtually Texas."[53] Therefore, he had opposed the Federal march up the coast of Texas with only token resistance until they neared Galveston but at that point, he determined to stop their advance. Magruder concentrated every available man around Galveston, expecting an all-out Federal attack. The Confederates nervously waited for months, but the expected enemy assault never materialized. Finally, there resulted a virtual standoff wherein the Federals held the lower coast of Texas, and Magruder the southeast portion of the state, with neither side anxious to advance upon the other.

Signs of nervous tension, mental fatigue, and physical exhaustion were evident among Magruder's soldiers in Galveston as a result of the endless waiting. The wearing effects of inactivity were compounded by poor living conditions and the fact that the troops were not paid regularly. A soldier wrote from Galveston that he had received no pay for eight months,[54] and another complained that, because of inflation "a Confederate soldier here, cannot buy his tobacco with his wages."[55] Food also remained of a disgracefully wretched quality as is evidenced in the diary of H. G. Medford, a Confederate soldier stationed opposite Galveston, at Virginia Point:

> Our rations are very scanty. The beeves that we eat here are so poor that they can scarcely stand. It is an outrage that Confederate soldiers should be compelled to live upon what we live upon . . . We have not drawn anything but poor beef in the way of meat since we have been in the state. . . . I am the last one to mutiny or desert; but if there are any justifiable causes for such things, it is here in our army.[56]

About one month after Medford complained of the substandard food and living conditions, the ladies of Galveston had a supper and ball in honor of General Magruder and other high-ranking officers of his command. When the party reached its "acme of joculary," about five hundred armed soldiers appeared and threatened to burn the house to the ground if General Magruder did not come forth and listen to their demands. The soldiers, aggravated by the miserable conditions under which they lived, protested that it was no time for "feasting, fiddling and dancing" because they were starving and the Confederacy was "bleeding at every pore." Magruder sympathized with their grievances, promising more food of a higher quality and better living conditions. Finally, however, when the mob of angry soldiers dispersed, "Prince John" returned to the party where he rallied the frightened participants and continued the ball in a grand manner.[57]

Although the military situation in southeast Texas had become calm enough in mid-1864 to permit General Magruder to attend an occasional party, the situation elsewhere remained desperate. General Robert E. Lee was hard pressed by Grant at Petersburg. Jubal Early, operating in the valley of Virginia, faced a numerically superior adversary and needed every available man. General John B. Hood had replaced Johnston at Atlanta and was confronted by the relentless Sherman. West of the Mississippi River, General N. P. Banks and Admiral David Porter organized a huge land-and-water enterprise whose main objective was to proceed up the Red River, enter Texas, and establish Union control over the state.[58] The Red River expedition (March 10-May 22, 1864) proved however, to be a costly fiasco for the Federals. General Richard Taylor defeated the Federals at Mansfield, Louisiana (April 8, 1864), forcing General Banks to begin a general withdrawal without having accomplished any of his objectives. As the Confederate strength in the southwest had hardly been shaken, General Kirby Smith reorganized his department in an effort to take some of the pressure off of the eastern theatre. Smith transferred General John G. Walker to Texas. General Simon Bolivar Buckner was sent to West Louisiana, and Magruder to command the District of Arkansas.[59]

Magruder performed admirably in Arkansas, holding his position against General Frederick Steele while Sterling Price attempted to obtain recruits and supplies for the Confederacy in Missouri. In March, 1865, however, there was a widespread rumor that a Federal force of over 40,000 men commanded by General Edward R. S. Canby was making final preparations for a landing on the coast of Texas.[60] Kirby Smith immediately ordered Magruder back to Texas,[61] but when he arrived on the coast he learned that Canby's expedition had been cancelled. The Federals needed no invasion; the Confederacy was crumbling.

> A feeling of gloom hung over the people of the South. They saw their brave armies, after a series of brilliant victories, drawn back, baffled and defeated. The iron began to enter their souls. . . . The future was filled with deep forebodings of evil. Their fate, their identity, as a people, hung in the balance and would soon be decided by that inexorable fiat, the sword. . . . The chivalric Lee was the central figure in this fearful drama. All hung upon his action. Under his masterly leadership his brave army of veterans had hotly contested the ground from the Wilderness to Petersburg, inch by inch, against overwhelming odds. If he could by masterly strategy overcome the great odds against him and achieve a decisive victory, there was hope; if not, all was lost. . . .[62]

General Lee, however, could not accomplish the impossible and on April 9, 1865, he surrendered his decimated army to Grant. Magruder and Kirby Smith realized the end was near but issued stirring appeals to their troops to maintain the struggle against the Federals.[63] The appeals, despite their eloquence and avowed patriotism, failed to arouse the enthusiasm of the soldiers who deserted in increasing numbers. They were war-weary and realized that with the surrender of Lee and Johnston in the eastern theatre, the struggle had in reality come to an end.[64] The Trans-Mississippi Department rapidly disintegrated until General Smith had no alternative except to surrender. Final terms were agreed to in New Orleans on May 26, by Major-General P. J. Osterhaus, chief of staff to General Canby and Kirby Smith's official representative, Lieutenant-General Buckner.[65] On June 2, 1865, Generals Smith and Magruder signed the document aboard the U.S.S. *Fort Jackson* in Galveston Bay,[66] thus officially ending the war in Texas and the Trans-Mississippi West.

The fighting was over for John B. Magruder but he was too proud and stubborn to admit defeat readily. When the Federals began arresting and imprisoning Confederate officials, he refused to submit to such personal humiliation and decided to escape Federal authority altogether by joining the Confederate exodus to Mexico. Shortly after the official surrender aboard the *Fort Jackson,* Magruder proceeded to San Antonio, then to Monterrey where hundreds of ex-Confederates had gathered.[67] Among the group were such outstanding leaders as Governor Pendleton Murrah of Texas, Governor Henry W. Allen, and former Governor Thomas O. Moore, both of Louisiana, former Governor Edward Clark of Texas, Governor Thomas C. Reynolds of Missouri and Generals Joseph O. Shelby, William Preston, Jubal A. Early, Sterling Price, Cadmus Wilcox, Thomas C. Hindman, Kirby Smith, and others.[68] They were cordially received by Archduke Maximilian, the puppet emperor of Napoleon III, who was sympathetic toward the Confederates and even assisted in their colonization schemes.[69] General Magruder was appointed chief of the Colonization Land Office with an annual salary of $3,000,[70] and soon established the first Confederate settlement in Mexico, naming it Carlota in honor of the Empress. The land was fertile, the climate excellent and initially the project was quite successful. However, in 1867, the settlement of Carlota was virtually abandoned in the wake of the political chaos which followed Napoleon's withdrawal from Mexico and the reinstatement of President Juarez. Magruder left Mexico in mid-1866 going first to Cuba and then on to the United

States where he traveled about the country, lecturing on his experiences in the Civil War. When his financial resources were exhausted he returned to Texas and established his permanent residence in Houston. Shortly afterwards, the gallant Magruder, broken in spirit and health and living in relative poverty, died on February 19, 1871.

Although given a pauper's burial in Houston, the citizens of Galveston had not forgotten the man who courageously wrested their city from the hands of the Federals on New Year's Day, 1863. Magruder's remains were transferred to Galveston and his grave marked by a magnificent tombstone. Ornately chiseled about its four sides were pictures of a general on horseback, a ship being sunk in Galveston harbor, a cannonball being fired, and a weary soldier with a tattered Confederate flag. A majestic spire rising toward the sky is draped with a cement replica of a Confederate cape. . . . A splendid monument, truly befitting an intrepid warrior, John Bankhead Magruder.

NOTES

[1]Dudley G. Wooten (ed.), **A Comprehensive History of Texas, 1685 to 1897** (2 vols.; Dallas: William G. Scarff, 1898), II, Part V, Chapter I, p. 526.

[2]Brigadier-General Paul O. Hebert to Judah P. Benjamin, Secretary of War, September 27, 1861. **The War of the Rebellion: A Compilation of the Official Records of the Union and Confederate Armies** (128 vols.; Washington, D. C.: Government Printing Office, 1880-1901). Series I, Vol. IV, p. 112. Hereafter cited as **Official Records.**

[3]Hebert to Colonel Joseph J. Cook, Commanding at Galveston, May 19, 1862, **Ibid.,** Series I, Vol. IX, p. 712.

[4]Special Order of Provost-Marshal J. C. Massie to the citizens of Galveston, May 23, 1862. Original MS in the Rosenberg Library, Galveston, Texas; Special Orders No. 471 from Headquarters Military District of Galveston, Cook to Lieutenant-Colonel J. H. Manly, May 14, 1862, **Official Records,** Series I, Vol. IX, p. 709.

[5]Thomas North, **Five Years in Texas; or What You Did Not Hear During the War from January 1861 to January 1866. A Narrative of His Travels, Experiences, and Observations, in Texas and Mexico** (Cincinnati: Elm Street Printing Company, 1871), p. 107.

[6]Special Orders No. 237 of the Adjutant and Inspector General's Office, October 10, 1862, **Official Records,** Series I, Vol. XV, p. 826.

[7]Richard Stoddert Ewell Papers. Typewritten copy of the originals [Library of Congress] in the Rosenberg Library, Galveston, Texas.

[8]George Francis Robert Henderson, **Stonewall Jackson and the American Civil War** (2 vols.; New York: Longmans, Green and Company, 1903), I, pp. 32-33.

[9]Herbert Lockwood, "The Skeleton's Closet." Unclassified manuscript given to author by Alice Murphy of the Houston **Post.**

[10]General Robert E. Lee to George W. Randolph, Secretary of War, August 14, 1862, **Official Records,** Series I, Vol. XI, Part II, pp. 679-680; Statement of Major-General J. Bankhead Magruder on Lee's remarks, September 5, 1862, **ibid.,** pp. 680-681.

[11]North, **Five Years in Texas,** pp. 107-108.

[12]Magruder to General Samuel Cooper, Adjutant and Inspector General, February 26, 1863, **Official Records,** Series I, Vol. XV, p. 212; Wooten, **A Comprehensive History of Texas,** p. 531.

[13]Magruder to Cooper, February 26, 1863, **Official Records,** Series I, Vol. XV, pp. 212-214; Charles Waldo Hayes, "The Island and City of Galveston," pp. 549-550. Unpublished MS in the Rosenberg Library, Galveston, Texas.

[14]Magruder to Cooper, February 26, 1863, **Official Records,** Series I, Vol. XV, p. 212.

[15]Hayes, "The Island and City of Galveston," p. 550.

[16]Magruder to Cooper, February 26, 1863, **Official Records,** Series I, Vol. XV, p. 213.

[17]In addition to being used by General Magruder, the bridge connecting Galveston with the mainland was used by Confederate scouts who maintained a continuous watch on the Union fleet anchored in Galveston Bay. The bridge had not been destroyed by the Federals because there had been several reports that an invasion of Texas would be launched from Galveston and in such a case, the bridge would have been a strategic necessity.

[18]Frank X. Tolbert, **Dick Dowling at Sabine Pass** (New York: McGraw-Hill Book Company, Inc., 1962), pp. 42-43.

[19]Magruder to Cooper, February 26, 1863, **Official Records,** Series I, Vol. XV, p. 214.

[20]Ibid., pp. 214-215.

[21]J. Thomas Scharf, **History of the Confederate States Navy from Its Organization to the Surrender of Its Last Vessel** (New York: Rogers and Sherwood, 1887), p. 507.

[22]Statement of Captain McCormick concerning the naval battle at Galveston. Published in the Houston **Telegraph,** January 5, 1883.

[23]Captain Henry S. Lubbock was the brother of Francis R. Lubbock, Governor of Texas, 1861-1863, Thomas S. Lubbock, and John B. Lubbock, prominent Texans of the Civil War era.

[24]Robert M. Franklin, **Story of the Battle of Galveston.** From Galveston News, May 8, 1911.

[25]Charles C. Cumberland, "The Confederate Loss and Recapture of Galveston, 1862-1863," **Southwestern Historical Quarterly,** LI (October, 1947), p. 125.

[26]Statement of Colonel Isaac S. Burrell in relation to the surrender of a portion of the 42nd Massachusetts Infantry Regiment, January 23, 1863, **Official Records,** Series I, Vol. XV, p. 226.

[27]Cumberland, "The Confederate Loss and Recapture of Galveston, 1862-1863," p. 126.

[28]Major William L. Burt to Major-General Nathaniel P. Banks, Commanding Department of the Gulf, undated letter, **Official Records,** Series I, Vol. XV, p. 203.

[29]Captain Law was court-martialed and found guilty of "leaving his station, in time of war, before regularly relieved "and "not doing his utmost to capture or destroy a vessel which it was his duty to encounter." The court dismissed him from the Navy, but in view of the gallantry displayed in his attack on the Confederate batteries at Fort Point, the sentence was commuted to a three-year suspension from the United States Navy. General Order No. 28, signed by Gideon Welles, Secretary of the Navy, January 7, 1864, **Official Records of the Union and Confederate Navies in the War of the Rebellion** (31 vols.; Washington, D. C.: Government Printing Office, 1894-1927). Series I, Vol. XIX, pp. 463-464. Hereafter cited as **Official Records of Navies.**

[30]Hayes, "The Island and City of Galveston," pp. 565-566.

[31]Magruder to Cooper, February 26, 1863, **Official Records,** Series I, Vol. XV, p. 216. For accounts of the Battle of Galveston consult the following correspondence, all of which can be found in **Official Records of Navies,** Series I, Vol. XIX, at the page indicated: Magruder to Cooper, February 26, 1863, p. 470; Spear to Farragut, January 2, 1863, p. 438; Henry Wilson of the USS **Owasco** to Farragut, January 2, 1863, p. 439; Report of Court of Inquiry to Farragut, January 12, 1863, p. 447. For additional information consult the following: Xavier B. Debray, **A Sketch of the History of Debray's 26th Regiment of Texas Cavalry** (1884); Clement A. Evans (ed.), **Confederate Military History,** XI (1899); Robert M. Franklin, **Story of the Battle of Galveston** (1911); Statement of Captain McCormick concerning the naval battle at Galveston, published in the Houston **Telegraph,** January 5, 1883; Alfred T. Mahan, **The Gulf and Inland Waters** (1883); David D. Porter, **The Naval History of the Civil War** (1885); J. Thomas Scharf, **History of the Confederate States Navy from Its Organization to the Surrender of Its Last Vessel** (1887); Dudley G. Wooten, **A Comprehensive History of Texas, 1685-1897,** II (1898).

[32]Rear-Admiral David G. Farragut to Acting Rear-Admiral Theodorus Bailey, April 22, 1863, **Official Records of Navies,** Series I, Vol. XX, p. 157.

[33]Farragut to Commodore Henry H. Bell, Commanding U.S.S. **Brooklyn,** January 3, 1863, **ibid.,** Series I, Vol. XIX, p. 479.

[34]Farragut to Welles, January 3, 1863, **ibid.,** p. 481.

[35]Although Bell arrived off Galveston on the morning of January 7, 1863, he did not officially announce the reestablishment of the blockade until January 20. Bell to Farragut, January 11, 1863, **ibid.,** p. 504; Proclamation of Commodore Bell announcing the blockade of the coast of Texas by United States naval vessels, January 20, 1863, **ibid.,** pp. 451-452.

[36]Frederick Thompson to Joseph Thompson, January 10, 1863, **Official Records of Navies,** Series I, Vol. XIX, p. 505. Thompson apparently believed the widespread rumor that the entire crew of the **Harriet Lane** had been massacred.

[37]Bell to Welles, January 13, 1863, **ibid.**, pp. 508-509.

[38]For accounts of the naval battle between the **Alabama** and **Hatteras** consult the following correspondence, all of which can be found in **Official Records of Navies,** Series I, Vol. II, at the page indicated: Blake to Welles, January 21, 1863, p. 18; Partridge to Farragut, January 12, 1863, p. 21; Semmes to Mallory, May 12, 1863, p. 483; Extracts from the journal of Raphael Semmes, commanding the CSS **Alabama,** Sunday, January 11, 1863 —Monday, January 12, 1863, p. 721. The following also contain excellent first-hand accounts of the duel between the **Alabama** and **Hatteras:** Raphael Semmes, **Memoirs of Service Afloat, During the War Between the States** (1869); Arthur Sinclair, **Two Years on the "Alabama."** (1895).

[39]Tolbert, **Dick Dowling at Sabine Pass**, p. 48.

[40]Joseph Howard Parks, **General Edmund Kirby Smith, CSA** (Baton Rouge, Louisiana: Louisiana State University Press, 1954), p. 347.

[41]Report of Lieutenant-Colonel Edward F. Gray, Texas Third Infantry, August 4, 1863, **Official Records,** Series I, Vol. XXVI, Part I, p. 241.

[42]Report of Acting Brigadier-General Xavier B. Debray, August 11, 1863, **ibid.,** p. 242.

[43]**Ibid.,** August 12, 1863, p. 243.

[44]Report of Acting Brigadier-General Philip N. Luckett, August 13, 1863, **ibid.,** pp. 245-246.

[45]Brigadier-General William R. Boggs, Chief of Staff to General E. K. Smith, to Magruder, August 28, 1863, **ibid.,** Series I, Vol. XXII, Part II, p. 982.

[46]Magruder to Boggs, September 4, 1863, **ibid.,** Series I, Vol. XXVI, Part II, pp. 203-204.

[47]Magruder to Boggs, September 9, 1863, **ibid.,** Series I, Vol. XXVI, Part I, pp. 302-303.

[48]For accounts of the Battle of Sabine Pass consult the following correspondence, all of which can be found in **Official Records,** Series I, Vol. XXVI, Part I, at the page indicated: Banks to Halleck, September 13, 1863, p. 288; Roe to Drake, February 2, 1864, p. 293; Franklin to Banks, September 11, 1863, p. 294; Weitzel to Hoffman, September 11, 1863, p. 298; Crocker to Bell, September 12, 1863, p. 301; Magruder to Boggs, September 10, 1863, p. 303; Smith to Turner, September 8, 1863, p. 307; Odlum to Mills, September 9, 1863, p. 309; Dowling to Odlum, September 9, 1863, p. 311. For additional information consult the following: Mrs. R. F. Pray, **Dick Dowling's Battle: An Account of the War Between the States in the Eastern Gulf Coast Region of Texas** (1936); Colonel Harold B. Simpson, "The Battle of Sabine Pass," in **Battles of Texas** (1967); Frank X. Tolbert, **Dick Dowling at Sabine Pass** (1962).

[49]Magruder to Boggs, September 10, 1863, **Official Records,** Series I, Vol. XXVI, Part I, p. 303.

[50]Magruder to Cooper, September 27, 1863, **ibid.,** pp. 305-306.

[51]Banks to Edwin Stanton, Secretary of War, April 6, 1865, **ibid.,** pp. 19-20; Report of Banks, October 22, 1863, **ibid.,** p. 292.

[52]Banks to Stanton, April 6, 1865, **ibid.,** pp. 20-21.

[53]Magruder to Smith, September 26, 1863, **ibid.**, Series I, Vol. XXVI, Part II, pp. 260-262.

[54]Houston **Daily Telegraph,** May 6, 1864.

[55]Rebecca W. Smith and Marion Mullins (eds.), "Diary of H. C. Medford, Confederate Soldier, 1864," **Southwestern Historical Quarterly,** XXXIV (October, 1930), p. 121.

[56]**Ibid.,** pp. 120-121.

[57]**Ibid.,** pp. 128-129.

[58]Banks left General Napoleon J. T. Dana in command of Union troops on the Texas coast. General Banks hoped that by forcing the Confederates defending the state to oppose the Federals on two fronts, the Red River and on the coast, he could divide their forces sufficiently to overpower them and seize control of the state.

[59]General Orders No. 60, August 4, 1864, in **Official Records,** Series I, Vol. XLI, Part II, p. 1039.

[60]General John G. Walker to Smith, March 7, 1865, **ibid.**, Series I, Vol. XLVIII, Part I, p. 1412.

[61]General Orders No. 30, March 31, 1865, **ibid.,** p. 1455.

[62]Hayes, "The Island and City of Galveston," pp. 629-630.

[63]Smith to the Soldiers of the Trans-Mississippi Army, April 21, 1865, **Official Records,** Series I, Vol. XLVIII, Part II, p. 1284; General Orders No. 20, April 23, 1865, **ibid.,** pp. 1284-1285; Magruder to People and Army of Texas, May 4, 1865, **ibid., p. 1294.**

[64]Brigadier-General James E. Slaughter to Magruder, May 19, 1865, **ibid.,** pp. 1313-1314; Walker to Smith, May 16, 1865, **ibid.,** pp. 1308-1309.

[65]Terms for surrender of the Trans-Mississippi Department, May 26, 1865, **ibid.,** pp. 600-602.

[66]Report of Acting Rear-Admiral Henry K. Thatcher, June 8, 1865, **Official Records of Navies,** Series I, Vol. XXII, p. 216.

[67]Alexander W. Terrell, **From Texas to Mexico and the Court of Maximilian in 1865** (Dallas: The Book Club of Texas, 1933), pp. 18-19.

[68]Carl C. Rister, "Carlota, A Confederate Colony in Mexico," **Journal of Southern History,** XI (February, 1945), pp. 36-39.

[69]William C. Nunn, **Escape from Reconstruction** (Fort Worth: Leo Potishman Foundation, 1956), pp. 38, 41; Rister, "Carlota, A Confederate Colony in Mexico," pp. 33-34, 40.

[70]J. Fred Rippy, "Mexican Projects of the Confederates," **Southwestern Historical Quarterly,** XXII (April, 1919), p. 316.

Pendleton Murrah

by

BENNY E. DEUSON

The campaign for governor of the Lone Star State in 1863 excited little enthusiasm among the Texas voters. Most Texans were involved in the war effort either directly or indirectly and this, of course, occupied the lion's share of their thoughts and their time. This preoccupation plus the fact that neither candidate for the gubernatorial office was a dynamic, exciting personality considerably dampened the political ardor of the electorate. General Thomas Jefferson Chambers, one of the two candidates, had campaigned for the office unsuccessfully on three previous occasions. The other candidate, Pendleton Murrah, an East Texan, was relatively unknown in other parts of the state.[1] This choice of candidates failed to bring out the vote, and only 29,966 Texans went to the polls on August 3, 1863. Murrah claimed 17,511 of the votes cast, and Chambers counted but 2,455.[2]

Murrah's obscurity as a state personality was revealed by the following statement which appeared in the *Tri-Weekly State Gazette* of Austin, two weeks prior to the election. "Who is Pendleton Murrah?" asked a resident of Brenham, Texas. "The objection raised against Mr. Murrah is not that he is not qualified, but we do not know who he is."[3] This was a justifiable question for Murrah's reputation as a lawyer and a legislator had not spread to all parts of the state. Many people had not come to know this attractive man—tall, slightly stooped, with a gentle demeanor but a lightning-quick temper and an unforgiving nature. Those who did know him admired his keen mind and dedication to his work. They also might have seen traces of depression in his behavior caused by events in his early childhood and marriage. They might also have noticed that he suffered from tuberculosis,[4] an ever-present companion that shortened a promising career and drove him to a lonely death in Monterrey, Mexico.[5]

Little is known of Murrah's early life in South Carolina, his birthplace. His parents and date of birth are unknown. Vivian Mitchell, Murrah's great-great-niece, stated in a letter to the librarian of the University of Texas that Murrah's only trace of an immediate family was a sister who died in 1921 and was buried at Clanton, Alabama.[6]

Although his education came from charitable sources, it was an excellent one. A society of the Baptist Church sent him to Brown University at Providence, Rhode Island.[7] After graduating from Brown in 1848, Murrah settled in Alabama and studied law at the old Driscoll Mansion located in Plantersville in Dallas County.[8] Soon after moving to Alabama, however, he contracted tuberculosis. With his health failing rapidly, Murrah decided to move to Texas and seek the relief of a dry climate.[9]

After arriving in the Lone Star State, Murrah settled in Marshall, the county seat of Harrison County. This East Texas city was the center of social refinement, wealth, and political influence in that part of the state. Too, the lawyers practicing in Marshall at the time were deemed to be some of the ablest in Texas. Working in this environment and competing with the best lawyers in the state, Murrah soon became a recognized leader in his profession, knowledgeable in theory, adept in practice and procedure, and forceful and persuasive in oratory.[10]

Murrah's reputation brought him in contact with leading businessmen and planters in the Marshall area. During a social affair he met Sue Ellen Taylor, daughter of Bayliss Taylor, a wealthy plantation owner. The Taylor family was also from the "Old South"; Sue Ellen had been born in Pendleton, South Carolina.[11] After a whirlwind courtship, the two were married on October 16, 1850.

After his marriage Murrah's law practice increased rapidly. By the mid-1850's, after having amassed a small fortune, his interest turned to politics.[12] He entered this capricious field gradually by giving campaign speeches for his friends who were running for office. It was not until 1855 that Murrah decided to run for office himself. He declared himself a candidate for the state legislature on the Democratic ticket. He campaigned bitterly and vigorously against the Know-Nothing Party and its candidate. During a speech given at the courthouse in Marshall, he made a vigorous attack on Know-Nothingism, resulting in a walk-out by prominent citizens—the few in the audience that remained were his close friends.[13] The Know-Nothing Party was strong in East Texas, particularly among the well-to-do and the landed gentry.

After this incident Murrah realized that he had little chance of winning and that the Know-Nothing Party would probably sweep the district. Shaken by this startling realization, he hurriedly announced his withdrawal. Only the persuasiveness of Colonel R. W. Loughery, editor of the *Texas Republican,* changed his mind.[14] Even though he was defeated, his campaign did strengthen the Democratic Party in his district and confirmed his political reputation.[15]

His efforts bore fruit in 1857. He ran successfully for the same office, and a year later (1858) served on the Democratic State Executive Committee.[16]

Tuberculosis again threatened his life. By 1860, his health had failed noticeably, and Murrah realized his life would probably be short, but the young lawyer was determined to make it a useful one. He had favored secession from the beginning and early in 1862 assisted ex-Governor Edward Clark in raising the 14th Texas Infantry Regiment. He acted as quartermaster for the regiment for several months,[17] but his illness precluded field service, so he returned home.[18]

Seeking a position that was less demanding physically, Murrah responded again to the call of politics. After Governor Lubbock declined to run for re-election, Murrah's friends convinced him that he could win the office. Accepting the nomination, he waged a successful campaign against thrice-loser Thomas Jefferson Chambers, and on November 5, 1863, was sworn in as the state's chief executive.[19]

The colorless inauguration on that dreary November day seemed appropriate for the times and conditions. The ceremonies were simple and devoid of any gaiety or splendor. The *piece de resistance* of the state dinner consisted of corn meal cakes made and served by wives of the new state officials. No inaugural ball had been scheduled, for none felt that dancing or frivolities were appropriate during such somber times.[20]

As a devotee to the theory of state rights, Murrah anticipated conflict with the Confederacy, but as a Democrat also, he reasoned that compromising solutions could be found to the major problems. In most instances his reasoning was correct, but several solutions resulted only with his complete compliance with Confederate demands. Many situations warranted arbitrary action by Confederate officials, and in extreme instances, they overrode decisions by state officials, including the governor. Hence, Murrah's administration in many respects became one of conflict and strife from beginning to end. The Civil War had been raging for over two years by the time the Marshall lawyer became governor, and conditions across the state had become so deplorable that little could have been done to improve them.[21]

The factor that caused the greatest conflict between Murrah and the Confederacy was the Impressment Act passed by the Confederate government in March, 1863. The Impressment Act provided that:

> Whenever the exigencies of an army in the field are such as to make impressment of forage, articles of subsistence, or other property absolutely necessary, then such impressments may be made by the officer or officers whose duty it is to furnish such forage, articles of subsistence, or other property for such army.[22]

Confederate officials in the Trans-Mississippi Department doubted the legality of the act, and resorted to it only occasionally during the early part of the war, however, by 1863 General E. Kirby Smith, the department commander, felt compelled to execute the measure fully. On June 27, he directed the impressment of all cotton and all transportation to meet the immediate needs of the department.[23]

After General Smith ordered the impressment of cotton, General John B. Magruder, Commander of the Texas, New Mexico, and Arizona District of the Trans-Mississippi Department, appointed a special quartermaster officer to carry out the order. It was not publicly stated what portion of the cotton crop was to be taken. The planters presumed that all of the cotton was to be impressed and protested to Governor Murrah.[24]

Prominent newspapers heatedly discussed, pro and con, the seizure of cotton. The *LaGrange Patriot,* on the one hand, expressed opposition to the impressment of cotton in a scorching editorial. The editor stated that cotton did not come under the head of "other property," it was not an army necessity, and that army officers were not legally empowered to buy or seize it.[25]

The *Houston Daily Telegraph,* on the other hand, supported the action of the Confederate government. The *Telegraph* stated that if the Richmond government could not impress cotton, then it could not impress anything.[26]

Murrah became concerned about the situation after the Confederate Cotton Bureau was created at a meeting in Houston in December, 1863.[27] Headquarters for the Bureau were established in Shreveport, Louisiana, with a branch office in Houston.[28] The bureau acted as the official Confederate agent in impressing cotton for the use of the army. Under its program the planter had to sell half of his cotton to the Richmond government, and then was given a permit to export the other half. By the middle of May, 1864, the bureau had realized the amount of $151,490 in specie for cotton.[29]

To combat and frustrate the efforts of the Confederate Cotton Agency, the New Military Board, created by the state on April 12, 1864, to carry on military affairs, appointed an agent to buy cotton.[30] The fact that the state agent paid higher prices for cotton than did his Confederate counterpart and Murrah's announcement in March, 1864, that he would not permit the impressment of cotton helped to stall the Richmond effort.[31] The state agent went on to purchase 266 bales during the remainder of 1864 and exported them to Mexico for sale.[32]

Under Murrah's direction, the state militia board offered another plan for purchasing cotton. Contracts were made with individuals to export their own cotton but in the name of the board. By this method the state accepted full responsibility of the cotton during its shipment.[33] Many men were willing to sell cotton in this way, but did not have wagons and teams enough to do the job as both were constantly being used by the Confederacy. B. H. Epperson of Clarksville wrote the governor that he would carry cotton for the state if Murrah could get an exemption from General Smith for twenty or thirty teams for his use.[34] A farmer from Brenham had also complained earlier to the governor that the transportation of cotton to Mexico was impossible for no planter had an extra team to use.[35]

The state was forced finally to stop its activity in cotton purchasing. Murrah had been under pressure from General

Smith for some time to cease his competitive operation. Calling the governor to a conference at Hempstead, Texas, Smith convinced him of the necessity of the new Confederate policy, instituted in June, 1864, for the army to impress half of all the cotton in the Trans-Mississippi Department. Murrah, reluctantly, ordered the Military Board to cease the purchase of cotton.[36] By the end of 1864, the Confederate Cotton Bureau had also suspended operations.[37]

Murrah's ideas also conflicted with Confederate policies concerning the impressment of wagons and teams to transport the impressed cotton. After May, 1863, orders to impress transportation went out to local military commanders by the authority of Magruder and Smith. The impressment of transportation was extensive and brought forth complaints from citizens of the state. John Gibbs of Huntsville protested the impressment of his teams, which left him unable to transport his cotton from Huntsville to Eagle Pass. Murrah sympathized but could do nothing to alleviate the situation.[38]

The impressment of slaves by Confederate authorities created still another problem. Governor Lubbock had left the matter entirely in the hands of Confederate military authorities.[39] In the summer of 1863, the Confederate Congress established the Bureau of Slave Labor to direct the impressment of Negroes. This organization found a "rocky road to travel" in Texas. Many Texans refused to give up their slaves for Confederate use because they feared the slaves would escape.[40] Others declined to cooperate unless they were declared exempt from service as long as their Negroes were used.[41] This impressment inflamed others because they feared that slaves would be used by private speculators.[24] The governor could do little but to try to pacify the citizenry and check on their claims of illegal slave impressment.[43]

Sometimes action by Murrah resulted in better treatment for Texas citizens. Confederate officials by law could also impress Texas beef. Cattle were regularly exchanged across the Rio Grande for food and supplies by Texas ranchers, but Confederate authorities also confiscated Texas cattle that had not been impressed but went across into Mexico illegally.[44] The governor objected to this practice and convinced the state legislature to pass a joint resolution condemning the practice of impressing cattle without payment. The resolution asked General Smith to prohibit cattle confiscation and to have all Confederate authorities strictly adhere to the impressment laws.[45] The resolution bore satisfactory results. Confederate agents were appointed, and under specific orders, bought beef at state scheduled prices, allowed cattle owners to gather their own stock, and made payment in old Confederate notes. When the citizens protested other impressment acts, Murrah acted accordingly.[46]

To try to bring some order out of the confusion caused by impressment, the chief executive cooperated fully with the price board, composed of two commissioners, one appointed by President Davis and one by the governor. The board tried to arrive at fair prices for those commodities whose value was influenced by Confederate impressment practices.[47] In most cases its work was satisfactory, but many times merchants drove the prices up by submitting inflated price lists.[48]

The chief executive then turned his attention to the urgent matter of restoring law and order. He made an appeal to the people in a message to the legislature to take steps to put down the wave of crime that tore at the vital organs of the state.[49] This plea was made in response to letters like the one the governor received from Sterling C. Robertson of Salado. Robertson stated that people were moving to Mexico because of volatile acts of deserters, robbers, and jayhawkers.[50] The governor's message stated:

> In some sections society is almost disorganized, the voice of the law is hushed, and its authority seldom asserted. Murder, robbery, theft, outrages against everything sacred to civilized people are frequent and general. Whole communities are under a reign of terror, and they utter their dreadful apprehension and their cry of distress in vain.[51]

His plea was mostly in vain because most of the able-bodied men, those capable of keeping law and order, were away at war, and the handful of enforcement officers could not or would not protect the scattered settlements.[52]

Another basic problem that resulted in a conflict of interest between the state and the Confederate government was the implementation of the Conscription Act. Much of this conflict arose from disagreement between Texas and Confederate authorities over control and use of state troops. Governor Murrah, in his message to the Tenth Legislature, disagreed with demands made by Confederate officials that members of the state militia should be discharged from state service and placed in the Confederate Army.[53] The governor recommended that those state troops between eighteen and fifty years of age who lived in border counties be made into a permanent body for service anywhere in the state, and those between fifty and sixty be organized into local defense companies for service in their own counties. The older men would also be held as a reserve force to meet emergencies. Thus a state militia corps materialized with James W. Barnes as colonel, and Elwood M. Bean, K. B. Dewalt, and C. C. Dewet as majors.[54]

Several of Murrah's recommendations on conscription became state law on December 15, 1863. This legislative act exempted from conscription all persons of military age who resided in the border counties of the northern, central, and western military sub-divisions, providing these men organized into companies for frontier defense.[55]

Murrah was drawn into a dispute with Confederate officials soon after the state law was passed. Many soldiers who lived in frontier counties but who were serving elsewhere in bona fide state units, interpreted the governor's proclamation for the organization of state troops under the new law as applicable to them. A large number left the units to which they had been assigned and went home. This action, according to General J. B. Magruder, resulted in the disintegration of the state units and lost for a time all conscripts.[56]

The governor appealed to President Davis for the exemption of state troops in eighteen western and northern counties from Confederate conscription. Davis refused to grant this appeal, citing an act of the Confederate Congress of February 17, 1864, as the basis for his refusal and stating he had no power to make exceptions for any state.[57]

When the Confederate high command learned that Federal troops were planning to advance up the Red River Valley in the spring of 1864, General Magruder received orders to send all troops to Louisiana except a few small garrisons that were to remain at important coastal points. Magruder requested that Murrah forward to him individual companies of state troops and promised that they would be organized into regiments.[58] Murrah objected to this organizational procedure. The governor wanted the state troops to be organized into brigades before being forwarded to Magruder, thus, they would serve under state-appointed generals rather than Confederate generals.[59] Magruder refused to accept them in this manner but reaffirmed the urgency of stopping the Federal forces before they entered Texas.[60] Magruder again contacted Murrah and asked him to abide by the acts of the Confederate Congress.[61] Murrah yielded and proclaimed the supremacy of the Confederate law to his troops.[62] But this Confederate-state controversy had caused such a delay that the state troops did not arrive in time to help check General Nathaniel P. Banks' advance.[63] Had the Confederates been opposed by a more aggressive general than Banks, this delay could have been catastrophic.

Still another problem that Governor Murrah faced during his short term was the financial insolvency of Texas. Again much of the difficulty stemmed from the policies of the Richmond government, but Murrah realized that most of these policies resulted primarily from insoluble Confederate problems and not always from improper courses of action. The basic underlying financial problem was the runaway inflation caused by the rapid depreciation of Confederate currency. In his message to the Tenth Legislature in the fall of 1863, Murrah had stated that the state would accept payment of taxes in Confederate money at par value, as the market value at that time was only three to four cents per dollar.

The problem continued to haunt the Murrah administration. Even though a special session of the legislature was called in May, 1864, to deal forcibly with the problem, little was solved. The legislators provided only for the exchanging of the old issue of Confederate bills for the new issue.[64]

A second called session was convened on October 17, 1864, to deal with the fast-deteriorating and almost embarrassing finances. Since the last called session, the state had exchanged one-half of its Confederate one-hundred-dollar bills in the state treasury for new issue. State treasury warrants also had been issued for the benefit of soldiers' families. Both of these issues had greatly depreciated. The governor showed good judgment when he suggested that the further issuance of treasury warrants be stopped to save the state from accumulating an onerous debt.[65]

Adding to the perplexity of the financial problem were the uncontrolled actions by county and city governments and individuals. Compounding the inflationary cycle was the paper money (or warrants) issued by numerous counties and cities across the state. This money was issued in denominations of from twenty-five cents to twenty dollars, and in such quantities that it soon became practically worthless. Individual merchants issued small denominational "shin-plasters" that were restricted as to use and questionable as to value.[66] Many citizens by this time would accept nothing but specie,[67] and there was little specie in circulation.[68]

Juggling of the state finances by Murrah and the legislature did little to stabilize the economy. By 1863, $1,753,317 had been taken from the public school funds by the legislature and lent to the railroads to finance the building of additional track. The railroads were not able to repay this loan nor the interest on it because of wartime impediments to their operations and the depreciation of their rolling stock. Governor Murrah transferred $1,285,327 from this same fund to the Military Board to finance its operation. The depletion of the public schools fund reflected the financial instability of the entire state government.[69]

The deplorable financial condition of the state was well reflected by the living conditions forced upon the state lawmakers when attending sessions of the legislature. They had no money with which to pay their bills, and some even brought nails and tobacco to use for bartering purposes for their room and board. Most of them, however, camped outside the state capitol in their wagons and cooked their own corn dodgers.[70]

Adding pathos to Murrah's term of office already wracked with civil crime, conflict with the Confederacy, and financial ruin were his personal problems. Murrah's health deteriorated rapidly under the demands of the office. These problems bore down on him with unrelenting force. But the catalyst which increased the magnitude of his troubles and made them even more unbearable was his relationship with his wife. Their marriage was never consummated. The governor had a terrible temper and an overly sensitive pride; many times small incidents moved him to anger. Irregularities in their relationship began on their wedding night. He felt she neglected him for her friends at the wedding reception held at the Bayliss Taylor plantation. Therefore, he remained in the parlor all night, never going to her room. For the rest of their marriage, she remained his wife in name only.[71]

The Governor's Mansion seemed to project an aura of unhappiness and futility for its occupants during the Murrah years. Contributing to this image was the ill-fated death of the chief executive's nephew, who along with a niece lived with the Murrahs. The two guests were not related, and the nephew fell in love with the niece. After purposely leading him on, she scoffed at his marriage proposal. His disappointment and humiliation vented itself in self-destruction later that night.[72]

With personal problems of this nature adding to his other woes, Pendleton Murrah might have considered the collapse of the Confederacy a certainty. If so, he did not reveal it to the people. In January of 1865, Murrah made a public address, enjoining the Texans not to give up hope and telling them that harmony and unity were prerequisites to success.[73]

His speech had little effect for signs of defeat were everywhere. In February, 1865, Charles S. West, an officer on the staff of General E. Kirby Smith (who still commanded the Trans-Mississippi Department), wrote a letter to James H. Raymond, a partner in the banking firm of John M. Swisher, in Austin, stating the cause east of the Mississippi was hopeless and that Texans should look after their own affairs. Thomas J. McKinney of Austin, a purchasing agent for the Confederacy, received a letter from Guy M. Bryan, Texas representative to the headquarters of Trans-Mississippi Department, suggesting the same thing.[74]

The hint of possible defeat did not come from the governor until late April. His proclamation of April 27 admitted that the struggle was hopeless. He confirmed the fall of Richmond and the surrender of General Lee and the Army of Northern Virginia. To keep the people from panicking, he expressed the desire that "they would not yield to hopelessness but would look to the army west of the Mississippi for help and to the law for deliverance from anarchy."[75]

Soon, however, even the governor had to admit defeat. Sensing the despondency of the people and being aware of the growing internal disorder, he felt that Federal occupation of Texas was the only answer to maintaining law and order. In May, Colonel Ashbel Smith and Judge William P. Ballinger were dispatched to New Orleans as official representatives of the governor. They informed General E. R. S. Canby of the Federal Army, who commanded there, that all Confederate military operations had ceased in Texas.[76] General E. Kirby Smith finalized the surrender of all organized Confederate forces west of the Mississippi when he signed the articles of capitulation on June 2, 1865, on board the Union warship *Fort Jackson* in Galveston harbor.[77]

After the surrender, and before the arrival of the Federal occupation force under General Gordon Granger on June 19, a condition of chaos and confusion existed in Texas. Confederate officers disbanded their troops before the surrender of the Trans-Mississippi Department. The men left their military units, taking their guns, ammunition, horses, and wagons with them.[78] At the state capital, company after company of soldiers arrived and milled around the capitol and adjoining grounds. The veterans were joined by white civilians, Negroes, and deserters. With no law and order and little government, the crowd soon turned to looting, smashing in the doors and windows of the stores and carrying away everything that they could carry. Many felt that they were salvaging some sort of repayment for their many sacrifices during the war. Others stole only because everyone across the state seemed to be doing the same thing. The countryside was picked clean of mules, horses, and wagons belonging to the government or to civilian owners. Rumors were everywhere; fear of murder was a constant companion.[79]

The governor pleaded with the sheriffs of the various counties to collect and preserve public property and try to restore order but the task was beyond their power and chaos reigned throughout the state. Murrah issued a call for the legislature to meet in special session on July 16, 1865, and at the same time called for a special election to take place on June 19 for delegates to a state convention to meet on July 10 to take steps to restore Texas to the Union so that Federal occupation could be avoided.[80] These plans never materialized, being preempted by the arrival of General Gordon Granger and Federal troops on June 19.

Rumors of all sorts constantly bombarded Murrah and other Confederate officials in early June. One of an especially alarming nature stated that terrible punishment awaited the state officials.[81] Word that a colony was to be formed by Southern leaders in Mexico under the sponsorship of Maximilian, the Austrian emperor of Mexico, had also reached Austin. On June 11, when General Joseph O. Shelby and some 500 of his men passed through the state capital on their way south of the Rio Grande, Murrah decided to forsake his office and join Shelby and his entourage.[82]

Even Murrah's last night at Austin was ill-fated. On June 11, 1865, a group of ruffians attempted to rob the state treasury. A number of Austin citizens and some of Shelby's men, who were camped across the Colorado River, arrived in time to abort the attempt. Most of the money was saved; one looter was killed inside the vault.[83] The following morning, June 12, Murrah vacated his office, leaving it in the hands of Lieutenant Governor Fletcher Stockdale.[84]

After reaching Monterrey, Mexico, Murrah's health failed completely and he was confined to bed. News of his condition was slow in coming back to Texas. The *Dallas Herald,* quoting from the *Matamoros Ranchero,* informed its readers that he was very, very ill with no hope for recovery.[85] On August 19, the *Herald,* listed his condition as still critical.[86] But Murrah actually died on August 4, 1865.[87]

Judge A. W. Terrell was at the governor's side during his last moments. Murrah called him to his bed and declared that, contrary to statements of many people, he had never taken a cent of the state's money—he wanted that understood.[88] His life could not have ended more incongruously. A man who ignored a terminal disease to serve his state during its most difficult years and who spent his personal fortune for the benefit of the state, died penniless in exile, denying that he had stolen from his state.[89]

An evaluation of Pendleton Murrah's term of office is very difficult to make. Many of his actions were dictated by his earlier indoctrination in the John C. Calhoun school of state rights and state sovereignty. Being a man of determination and positive convictions, he could not adjust to the actual situation that existed when he became governor. His lack of cooperation with Confederate authorities concerning conscription and cotton purchasing, no doubt, hindered the Southern cause at a time when the state was in serious danger from a Federal invasion. Under different conditions he could have been a good, even a great governor. As it was, his administration did not fulfill his own ambitions, was offensive to the Confederate military commanders in the state, and of little benefit to the state as a whole.[90]

NOTES

[1]James T. DeShields, **They Sat in High Place** (San Antonio: The Naylor Company, 1940), p. 241.

[2]Louis J. Wortham, **A History of Texas from Wilderness to Commonwealth**, IV (Fort Worth: Wortham-Molyneaux Co., 1924), p. 361.

[3]**Tri-Weekly State Gazette** (Austin, Texas), July 21, 1863.

[4]DeShields, **High Place**, pp. 248-49.

[5]W. C. Nunn, **Escape from Reconstruction** (Fort Worth: Leo Potishman Foundation, 1956), p. 37.

[6]Letter from Vivian A. Mitchell to Librarian of University of Texas, June 19, 1962.

[7]DeShields, **High Place**, p. 247.

[8]Letter from Vivian A. Mitchell, **op. cit.**

[9]DeShields, **High Place**, p. 247.

[10]**Ibid.**

[11]Pearl Cashell Jackson, **Texas Governors' Wives** (Austin: E. L. Steck, 1915), pp. 50-53.

[12]DeShields, **High Place**, p. 248.

[13]"Pendleton Murrah," **National Cyclopedia of American Biography**, IX (New York: James T. White and Co., 1907), 70.

[14]L. E. Daniel, "Murrah," **Texas, The Country and Its Men** (Austin: Press of City Printing Co., n.d.), p. 101.

[15]"Pendleton Murrah," **National Cyclopedia of American Biography**, IX, 70.

[16]Norman G. Kittrell, **Governors Who Have Been and Other Public Men of Texas** (Houston: Dealy-Adey-Elgin Co., 1921), p. 45.

[17]**Dallas Herald,** May 13, 1863.

[18]Dudley G. Wooten, **A Comprehensive History of Texas,** II (Dallas: William G. Scarff, 1898), 143.

[19]DeShields, **High Place,** p. 248.

[20]**Ibid.,** pp. 241-42.

[21]Walter Prescott Webb (ed.), **Texas Handbook,** II (Austin: Texas Historical Association, 1952), 251.

[22]**Statutes at Large, C.S.A.,** 1st Cong., 3rd Session, p. 102.

[23]**Official Records,** Ser. I, XXVI, Part 2 (Washington: Government Printing Office, 1907), pp. 89-94.

[24]Hutchins to Murrah, May 14, 1864, **Executive Correspondence,** Texas Archives.

[25]**LaGrange Patriot,** August 16, 1864.

[26]**Houston Daily Telegraph,** October 19, 1864.

[27]A. M. Thrall, **A History of Texas** (New York: University Publishing Co., 1892), p. 151.

[28]Florence Elizabeth Holladay, "The Powers of the Commander of the Confederate Trans-Mississippi Department, 1863-65," **Southwestern Historical Quarterly,** XXI (Jan.-April, 1918), pp. 349-50.

[29]Thrall, **A History of Texas,** pp. 151-52.

[30]Holladay, "Trans-Mississippi Department," pp. 349-50.

[31]**Official Records,** Ser. I, Vol. LIII, Part 2, p. 972.

[32]Edmund Thornton Miller, **A Financial History of Texas** (Bulletin of University of Texas, 1916: No. 37; Austin, The University of Texas, 1916), p. 136.

[33]**Ibid.,** p. 137.

[34]Epperson to Murrah, January 20, 1865, **Executive Correspondence,** State Archives.

[35]Flewellen to Murrah, March 18, 1864, **Executive Correspondence,** State Archives.

[36]Holladay, "Trans-Mississippi Department," pp. 349-50.

[37]Thrall, **A History of Texas,** pp. 151-58.

[38]Gibbs to Murrah, Feb. 19, 1864, **Executive Correspondence,** State Archives.

[39]**Official Records,** Ser. I, Vol. XXVI, Part 2, p. 36.

[40]**Ibid.,** pp. 105-06. [41]**Ibid.,** pp. 154-55.

[42]**LaGrange Patriot,** August 20, 1863.

[43]Magruder to Murrah, January 13, 1864 and Glass to Murrah, February 25, 1864, **Executive Correspondence,** State Archives.

[44]Aldrich to Hunter, October 17, 1864, **Executive Correspondence,** State Archives.

[45]H. P. N. Gammel, (comp.), **Laws of Texas 1822-1897** (Austin: The Gammel Book Company, 1898), V, pp. 829-30.

[46]**Daily Telegraph** (Houston), June 1, 1864.

[47]**Weekly State Gazette** (Austin), February 22, 1865.

[48]B. H. Epperson to Murrah, June 14, 1864, **Executive Correspondence,** State Archives.

[49]Iron Department to Murrah, February 27, 1864, **Executive Correspondence,** State Archives.

[50]Robertson to Murrah, March 9, 1865, **Executive Correspondence,** State Archives.

[51]**Messages of Governor Murrah to the Legislature of the State of Texas** (Austin: State Gazette Book and Job Office, 1864), no page.

[52]Hubert Howe Bancroft, **North Mexican States,** pp. 473-74.

[53]James M. Day (ed.), **House Journal,** Tenth Legislature, Regular Session of the State of Texas (Austin: Texas State Library, 1965), pp. 8-17.

[54]O. M. Roberts, "Texas," Clement A. Evans (ed.), **Confederate Military History,** XI (Atlanta: Confederate Publishing Co., 1899), p. 121.

[55]H. P. N. Gammel, (comp.), **Laws,** pp. 677-79.

[56]Robert Pattison Felgar, "Texas in the War for Southern Independence," (Unpublished Ph.D. dissertation, Dept. of History, University of Texas, 1936), p. 212.

[57]Davis to Murrah, April 26, 1864, **Official Records,** Ser. I, Vol. LIII, Part 2, p. 985.

[58]Magruder to Murrah, March 14, 1864, **Official Records,** Ser. I, Vol. XXXIV, Part 2, pp. 973-75.

[59]Murrah to Magruder, March 17, 1864, **Official Records,** Ser. I, Vol. XXXIV, Part 2, pp. 1091-92.

[60]Magruder to Murrah, March 23, 1864, **Official Records,** Ser. I, Vol. XXXIV, Part 2, pp. 1093-95.

[61]Magruder to Murrah, April 2, 1864, **Official Records,** Ser. I, Vol. XXIV, Part 3, pp. 739-41.

[62]Bancroft, **North Mexican States,** p. 472.

[63]Murrah to Magruder, April 7, 1864, **Official Records,** Ser. I, Vol. XXXIV, Part 3, p. 747.

[64]Homer S. Thrall, **Pictorial History of Texas** (St. Louis: N. D. Thomas and Co., 1879), pp. 400-05.

[65]Frank Brown, "Annals of Travis County and of the City of Austin," (Austin: Typed copy at the State Archives), pp. 43-47.

[66]**Ibid.,** pp. 43-44.

[67]James M. Day (ed.), **House Journal,** Tenth Legislature, Second Called Session of State of Texas (Austin: Texas State Library, 1965), pp. 5-12.

[68]Brown, "Annals," pp. 43-44.

[69]Frederick Eby, **Education in Texas, Source Materials** (Bulletin of University of Texas, 1918: No .184; Austin: The University of Texas, 1918), pp. 150-51.

[70]Brown, "Annals," p. 66

[71]Jackson, **Wives,** pp. 50-53.

[72]**Ibid.**

[73]Brown, "Annals," p. 4.

[74]**Ibid.,** p. 5.

[75]**Ibid.,** p. 9.

[76]Wooten, **History of Texas,** p. 150.

[77]**Houston Tri-Weekly Telegraph,** June 20, 1865.

[78]D. Appleton (ed.), **The American Annual Cyclopaedia** (New York: D. Appleton and Co., 1872), Vol. V, p. 786.

[79]Brown, "Annals," pp. 11-14.

[80]Appleton (ed.), **Annual Cyclopaedia,** Vol. V, p. 786.

[81]Paul Bolton, **Governors of Texas** (Corpus Christi: **Corpus Christi Caller-Times,** 1947), no page.

[82]Nunn, **Escape,** pp. 31-32.

[83]Hal Bourlan, "A Bold Attempt to Rob the State Treasury," **Confederate Veteran,** XXXI (November, 1923), p. 415.

[84]**Flakes Daily Bulletin** (Galveston), June 23, 1865.

[85]**Dallas Herald,** August 12, 1865.

[86]**Dallas Herald,** Aug. 19, 1865.

[87]**Flakes Daily Bulletin** (Galveston), August 30, 1865.

[88]**Dallas Herald,** October 14, 1865.

[89]**Ibid.,** March 30, 1867. On January 16, 1869, the **Dallas Herald** noted the death of Mrs. Murrah who died on January 9, 1869, at the residence of Judge Samuel Earle near Tyler, Texas.

[90]Thrall, **Pictorial History of Texas,** p. 408.

Williamson Simpson Oldham

by

LAURA N. HARPER

> The man who, from the obscurity of a boyhood of poverty, with no legacy from his father by honesty and industry, with no education, and reared in the interior of a State remote from any advantages of position such as great cities afford, could rise to the highest eminence as a jurist, legislator, orator, and representative and leader of States and a whole Republic, was certainly no ordinary character.[1]

In Franklin County, Tennessee, on June 19, 1813, Williamson Simpson Oldham began life as the fourth child in a large family of fourteen. His parents, Elias and Mary Bratton Oldham, were farmers—poor, but honest—unable to provide other than the necessities of life.

Ambitious, even as a child, Williamson S. Oldham persisted in procuring an education for himself. He studied at night by the light of the fire even after a full day of labor on the farm. His ambitions lay in the study of law.

At twenty, finding teaching monetarily unsuccessful, W. S. Oldham turned his energies to the position of deputy clerk in the office of the district clerk of Franklin County, Tennessee. Here Oldham attracted the attention of Judge Nathan Green by his "energy, sprightliness, and aspirations."[2]

Judge Green, later Chief Justice of Tennessee, guided Oldham's studies in law. In the fall of 1836, at the age of twenty-three W. S. Oldham was admitted to the bar. Judge Green, on signing the license, not only predicted a brilliant career, but furnished a law library for Oldham. In later years when Oldham offered to repay the kindness, the Judge told him to "go and do likewise for some worthy young man."[3]

In 1836 young attorney Oldham moved to Fayetteville, Arkansas, seeking greater opportunities. Here he proceeded to establish a solid legal reputation. His knowledge of law, his marriage to Mary Vance McKissick, the daughter of an influential citizen of Arkansas, and the wealth that came as a result of his business success made Oldham a logical candidate for political office. Soon after moving to Arkansas, he was successful in his bid for a seat in the state legislature. His record in the lower house (where he was the youngest member) was so able that he won the admiration and approval of the more experienced members. W. S. Oldham was only twenty-nine when he was chosen to be the Speaker of the Arkansas House of Representatives in 1842.

From 1844 to 1848, Williamson S. Oldham held the position of associate justice of the Supreme Court of Arkansas. During his tenure, he settled many trying questions, and his decisions were noted for their "logical clearness, legal erudition, and their wise application, and development of legal principles."[4]

However, Oldham preferred a political career to one in the judiciary, and in 1848 he again sought political office. After a series of political defeats, capped by an unsuccessful bid for the United States Senate in 1848, and threatened with tuberculosis, Oldham decided to move to Texas. In the Lone Star State he hoped to recoup his political fortunes and to regain his health. Austin was selected as the new home for the Oldhams, and in 1849, Williamson Simpson Oldham, accompanied by his wife and five children, left Fayetteville. Unfortunately a tragedy marred the move, for near Waco, Mary Oldham became suddenly very ill and died.

Austin in the early 1850's was a comparatively small town of about two thousand people. Even so, it was already a haven for those trained in the legal profession, boasting twenty-five lawyers—a profession that outnumbered all others. Soon after arriving there, Oldham was initiated into the legal and public affairs of the capital city and the state of Texas.[5]

The atmosphere of Austin proved to be just the tonic for Oldham. He entered wholeheartedly into its business and social life, and on December 26, 1850, married Mrs. Anne Kirk of Lockhart. In their two-story house (one of the first such houses in Austin) he had time to enjoy his children and to play his violin, often to the accompaniment of his wife or daughter. He entertained others of his profession and was not above meeting his cronies at the corner of Sixth and Congress from whence they would ride horseback out to Barton's Creek to swim.

Still holding his interest in politics, Judge Oldham held many political discussions in the library of his home. The subject most often discussed was that of state's rights, and Oldham would grow excited as he proclaimed the principles that he would advocate in later years from Austin to Richmond. At the stroke of nine, all activities would cease; his guests would leave, and Oldham would retire to study or read until almost four in the morning.[6]

In August, 1854, while still practicing law as a partner in the firm of Oldham, Marshall and Terrill, Judge Oldham purchased the interest of Major William R. Scurry in the *Texas State Gazette* and became one of the co-owners and editors of the leading Democratic paper in the state. He was associated in this venture with John Marshall who had just a few months before purchased the interest of J. W. Hampton.

Oldham's salutatory, published August 19, 1854, read as follows:

> My connection with the *State Gazette* will not change its political complexion. Being a Democrat of the strictest sect, I conceive the only safeguard of the rights of the states is in a strict adherence, by the general government, to the powers specifically delegated by the constitution and those absolutely necessary to carry into effect those delegated powers.[7]

During a period when Marshall was absent on a trip to Mississippi, the *State Gazette* printed some very radical Southern statements. On May 12, 1855, the *Gazette* declared that the prosperity and happiness of the South depended on slavery. The Negro was an "inferior being and God intended him to be a hewer of wood and drawer of water" for the white race. As a slave, the Negro was "happy and well provided for, but as a laborer he would be neglected and despised." The statements were allegedly written by Oldham.[8]

A speech on the "Rights of the South in Opposition to 'Squatters Sovereignty' " was Williamson S. Oldham's first major oration at the capitol. Delivered on August 27, 1856, the speech attempted to clarify the Democratic Party's stand on the question of slavery and began:

> If there ever was a time when the true theory of our government should be ascertained and its just powers defined, it is the present. The times are portentious of evil. . . . Parties divided by geographical lines . . . are destroying the fraternal feeling of our people, and threatening to overturn our free institutions.

Oldham further expounded that the United States had no power over slavery in the territories; that the sovereign states had the power to say what was property in the state; and that the power to determine the question of slavery in the territories was a reserved right of the state. He concluded with the statement:

> With us in the South, the case is different . . . "the union of the States, and the rights of the States under the constitution," is our motto. It is only by observing a strict rule of constitutional construction, and an unyielding adherence to the reserved powers of the state, that our rights can be secured and our Union preserved.[9]

An act passed by the Texas legislature in 1858 authorized the governor to seek the preparation of a digest of all the general statutes of the state. The digest would contain, along with these statutes, all the repealed laws of the Republic and the state; the colonization laws of Mexico and of the state of Coahuila and Texas in force at the declaration of Texas independence. The contract for preparing the digest was awarded to Williamson S. Oldham and George W. White. The work, *A Digest of the General Statute Laws of the State of Texas,* still holds a prominent place in the jurisprudence of the state.[10]

One afternoon in the fall of 1860, General Sam Houston gave an address expressing his views on secession. His entire address appealed to reason. He depicted the horrors of civil war and foretold its progress and results with prophetic truth. He warned that civil war would follow secession and would result in the destruction of slavery. He admitted that, at first, the South would triumph, but defeat would follow with certainty. He went into detail on the North's superiority in people and munitions. The South, he deplored, had made no preparation for war. Houston correctly prophesied that the boys from Texas would be sent across the Mississippi River, and that the North would capture the Mississippi and cut the Confederacy in two. He questioned whether the people of Texas wanted their boys to die on distant fields.[11]

W. S. Oldham debated the opinions expressed by Sam Houston and called his statements distortions of fact in order to frighten the people. Oldham advocated that the Southern states secede and set up a new federation for their own protection. If war came, it would be conducted by the officials appointed to conduct it, and their duties would be defined by law. The state governments, he said, surely would continue to function as before.[12]

During September, 1860, Oldham and his family took up residence in Brenham. At a mass meeting held in this predominantly German community on November 17, 1860, Oldham was elected a member of a committee to draw up resolutions advocating secession. The resolutions drawn up suggested that Governor Houston call a special session of the legislature for the purpose of sitting as a secession convention. The committee, fully aware of Houston's views on secession, stated that if the governor refused to call such a convention, the judges of the Supreme Court and other state officers should call the meeting. The officers of the United States government in Texas were asked to resign before March 4, 1861, and the senators and representatives of Texas in the United States Congress were requested not to attend legislative sessions. In several speeches in and around Brenham, Oldham spoke in favor of these resolutions. Other parts of the state were also passing similar resolutions and asking the governor to call a special session of the legislature.

Governor Houston refused to call the special session. After a long discussion with the attorney general of Texas, George M. Flournoy, a group of men in Austin on December 3, decided to make a citizens' call for the convention. The committee drew up the call and sent copies of it throughout the state to be read at public meetings. The *State Gazette* carried the call on December 8, 1860.[13]

On the same date as the call, Oldham addressed the citizens of Austin at two o'clock in the courthouse. The speech on "the grave issues before the people" favored secession. He reviewed the history of slavery from the formation of the United States to 1861. He cautioned that, as a result of being taught from childhood to hate the people of the South, that many persons in the North would not consent to compromise. The last part of the address was a plea to the people not to submit, and for Texas to exercise her power of sovereignty in withdrawing from the Federal government. Secession could not mean war, Oldham said, because the closing of markets in the South would bring ruin to Northern commerce.[14]

On December 15, 1860, *Harper's Weekly* in a dispatch from New Orleans reported on the citizens' committee held at Austin:

> A committee of citizens of Texas petitioned Governor Houston to convene the Legislature. The Governor responded that viewing the proposed measure as unwise, he could not call the Legislature together; but if a majority of the citizens of the state petition for it he could not stand in their way. A circular letter signed by a number of gentlemen urged citizens to a convention on the 8th of January. The movement seems to meet popular sanction.

Oldham was one of those who signed the circular letter referred to in the *Harper's* article.[15]

On December 19, 1860, Oldham made another speech in which he said there was no longer any feeling of "brotherly love and kindness" between the North and the South; therefore, the South "must shift for herself."[16]

South Carolina, Georgia, Florida, Alabama, and Mississippi had already seceded when Houston opened the extraordinary session of the legislature on January 21. Williamson S. Oldham, James E. Shepard, and Jerome B. Robertson attended as the delegates for the Secession Convention from Washington County.

Even while the legislature was making up its mind about the Secession Convention, the convention had become a fact as of January 28, 1861, and Oran M. Roberts had been elected to preside.

The Secession Convention of Texas met in the hall of the House of Representatives, and Williamson S. Oldham was seated as a delegate from Washington County. It took this gathering of Texans only four days to seal the fate of the Lone Star State. The convention took a vote at eleven o'clock on the first day of February on the Ordinance of Secession. As some of the delegates rose to vote, they gave a reason for their stand. The Ordinance of Secession passed overwhelmingly by a vote of one hundred and sixty-six to eight. Oldham voted for the ordinance, and, at seven-thirty on the same day, signed the ordinance as a member of the Secession Convention.[17]

With the secession of Texas guaranteed (at least by the convention), the members concerned themselves with other details. They prescribed the date and manner in which the popular election was to be held to ratify the ordinance, and the body selected a Committee on Public Safety. The purpose of the committee was to deal with any armed resistance that might be met (from United States troops in the state), while carrying out the process of secession.

One other important action was taken before adjournment. A delegation of seven members was elected on February 4, to represent Texas at the forthcoming convention of Southern states at Montgomery, Alabama. The purpose of the delegation was to act for Texas at the Montgomery convention as soon as the popular vote for the secession had been taken. Louis T. Wigfall, John H. Reagan, John Hemphill, T. N. Waul, John Gregg, W. S. Oldham, and William B. Ochiltree were elected as the delegates. Oldham was elected on the third ballot by a vote of sixty-seven out of one hundred thirty-three votes cast.[18]

The convention adjourned on February 5, 1861, to meet again on March 2, following the popular vote which had been set for February 23. The ratification of the Ordinance of Secession was passed by the voters of Texas by a three-to-one majority, with 39,415 voting for the ordinance, and 13,841 against it. Texas was now out of the Federal Union and was accepted into the Confederate States of America.[19]

The Provisional Congress of the Confederate States met at Montgomery, Alabama, on February 4, 1861. At first the delegates of Texas were not allowed to participate actively in the deliberations of Congress. They were permitted only to advise on matters concerning their state until Texas was officially out of the Union.

On March 2, Oldham and Reagan took their seats in the Congress along with the other five Texas representatives. On the same day, Texas was admitted as a bona fide member of the Confederacy and the delegates from Texas affixed their signatures to the Provisional Constitution of the Confederate States of America.[20]

On March 2, W. S. Oldham voted for the first time at the Provisional Congress. On February 28, 1861, President Davis had vetoed an act concerning the reopening of the African slave trade. An attempt was made to pass the act over Davis' veto. Oldham cast his vote to sustain the veto of the President, and thus helped to defeat the attempted override.

Oldham did not have an opportunity to assume a very important part in the first session of the Provisional Confederate Congress. He was appointed a member of the Judiciary Committee and a member of the Committee on Naval Affairs by the Congress on March 6. President Davis named Williamson S. Oldham the commissioner to Arkansas on March 9, 1861, and Oldham departed to do his part for secession in his old stamping grounds.[21]

In a letter dated March 13, 1861, the appointment of Oldham as the commissioner to Arkansas was made known to the Texas Convention. The letter was addressed to the person of O. M. Roberts and signed by the Texas delegates to Montgomery.

> It being considered by this government necessary to send a commission to the Convention in Arkansas, our Colleague and Fellow Citizen the Hon. W. S. Oldham was nominated to the highly responsible position. He accepted under the advice and solicitation of such of our delegation as was here.[22]

It had been concluded that since Arkansas was the former residence of Oldham he would have some influence in bringing the state into the Confederate orbit. Oldham arrived in Little Rock in mid-March, 1861. The Arkansas Convention was already in session when he presented his credentials and a letter from President Davis. Neither the missive nor W. S. Oldham caused much of a stir in the convention, for the Unionists were in the majority and were dominating the proceedings. On March 18, Oldham addressed the convention. He invited Arkansas to join with the seven states that had already withdrawn from the Union. Oldham summarized the causes that had led to the separation of the states and refuted the fact that the action of the

Southern states was a hasty step. Oldham said it was the work of a "free people, determined to maintain, defend, and preserve their liberties." The separation was final and complete, for the intersts of the two sections differed and the Federal governmnt had ceased to protect the Southern people.

When questioned on how the new Confederacy was to be maintained, Oldham replied that he did not think it would be held together by force, but that "mutual interests, sympathies, and common institutions of the Confederate States, with wise and just administration . . . are the cohesive powers that will bind its parts together."

Oldham concluded his address with this appeal to the people of Arkansas:

> Your institutions are the same as ours, your productions the same . . . we have common interests, mutual sympathies, and are exposed to a common danger . . . hence the government from which I come, desires not to dictate to, but to consult, and confer with you for the advancement of our mutual interests, to invite you to be an equal, and not as an inferior, as a sovereign state, and not as a degraded province, to unite and share with us a common destiny. And may I not be permitted to add my individual hope, that the State in which I spent my early manhood, who conferred upon me her honors, and whose favors I shall ever cherish with gratitude, will assume that position which I believe is alike demanded by her honor and her safety? . . . It seems clear that every consideration of interest, safety, affection, resulting from similar institutions, exposed to the same dangers, would induce the people of Arkansas to unite with us in the government we have formed and share with us its protection and its blessings.[23]

Ignoring Oldham's plea, the members of the convention on the same afternoon as the speech, defeated the motion for secession. However, in less than three days the Unionists had backed down, and eventually Arkansas aligned with the Confederate States of America. How much influence Oldham had upon Arkansas reversing itself is difficult to determine.

The Provisional Congress had adjourned on March 16, 1861, prior to Oldhams return to Montgomery from Arkansas. He remained in Montgomery however, to see the Secretary of War,

L. P. Walker, upon the subject of the defense of the Texas frontier. Little was immediately accomplished, and Oldham was back in Texas by early spring, where the problems of state defense continued to perturb him. On April 16, four days after the fall of Fort Sumter and the beginning of the Civil War, he penned a letter to Governor Edward Clark insisting that Texas prepare herself against being invaded. He suggested that Clark call for volunteers who could be ready at short notice. The following day, he again wrote to Clark, as he was certain that Texas was programmed for an early invasion. In the second letter he theorized on the strategy to be used by the North:

> 1st. They intend, to hold if they can the Southern forts and drive the South to attack them as at Sumter.
>
> 2nd. They intend to blockade the Southern ports, so as to cut off their commerce. If the Southern ports remain open, the commerce of the North will be destroyed. Hence as a matter of self-preservation, they are forced to the necessity of attempting a blockade and
>
> 3rd. Under the invitation of the disaffected in Texas they intend to invade our State.[24]

Still vitally concerned with the state of preparedness of Texas, Oldham again urged Governor Clark to call for volunteers, as he was certain that Texas would be an early battleground. Clark made the call at once, not only because of Oldham's insistence, but because of the demand of the Confederate government for men at the beginning of the war.

In the called session of the Provisional Congress that met from April 29 to May 21, 1861, Oldham participated but little in the debates and congressional actions that followed. On May 3, he was placed on the Committee on Territories, but no important action was taken by this committee. He endorsed a letter written by W. B. Ochiltree, requesting that the Secretary of War levy a call on Texas for troops to fight east of the Mississippi. Oldham was one of the members who voted on the move of the seat of government to Richmond.[25]

Following the adjournment of the called session, Oldham returned to Texas where on July 6, 1861, he reviewed for the citizens of Austin the actions of Congress and the policies of the states' rights group. He was critical of General Houston and his followers, and made every effort to see that Texas was united behind the Confederacy.[26]

On his journey to Richmond, after a short sojourn in Texas, Oldham described the attitude of the Southerner as he crossed the breadth of the Confederacy in July, 1861:

> The war spirit was universal, and inspired alike the old and the young, men, women, and children, white and black. There was not an opposing sentiment uttered, not a discordant voice raised. The young men were hastening to the army . . . those who were not in condition to go immediately, were busily preparing to do so as soon as possible. The most undoubted confidence prevailed and a shout of defiant determination echoed from one end of the land to the other.[27]

The Texan arrived in Richmond, Virginia, to find the Confederate Congress meeting in a small, dingy room, furnished with a wicker seat for the President and rude timber seats for the others. The Congressional debates and discussions were secret, but it was common knowledge that Congress had provided for a permanent government and an army, and other machinery to carry on the conflict.

In the fall of 1861, Oldham was rewarded for playing his part as a secessionist and a representative of his state. On November 16, 1861, Louis T. Wigfall and Williamson S. Oldham were elected to the Confederate Senate. Wigfall was elected without opposition, but Oldham defeated two opponents in a close race. Oldham would represent Texas in the Senate until 1865, but he would be overshadowed by his vociferous and flamboyant colleague, Louis T. Wigfall, in the legislative hall of the Confederate Congress.[28]

Senators Oldham and Wigfall took their oaths of office on February 18, 1862. On February 21, the members of the Senate drew for their terms of office. Oldham drew a term of six years, and Wigfall drew the four-year term.[29]

During his days in the Confederate Senate, Oldham championed for states' rights and free trade. Every issue involving the safeguard of these two sacred principles gained his support. Early in March, 1862, he opposed a proposed measure restricting the planting of cotton to three acres for each laborer. Oldham felt that the central government was usurping too much authority and that the state governments would be of no use if measures like this one and others were passed. He argued his point using Texas as an example. Texas was an independent nation, he said, and when she became a state, she did not give up any of her state rights. On March 17, Oldham inferred that the "three-acre" bill was unconstitutional because of the restrictions in the Constitution that gave Congress only the power to carry on war, make and buy arms, and obtain supplies. He did not believe in setting a precedent which could be used and abused after the war. He did not want his name linked with an act that violated the Constitution. According to Oldham, the bill was an assumption of power by the central government, and he thought that the Confederate States should avoid the mistakes made by the old Union.[30]

General Sam Houston wrote to Oldham and praised him for his free trade stand in the Senate:

> . . . so far as I understand your senatorial action. I entirely approve it. Your advocacy of free trade, I regard not only as a statesmanship-like measure, but indispensable to the wants, and conditions of the country, and I most heartily wish you success.[31]

During 1862, the Confederate Congress found several flaws in the exemption clauses of the conscription law. Congress found it difficult to strike a balance of manpower needs between the home front and the army. The leading objection to conscription in the South was that it would weaken the local defense. The states in the Trans-Mississippi area particularly felt that their defense suffered by the concentration of armies east of the Mississippi and by frequent drafts of its militia. Texas feared Indian trouble and felt that the Richmond government should suspend conscription and accept Texas volunteers to be used only for frontier defense.[32]

On April 1, 1862, Senator Wigfall reported on a bill he had authored to raise an army by conscription. Oldham objected. He and Wigfall quarreled vehemently over the constitutionality of such an act. Conscription was contrary to Oldham's states' rights doctrine. His thinking was that if Congress had the power to force men into the army in time of war, the same power could be wielded in time of peace. He feared the Confederate government would turn into a military dictatorship. Other than voicing his opinions privately, Oldham took no active part in the floor discussions concerning the bill, but voted with five other senators against it on April 11, when it came up for a vote.[33] Despite his opposition, this first conscription act became a law that same week. Such a measure proved to be necessary as volunteering had greatly declined.

In August, 1862, Oldham took an active part in a discussion of exemptions, offering an amendment by which the frontier regiment in Texas would be exempted from conscriptions. He was outspoken in the Confederate Congress concerning what he thought to be improper assignment of Texas troops.

> The section west of the Mississippi was as important as any part of the Confederacy; but regiments after regiments have been transported east of the Mississippi, and far beyond the Alleghany mountains, to fight battles in Virginia. I am proud of the fact that they were brought here, inasmuch as they were not needed at the time and were an enormous expense to the Government. The enemy are going to make one convulsive movement and I think it will be their last. My impression is that they will make an effort soon west of the Mississippi. . . . The best troops of Texas you have transported east of the Mississippi, brought to Virginia, put into the hottest part of contests, where they have been decimated. . . . Let this Government continue to draw on the fighting population of Texas to keep up these regiments and Texas will be ruined, irretrievably ruined. I think it is wrong and impolitic and unjust. My constituents have families, property, and homes to defend, and I protest against the men west of the Mississippi being transferred east of it, leaving their country open to the incursions of the enemy north, east, west, and south.[34]

In this battle, Oldham was unsuccessful, for later the conscription of state frontier troops was legalized by the Confederate Congress.

Oldham was a member of a small group of legislators who were opposed to the suspension of the writ of habeas corpus and investing too much power in the provost marshals. On April 19, 1862, President Davis was given the authority to suspend this writ for thirty days after the next session of Congress. Oldham was the only senator who opposed such action at the time that it was taken. An example of military officers assuming too much power under the act had been observed by the Texas senator. The provost marshal of Texas had proclaimed martial law in areas of the Lone Star State where there were no Unionists. Oldham thought the office of the provost marshal should be abolished, because the President and Congress did not have the power to establish martial law in such cases. On August 27, 1862, a resolution introduced by Oldham requested that the President give to the Senate information on what authority provost marshals were appointed. The resolution was passed by the Senate. When Oldham voted for the act of suspension, he did so only to limit the power to suspend the writ to Congress and no one else. The April 19th bill, Oldham stated, granted the President the power to suspend civil government. Oldham wanted to fight for the independence of the individual and his own personal freedom. The Texan had observed many objectionable things on trips to and from Richmond. People who did not possess passes to travel on trains had been pushed aside by the armed guards. Such actions infuriated Oldham. Many of the people denied admittance did not know they were required by the provost marshals to have a pass, and did not know how to obtain one. While trying to find where and how to get such a pass, many travelers missed their trains. He reported the officers as being both rude and despotic.

On one occasion, Oldham and his daughter were boarding a train with their arms full of blankets and luggage when they were stopped for a pass. He could not reach into his pocket for the pass without dropping his bundles. He told the guard that he would be back. On his return with the pass, the guard was so unpleasant that Oldham decided to take legislative action to combat the problem when he returned to Richmond. On September 24, 1862, Oldham brought the issue before the Senate. He pointed out that in Richmond the provost marshals appeared to have unlimited power. A resolution was offered by Oldham providing that the War Department had no authority to appoint provost marshals and invest them with power over civilians. The resolution passed the Senate but never reached a vote in the House.[35]

On February 15, 1864, a bill passed in which there were certain instances when the writ of habeas corpus could be suspended. An arrest could be made by order of the President, the Secretary of War, and the General in command of the Trans-Mississippi Department without a writ. Oldham again objected to the bill as he claimed that some of the offenses listed in the act were not offenses under any law of the land.[36]

Early in January, 1865, Oldham, along with two other senators, was appointed to a committee to assess the resources of the Confederacy in relation to ultimate victory. On January 25, the committee reported, finding that enough men and supplies were available to continue the war. With the careful marshalling of these resources, the South was capable of resisting, the senators thought, until the North grew weary of war.[37]

On January 30, 1865, W. S. Oldham introduced in the Confederate Senate, certain resolutions passed in Texas in November, 1864, concerning peace, reconstruction, and independence. He admitted the military events were cause for despondency, but appealed to the people to continue the struggle for independence, as submission would mean degradation and humiliation.

> Subjugation! What does it mean? Do Senators, do our people comprehend what it means? It means the erasing of our name and country from the map of the world; the conclusion of our history, with no future; the destruction of our governments, both State and Confederate, and the provincializing of our States, to be governed by a triumvirate consisting of the shining, canting, hypocritical Yankee, the red republican, and the infidel German, and the superior of the trio, the African negro.[38]

Oldham was never to understand why the Confederacy failed. He seemed to feel that the people and politicians merely grew tired of the war and had settled down to hopelessness. When the suggestion was broached in Congress that a cessation of hostilities take place, Oldham pledged that he would never live as a conquered subject, but would emigrate to a foreign country. He pledged, however, that until this time came, he would stay at his post and do all that he could to save his country.[39]

True to his word, and although the Congress adjourned on March 18, 1865, Oldham remained in Richmond until the last day of March. He left the Confederate capital just a few days before

Davis fled with his cabinet. Oldham's trip back to Texas was a most difficult one. He finally arrived in Houston in early June, but found only disorder and confusion. In June, 1865, he fled to Mexico where he joined other Southerners who had taken up residence at Cordoba.

Concerning Oldham's residing in Mexico a correspondent of the *New York Herald* reported:

> Judge Oldham, formerly Chief Justice of Texas, has turned photographer and is in business in this city [Cordoba]. The Judge has also turned author and is engaged upon the last sheets of a work entitled "A History of a Journey from Richmond to the Rio Grande from March 30 to June 26, 1865, or the Last Days of the Confederate States."[40]

Oldham left Mexico and went to Canada in 1866. When he saw his name listed in a New York paper as having been pardoned, he started home to Texas. He found, much to his chagrin, the pardon was for a relative who bore his name, but upon the assurances of Colonel G. W. White, his former associate, he continued on to Texas.

After returning to the United States, Williamson Simpson Oldham settled in Houston, but he took no further part in the politics of Texas. He continued in the practice of law. On May 8, 1868, at the age of fifty-four, Oldham succumbed to typhoid fever.

The Houston Bar Association wishing to honor Oldham passed a complimentary resolution on May 22, 1868. Judge C. B. Sabin, the military judge of the court, refused to allow the resolution, and it was later withdrawn. It read:

> Resolved, We recognize in W. S. Oldham, a distinguished and indefatigable public servant and patriot, sincerely, purely, and wholly devoted to the happiness and honor of our State.[41]

Oldham, bitter, disillusioned, and unreconciled to the downfall of his country and state, had accomplished, in his own way, the aims of a patriot of the South and of Texas.

NOTES

[1]Edward Fontaine, "Hon. Williamson S. Oldham," **De Bow's Review,** XXXVII (New Orleans: After the War Series, 1866-1870), p. 880.

[2]James D. Lynch, **Bench and Bar of Texas** (St. Louis: Nixon Jones Printing Co., 1885), p. 254.

[3]Alma Dexta King, "The Political Career of Williamson Simpson Oldham," **Southwestern Historical Quarterly,** XXXIII (July, 1929 to April, 1930), p. 112.

[4]Lynch, **The Bench and Bar of Texas,** p. 255.

[5]King, "Political Career of Williamson Simpson Oldham," p. 116.

[6]King, "Career of Williamson Simpson Oldham," p. 115.

[7]**Texas State Gazette** (Austin), August 19, 1854, p. 1.

[8]W. S. Oldham, "Colonel John Marshall," **Southwestern Historical Quarterly,** XX (July, 1916 to April, 1917), p. 113.

[9]**Texas State Gazette,** July 21, 1860, pp. 1-4.

[10]Lynch, **Bench and Bar of Texas,** p. 255.

[11]A. W. Terrell, "Recollections of General Sam Houston," **Southwestern Historical Quarterly,** XVI (July, 1912 to April, 1913), pp. 133-134.

[12]W. S. Oldham, **The Last Days of the Confederate States** (Manuscript, University of Texas, Archives), pp. 247-249.

[13]Dudley G. Wooten (ed.), **A Comprehensive History of Texas,** Vol. 2 (Dallas: William G. Scarff, 1898), pp. 87-89.

[14]Oldham, **The Last Days of the Confederate States,** p. 85.

[15]**Harper's Weekly** (New York), December 15, 1860.

[16]Wooten, **A History of Texas,** p. 99.

[17]James Farber, **Texas, C.S.A.** (San Antonio: The Jackson Company, 1947), pp. 3-8.

[18]E. W. Winkler (ed.), **Journal of the Secession Convention of Texas, 1861** (Austin: Austin Printing Company, 1912), p. 80.

[19]Wooten, **A History of Texas,** pp. 103-112.

[20]Winkler, **Journal of the Secession Convention,** p. 208.

[21]**War of the Rebellion, Official Records,** Ser. I, Vol. 53, p. 635.

[22]Winkler, **Journal of the Secession Convention,** p. 208.

[23]**Texas State Gazette,** April 27, 1861.

[24]Alma Dexta King, "The Political Career of Williamson Simpson Oldham," (unpublished Masters thesis, University of Texas, 1929), pp. 100-101.

[25]**Journal of the Congress of the Confederate States of America,** 1861-1865 (Washington: Government Printing Office, 1904-1905), pp. 213-257.

[26]King, "Williamson S. Oldham," (Thesis), p. 102.

[27]Oldham, **The Last Days of the Confederate States,** p. 194.

[28]King, "Williamson S. Oldham," (Thesis), pp. 106-107.

[29]**Journal of the Confederate Congress,** Vol. 2, p. 96.

[30]King, "Williamson S. Oldham," (Thesis), p. 114.

[31]E. W. Winkler, "Sam Houston and Williamson Simpson Oldham," **Southwestern Historical Quarterly,** XX (July, 1916 to April, 1917), pp. 148-149.

[32]W. B. Yearns, **The Confederate Congress** (Athens: The University of Georgia Press, 1960), pp. 79-83.

[33]King, "Williamson S. Oldham," (Thesis), p. 114.

[34]"Texas," **Appleton's Annual Cyclopaedia,** Vol. 2, 1862, p. 773; **Official Records,** Series I, Vol. LIII, Part 2, p. 985.

[35]King, "Williamson S. Oldham," (Thesis), p. 137.

[36]**Journal of the Congress of the Confederate States,** Vol. II, pp. 241-244.

[37]Lynch, **The Bench and Bar of Texas,** p. 256.

[38]W. S. Oldham, **Speech on the Resolutions of the State of Texas Concerning Peace, Reconstruction and Independence,** delivered in the Confederate Senate, January 30, 1865, p. 13.

[39]Oldham, **The Last Days of the Confederate States,** pp. 416-419.

[40]W. C. Nunn, **Escape from Reconstruction** (Fort Worth: Leo Potishman Foundation, 1956), pp. 65-66.

[41]**Texas Republican** (Marshall), May 22, 1868, Archives of the Texas State Library.

John H. Reagan

by

S. W. Schuster

On the night of October 16, 1859, an abolitionist fanatic attacked and captured the Federal arsenal at Harper's Ferry, Virginia. An act of violence! An invasion of Southern territory! An attempt to incite slave insurrection!—so most Texans viewed the actions of John Brown. Nor did events of the following year quiet their fears and suspicions. A wave of fires, poisonings, and abortive slave uprisings heightened the tension and provoked violent reaction. Vigilance and citizens' committees, organized in almost every county, prowled their districts, interrogated strangers, and hanged a few Negroes and suspected abolitionists. With great apprehension Texans also noted what was to them a worsening political situation. For at the Charlestown Convention in April a split weakened the Democratic Party; in the November elections the Republicans gained control of the government, and Lincoln was elected President. By late 1860, after a year of violence, uncertainty, and political frustration, Texans found themselves confronted with the dreaded question of secession.[1]

To one Texas leader, Congressman John H. Reagan, secession posed a particularly difficult decision; in fact, it required the complete reversal of a professed political attitude. For during the summer of 1858 in a successful bid for re-election, Reagan had run on a Unionist platform and had emphatically stated: "I am for a policy of Union."[2] At that time most Texans apparently had shared his moderate viewpoint, since they returned him to Congress by an overwhelming vote.[3] Yet in Congress, throughout 1859 and 1860, Reagan had found little moderation or willingness to compromise. He had witnessed an ever-increasing sectional breach, caustic and derogatory debates, haughty attitudes of Republicans who seemed determined to destroy the Democratic Party and degrade the South. He too had received the news of John Brown's raid and had watched the deterioration of Texas' domestic harmony with horror and foreboding.

He too believed that once the Republicans gained control of the government secession was the only course for Southerners to take. So on January 15, 1861, he took leave of Washington, his destiny linked with that of Texas and the South.[4]

Looking at his background, some of Reagan's fellow citizens might have been surprised when he joined the extremists and states' righters. After all, he had spent his early life in eastern Tennessee which was a Union stronghold. Then upon migrating to Texas he had advocated annexation, and soon thereafter, war with Mexico. Never had he sacrificed conviction for political expediency—not in 1848 when he had championed reapportionment of state representatives and senators; not in 1854 when he had fought against the Know-Nothings who were preaching hatred and bigotry; and certainly not in 1858 when he and Sam Houston had defeated the firebrands and had brought Texas into the Union camp.[5]

A closer examination of Reagan's background, however, would indicate that his secessionist stand was neither a drastic nor contradictory change. Born on the frontier near Sevierville, Tennessee on October 8, 1818, John Henniger Reagan was the eldest of Timothy Richard and Elizabeth Reagan's six children. Although desiring to learn and to improve himself, he was forced to forego a formal education because his family was extremely poor. So he worked during most of his youth, as a tanner, a clerk, a miller, and even a slave overseer. But in off-season or when work was slack, he attended a local academy and later Southwestern Seminary at Maysville, Tennessee. His finances permitted only a year's residence at the seminary, but he studied diligently, concentrating and excelling in logic and rhetoric, tools that were so important in his later endeavors.[6]

In search of great opportunity, Reagan migrated to the raw, turbulent frontier that was Texas in 1839. Within the next twenty years, he compiled a noteworthy record; first as an Indian fighter, surveyor, and scout; then as a self-taught lawyer, a founder and leader of the state Democratic Party, a state legislator, a county and district judge, and a congressman.[7]

During this early phase of his career, Reagan developed into an able statesman of admirable character. He became known and respected for his honesty and integrity; his diligent and hard-working nature; his straightforwardness which was often brutally blunt; his stubbornness when fighting for what he considered right and just, regardless of personal consequences; and his overall ruggedness, evidenced by a weatherbeaten face, dark unruly hair, coal-black eyes, and huge, six-foot-plus frame. He also established a reputation as a firm believer in the law; yet his was a legalism based on logic. Although always eager to learn more, to compromise, to change his mind if the argument warranted, he remained immovable unless convinced, no matter how intense the pressure, no matter how formidable the opposition.[8]

To such a man the events of 1859 and 1860—on the national scene, in Texas, and particularly in Congress—had a tremendous impact; in fact, they forced Reagan into the extremists' camp. They convinced him that the Southern cause was both logical and just; that the Republicans intended to destroy the South; that Southerners must seek security and freedom outside the Union.[9] By late 1860 he was corresponding with O. M. Roberts, a leading Texas secessionist, on the legality of calling a secession convention.[10] By early 1861 he decided to leave Washington, and on January 15 he delivered his farewell address to the House, a speech concluded with a plea and a warning: "Remember that we only ask you to let us alone—nothing else. Give us security in the Union. Respect our rights in the common Territories."[11]

Even before Reagan left Congress, however, the secession movement in Texas was well under way. Bombarded by letters, petitions, resolutions, and newspaper editorials, Governor Sam Houston was urged to call either a special legislative session or a special convention to consider the secession crisis.[12] Disregarding these numerous demands, the governor remained adamant in his support of union, but, even though he wielded considerable influence over the people as well as control of state government, he was outmaneuvered by the separatists. On December 3, 1860, O. M. Roberts, Attorney General George M. Flournoy, John S. Ford, and W. P. Rogers issued a call for a secession convention to be held at Austin on January 28, 1861.[13]

Reagan, meanwhile, was sailing homeward. When he reached New Orleans, he received word that he had been elected a delegate to the State Secession Convention. He went immediately to Austin therefore, instead of proceeding to his home at Palestine, Texas.[14]

By the time Reagan arrived at the capital on January 30, the extremists were in complete control of the convention.[15] Houston, in an attempt to forestall the separatists, had called the legislature into special session on January 21 and had pleaded for union. But the legislature had quickly granted complete authority and even residence in its chambers to the convention, requiring only that its actions be approved by a statewide referendum. O. M. Roberts had been unanimously elected convention president; the great majority of the assembled members were secessionists; and Houston had gone into virtual isolation, refusing to lend even his presence to the proceedings.[16]

While Reagan recognized that secession was practically assured, he also believed that unless Houston would lend his cooperation as well as that of the administration the opposition would remain formidable.[17] So after breakfast on the day of his arrival, he went to the governor's office and requested "a conference about a matter of great moment."[18] After waiting for the governor to finish some routine business, he began to explain the purpose of his visit. Houston, however, immediately interjected: "You know I am opposed to secession."[19] In answer to this somewhat disruptive thrust, Reagan replied that he was aware of the governor's position, but that secession "had reached a point which involved the future of the State, and had passed beyond the consideration of individual interests; that he [Houston] had long been recognized in Texas and the South as one of the leaders of public opinion;"[20] and that Texans now needed his help and hoped to acquire it. Houston, in turn, conceded only that he "had been born and reared in the South, had received all his honors from the South, and . . . would not draw his sword against his own people."[21]

The conversation then moved on to the problems of slavery and secession, the possibilities of war, and the possible reactions and policies of Great Britain and France if hostilities occurred. As the discussion neared its close, Reagan renewed the question of cooperation between the state government and the secessionists, and then asked Houston if he would receive "in a friendly spirit" a committee from the convention. With the governor's assurance that he would, Reagan left.[22]

Events moved swiftly thereafter. Reagan went immediately to the convention hall, submitted a motion for a committee, and was appointed head of a delegation to confer with Houston.[23] The next morning, the governor recognized the convention.[24] On February 1 the delegates passed the ordinance of secession; the next day they enumerated the causes for Texas' withdrawal from the Union; and two days later they elected seven representatives, including Reagan, to the Secession Convention at Montgomery, Alabama.[25] Their work completed, they then adjourned to await approval of their actions in the forthcoming referendum.[26]

Although a delegate to Montgomery, Reagan was forced to pay attention to private affairs and, unable to attend the convention immediately, returned to Palestine. But with news of the formation of the Confederate States of America and later the election of Jefferson Davis to the presidency and Alexander H. Stephens to the vice-presidency of the new republic, he could no longer restrain his enthusiasm. He hurriedly prepared for his departure to the Confederate capital. By late February he was on his way and on the night of March 1 he arrived at his destination.[27]

Reagan was once again in the midst of the turmoil of political life, but now in a more congenial atmosphere. He immediately set to work. Assuming his seat in Congress the morning of March 2, he took an active part in legislation.[28] Later in the day he called on President Davis to offer his congratulations—in his usual straightforward manner. Rather bluntly, he informed the new executive that if present at the time of election he would not have voted for him for President. "Not, however, because I distrusted . . . [your] fitness for the high office," he explained, "but because I wanted . . . [you] at the head of the Army." Davis, highly flattered, readily admitted that an army command "would have been more agreeable to him."[29] Thus began an enduring friendship.

Within a few days Reagan had an even more significant interview with Davis. On March 6, 1861, much to his surprise, he was asked to accept the position of postmaster general. But he flatly refused and steadfastly declined a second offer,[30] for this particular cabinet post was highly unattractive. Davis had already appointed, without regard to friendship but according to ability, recommendation, and geographic representation, Robert Toombs of Georgia as secretary of state; Christopher G. Memminger of South Carolina, secretary of the treasury; Judah P. Benjamin of Louisiana, attorney general; Leroy Pope Walker of Alabama, secretary of war; and Stephen R. Mallory of Florida, secretary of the navy.[31] But he thus far had been unsuccessful in enlisting a postmaster general. Mississippians Henry T. Ellett and Colonel Wirt Adams had both declined the post "on the ground of insuperable difficulties,"[32] and so Reagan's refusal was understandable.

Yet Davis was determined to secure the services of the stubborn Texan. He sent a special delegation to escort Reagan to a conference, then assembled in his office prominent congressmen and cabinet officers, and before this distinguished company once again tendered the post. Reagan, though deeply impressed, explained that to re-establish an effective postal system in the South would take considerable time, that because of lack of facilities, countless delays, and personal inexperience, the postmaster general would undoubtedly receive criticism and might even be branded an incompetent. In conclusion, he remarked that while he "would gladly perform . . . [his] duty to the Confederacy," he "did not desire to become a martyr."[33] Davis, on the other hand, insisted that they must not concede that there was a governmental department which they could not organize. Then, after Davis and the others present assured him that they would aid and sustain him against all unjust criticism, Reagan reluctantly accepted.[34]

Alone and rather despondent, Reagan walked from the meeting to his hotel. He was now a cabinet member, a leader of the new Confederate republic, but, as he later recalled, "instead of feeling proud of the honor . . . I felt that I was to be condemned by the public for incapacity."[35] At the same time, he was wondering where he should begin, how he could obtain the necessary information for organizing an efficient postal system. Then he met an old friend, H. P. Brewster of South Carolina, and he suddenly had the answer. He would send a personal agent to Washington and raid the United States Post Office of its Southern personnel as well as the necessary information. Writing to various department heads and appealing to their Southern loyalties, he offered them similar positions in his new department; and, should they accept, he urged them to bring all available data such as postal maps, reports, personnel books, and examples of all forms then in use. To facilitate the movement of men and material southward, Reagan put Brewster on the afternoon train with instructions to act as his emissary, to deliver the letters, and to take charge of shipping the acquired materials to Montgomery.[36]

Having posed the question of supreme loyalty to Southern members of the United States Post Office—a question that had agonized the military, the statesmen, and government officials—Reagan, with his hastily acquired staff of three assistants, anxiously awaited his reply.[37] His wait was short-lived; his success substantial. For within two weeks the exodus of Federal personnel southward had begun. Leading it were experienced postal officials such as Henry St. George Offutt, chief clerk in the office of sixth auditor; Benjamin N. Clements, chief clerk of the postmaster general's office; and departmental heads Joseph F. Lewis of the bond division; Captain Gustav A. Schwartzman of the dead letter office; and McNair of the finance bureau. Behind them came numerous minor employees and workers. Of those solicited, only two refused,[38] and Reagan found ample compensation for their absence in J. E. Harrell of Alabama, a well-known, able financier, and a capable Texan, W. D. Miller.[39]

Under the skillful administrative guidance of Reagan, the postal department was quickly taking shape. To replace the temporary headquarters which had been Reagan's hotel room, the government purchased a newly-completed, three-story building,[40] and with adequate housing facilities, the new postmaster general rapidly expanded his department's operations. To process and instruct prospective applicants, and to broaden his own knowledge, he opened an evening school;[41] as the needed materials arrived from Washington, clerks began preparing contracts, compiling postmaster lists, and revising the mail route network;[42] Regan began advertising for bids on required postal supplies, including mailbags, twine, sealing wax, and paper;[43] and he also negotiated with private engraving firms for stamps and stamped envelopes.[44]

The most critical problem, however, was that of finance. Optimistically, the framers of the Confederate Constitution had required the post office department to be self-sufficient by March 1, 1863;[45] optimistically, because most national postal systems, including that of the United States, were notorious for their inability to avoid deficits.[46] Reagan's difficult, perhaps impossible task was thus to make his department pay for itself.

Yet conditions, at least at first, were not completely unfavorable. The Confederate Congress had already abolished franking privileges, required postage on newspapers and magazines, and set postage rates at a high level.[47] In turn, the advent of war immediately eliminated the costly overland mail to the West Coast and later, as the Union blockade tightened, the equally expensive trans-Atlantic route was no longer feasible. As a result, the bulk of postal material was reduced, all that remained paid postage, and the postal network was greatly constricted.[48]

Helpful—but not enough. Reagan therefore took measures both to increase revenue and to cut expenses. With the consent of Congress, he doubled the rates on newspapers and printed material, included books as mailable items, and provided both stamps and stamped envelopes to the public.[49] To pare expenses to the minimum, he attacked the formidable problem of transportation, the major drain on postal revenue. Overhauling the mail route system, he eliminated costly star routes, discontinued duplicate services, and shortened needlessly long mail runs in order to stimulate competition.[50] Realizing that solvency depended largely upon reducing railway rates, he called a conference of Southern railroad executives at Montgomery in April, 1861. To the thirty-five representatives who responded, he spoke of the growing national emergency, of the critical days ahead, and, appealing to their patriotism, asked them to help in reducing costs. He then made three proposals: one daily mail service was to replace the normal two; rates were to be reduced by half; and payment in whole or in part was to be in Confederate government bonds. His appeal was successful, for within a few hours the executives accepted his plan.[51]

The railroad negotiations were what crowned Reagan's administrative achievements. For in less than two months he had completely organized the postal department and was able to issue on May 13, 1861, a proclamation declaring that as of June

1 the Confederacy would assume all postal responsibilities.[52] Shortly thereafter, Montgomery Blair, postmaster general of the United States, announced that all service would be suspended in the South on the same date. Thus, whether by design or by accident, the two departments made a peaceful transition.[53]

Despite his commendable efforts and substantial achievements, Reagan's work, his problems, his difficulties had only begun. It was one thing to organize a department, another to make it operate effectively. Against vested interests, against demands of his own and other departments, Reagan was forced to wage a continuous struggle. And above all, he was forced to do so in wartime, a time when his government was fighting for its very existence.

One of the most formidable obstacles facing Reagan was the bitter opposition of vested interests—the railroads, the express companies, the editors and publishers—who suffered financial loss as a result of postal regulations. Sometimes he was successful, sometimes not. In dealing with the railroads he perhaps enjoyed the greatest success. Although the railroad executives had agreed at the Montgomery meeting in 1861 to support those measures necessary for the functioning of the postal system, at least as long as the republic was threatened, their patriotic fervor quickly waned when confronted with inflation, rising wages, and general economic instability resulting from the war. Believing that they had been duped, some refused to negotiate contracts, many sought to evade postal regulations, and all fought to raise rates.[54] Reagan, however, remained obstinate and uncompromising. Charging that the railroads were not only doing a better business as a result of the war[55] but were also selfish monopolies in need of "wholesome and necessary reform,"[56] he used every possible form of legal and economic coercion against them. Withholding government payments and threatening a postal boycott, he forced most of the companies to submit, and by 1863 nearly all of them were fulfilling their contracts.[57]

Of lesser importance was Reagan's losing battle with the express companies, one of these, the Adams-Southern, was the postal system's chief rival. Hoping to eliminate competition, he attempted to exclude them by using both the courts and Congress. Yet, even with this powerful support, Reagan was unsuccessful; the Adams-Southern and others continued to operate.[58]

At the same time, Reagan waged a constant, abusive, and obstinate fight with editors and publishers. A rumbling of discontent turned into a roar of anger when postage rates were doubled. With an arsenal of propaganda weapons, the newspapers unleashed a furious barrage against the postmaster general and his department. Reagan had turned the post office into "an engine for the suppression of intelligence," charged the *Richmond Daily Examiner;*[59] the government had levied a direct tax for revenue, declared the *Montgomery Advertiser*;[60] the postal laws were an "outrage on a free people," claimed the *Atlanta Southern Confederacy.*[61] Against such an onslaught Reagan had little means of defense except to work hard and to correct abuses whenever and wherever he could. But the postal laws remained in effect, and as his department became increasingly self-sufficient, the attacks gradually diminished.[62]

Throughout the war Reagan also had to guard constantly against encroachments by other government agencies—especially the powerful Treasury and War Departments. While brief, the conflict with the treasury was extremely bitter. The dispute erupted violently in 1863 when Reagan, having deposited a considerable surplus of postal funds in specie, demanded withdrawal in kind. Hard-pressed at the time, Treasurer Christopher Memminger wanted to make payment in inflated paper money. This Reagan would not accept and, amid reciprocal threats of impeachment and with the support of President Davis, he won his point.[63] Not so with the military, for the War Department was pre-eminent, and, in the name of national security, repeatedly infringed upon the Postal Department. Particularly disastrous was the impressment of vital mail-carrying transportation facilities and the conscription of postal personnel and contractors. And against the military, the civilian-minded Postal Department was seemingly defenseless. The postmaster who wrote Reagan complaining of an officer "turning him out of the post office and using it as a dancing salon, and as a storehouse for forage,"[64] was certainly aware of this fact. Only the end of the war terminated the bitter inter-departmental conflict between Reagan and Secretaries of War George W. Randolph and James A. Seddon.[65]

Even within Reagan's own department, harmony was not

always the rule. Operating on a low budget and insisting on stringent economical operation, the postmaster general faced a growing discontent among his employees over low wages and long hours; in fact, the discontent grew until it erupted in postal strikes like the one in August, 1863, at Richmond, Virginia,[66] and, while Reagan was able to secure salary raises, the dissatisfaction continued.[67]

Permeating all of Reagan's difficulties were the chaotic effects of the war. As victorious Union armies advanced, penetrating ever deeper into Southern territory, communication routes were cut, postal facilities were destroyed, and the mail was frequently intercepted or interrupted. Then, with the fall of Vicksburg, Mississippi in July, 1863, the South was severed. Reagan, in an attempt to restore service to Arkansas, Louisiana, and Texas, reorganized the postal system, establishing the Trans-Mississippi Post Office Department under the separate authority of the capable Texan, Dr. James H. Starr.[68]

Under such circumstances, it was hardly surprising that, despite Reagan's strenuous efforts, the public was never satisfied. As wartime conditions exerted their mounting strain, service declined in quality and aggravating delays and losses increased. Yet Reagan, constantly beset with problems, constantly confronted with criticism, never slackened his pace. He worked feverishly to maintain the faltering postal system, and, considering the obstacles before him, performed admirably.[69]

Despite criticism, despite his grueling schedule, Reagan actually enjoyed the first two years of his tenure, particularly the association with the South's leading statesmen. A frontiersman in both appearance and attitude, however, he felt ill at ease in Richmond society. He therefore seldom attended official social functions, but, on occasion, held small dinner engagements with friends and other cabinet members. He preferred instead the privacy of his home, devoting most of his leisure time to his children and his wife, Edwina, on whom he relied especially for both personal support and judgment. But after 1863—that year of decision—his happiness vanished as every passing month made defeat seem inevitable.[70]

Reagan had participated in the critical decision of 1863, the invasion of the North. At that time, the Confederate government had the choice: relieve the beleaguered General John C.

Pemberton and thus save Vicksburg, the key to the West; or take the offensive in the East, turn the Army of Virginia loose on the Federals. At the cabinet meeting on the weekend of May 15-16, the members, swayed by the presence of Robert E. Lee, by the desire to strike at the North, by the belief that such an offensive would end the war, voted for invasion—all but Reagan. As a Westerner and perhaps more inclined to recognize the strategic value of that area, he adamantly supported the relief of Vicksburg and opposed the cabinet's final decision, not only voting against it in the meeting, but also later writing President Davis to persuade him to rescind the decision.[71]

But Lee invaded the North, as far north as Gettysburg, and Vicksburg fell. By 1864 the fruits of the decision of 1863 were apparent and by 1865 the Confederacy was doomed. Amid the chaos of a falling state, Reagan, along with other government leaders, fled the capital on April 2, 1865, hoping at first to re-establish the government, then later seeking only to escape. The pursued officials fled first to Danville, Virginia, where they remained only a week because news of Appomattox reached them on April 10; by nightfall they were again hastening southward, through a now hostile and fearful North Carolina. Arriving in Charleston, South Carolina on April 19, they received a short respite, but on April 26, with the surrender of Joseph E. Johnston's army to William T. Sherman, the fugitives were forced to continue their flight. They traveled on into Georgia until on May 10, 1865, near the small town of Irwinville, what remained of the Confederate government awakened to the sound of gunfire; all around them were Union soldiers—for them the war was over.[72]

Reagan's ordeal, however, was about to begin. He, like the other prominent Confederate leaders, received news of his fate on May 20—Federal prison. So he was taken by ship to Fort Warren, a bleak, foreboding fortress on a rock in Boston harbor, where he was placed in solitary confinement and on a stringent diet. He soon found prison life intolerable, but his indomitable will sustained him.[73]

During the long months of loneliness, he had ample opportunity to reflect upon the events of the past four years, and he recorded his thoughts in several letters, two of which were particularly interesting and significant. Writing to President Andrew Johnson on May 28, 1865, he admitted that arms had decided forever the questions of secession and slavery and he pleaded for a policy of friendship toward the South, rather than military rule and retaliation; for the harmonious assimilation of the South back into the Union, rather than the creation of another Poland, another Ireland.[74] To the people of Texas he addressed a second letter. Calling upon them to admit defeat, he advised that they submit to Federal authority, and, if necessary, admit the freed slaves to suffrage. Only by these actions, he warned, could Texans avoid the dual disasters of military rule and universal Negro suffrage.[75] This letter, once made public, was to have an effect totally unexpected by its author.

As the transition to peace was made, restrictions were gradually lifted, and Reagan began to hope for parole and release. Then on October 12, 1865, the long-awaited news arrived. After twenty-two weeks of imprisonment, Reagan was free; he could return to Texas.[76]

Following a visit with friends in New England and New York, a conference with President Johnson in Washington, and a long, leisurely journey homeward through the South, Reagan arrived at Galveston, Texas, in early December.[77] But his reception was cold and unsympathetic, for his fellow Texans had misunderstood his letter; they believed that he had lost his devotion to the South, that he was now espousing Negro suffrage. An exile in his own land, a saddened Reagan continued on to his home in Palestine.[78] His future looked dark and foreboding, his public career seemed ended, his private life a shambles. Few would have suspected that in the following decades John H. Reagan would be returned to Congress in 1875, continually reelected to the lower house until his selection for the Senate in 1887, serve as chairman of the House Commerce Committee for ten years, co-author the bill to establish the Interstate Commerce Commission, and serve as chairman of the Texas Railroad Commission from 1891 to 1899. Few would have imagined that following his death on March 6, 1905, Reagan's funeral would be attended by the State Legislature in a body—a great tribute to a great Texan.[79]

NOTES

[1]For the background of secession in Texas see Anna Irene Sandbo, "Beginnings of the Secession Movement in Texas," **Southwestern Historical Quarterly,** XVIII (July, 1914), pp. 43-73; Ralph A. Wooster, The Secession **Conventions of the South** (Princeton: Princeton University Press, 1962), pp. 121, 123; also see Wendell G. Addington, "Slave Insurrections in Texas," **Journal of Negro History,** XXXV (October, 1950), pp. 419-424; Clement Eaton, "Mob Violence in the Old South," **Mississippi Valley Historical Review,** XXIX (December, 1942), pp. 366-368; and William W. White, "The Texas Slave Insurrection of 1860," **Southwestern Historical Quarterly,** LII (January, 1949), pp. 259-285.

[2]Ben H. Procter, **Not Without Honor: The Life of John H. Reagan** (Austin: University of Texas Press, 1962), p. 110.

[3]**Ibid.,** p. 112.

[4]**Ibid.,** pp. 113-121; John H. Reagan, **Memoirs: With Special Reference to Secession and the Civil War,** ed. by Walter Flavius McCaleb (New York: Neale Publishing Company, 1906), pp. 76-82.

[5]Procter, **Reagan,** pp. 17, 52-54, 67-70, 106-112; Reagan, **Memoirs,** pp. 50, 54-57, 61-75.

[6]Procter, **Reagan,** pp. 7-41; Reagan, **Memoirs,** pp. 23-24.

[7]Procter, **Reagan,** pp. 15-98; Reagan, **Memoirs,** pp. 29-82.

[8]Procter, **Reagan,** pp. 55, 70-71, 101, 108, 145n, 167-168.

[9]**Ibid.,** pp. 118-119.

[10]**Ibid.,** p. 120; Letters, Reagan to Roberts, November 1, 20, December 7, 1860; University of Texas Archives, Oran Milo Roberts Papers, 1844-1895; Letter, Roberts to Reagan, November 25, 1860, Texas State Archives, John H. Reagan Papers, 1840-1905.

[11]Procter, **Reagan,** p. 121.

[12]Wooster, **Secession Conventions,** p. 123; Dudley Goodall Wooten (ed.), **A Comprehensive History of Texas, 1685-1897** (Dallas: William G. Scarff, 1898), II, pp. 86-87.

[13]Llerena Friend, **Sam Houston: The Great Designer** (Austin: University of Texas Press, 1954), pp. 330-333; Edward R. Maher, Jr., "Sam Houston and Secession," **Southwestern Historical Quarterly,** LX (April, 1952), p. 452; Anna Irene Sandbo, "First Session of the Secession Convention in Texas," **Southwestern Historical Quarterly,** XVIII (October, 1914), pp. 179-180; Ernest William Winkler (ed.), **Journal of the Secession Convention of Texas, 1861** (Austin: Austin Publishing Co. ,1912), pp. 9-13; Wooster, **Secession Conventions,** pp. 123-124; Wooten, **Comprehensive History,** II, p. 88.

[14]Procter, **Reagan,** p. 125, **Memoirs,** p. 104; John H. Reagan, "A Conversation with Governor Houston," **Quarterly of the Texas State Historical Association,** III (April, 1900), p. 279.

[15]Procter, **Reagan,** p. 125; Reagan, **Memoirs,** p. 104.

[16]Friend, **Sam Houston,** pp. 333-335; Maher, "Houston and Secession," pp. 453-455; Winkler, **Journal of Secession Convention,** pp. 13-16; Wooster, **Secession Conventions,** pp. 124, 129.

[17]Procter, **Reagan,** p. 126.

[18]Reagan, "Conversation with Houston," p. 279.

[19]**Ibid.,** p. 280.

[20]**Ibid.**

[21]**Ibid.**

[22]**Ibid.,** pp. 280-281; Procter, **Reagan,** p. 126; Reagan, **Memoirs,** pp. 105-106.

[23]Reagan, "Conversation with Houston," p. 281. Members of the committee were Reagan, P. W. Grey, John D. Stell, Thomas J. Devine, and W. P. Rogers. Winkler, **Journal of Secession Convention,** p. 34; Procter, **Reagan, p. 127n.**

[24]Winkler, **Journal of Secession Convention,** pp. 34, 46-47; Wooster, **Secession Conventions,** p. 129; Houston later repudiated the convention. Friend, **Sam Houston,** pp. 336-339.

[25]The other delegates included Louis Trezevant Wigfall, John Hemphill, William Beck Ochiltree, Williamson Simpson Oldham, John Gregg, and Thomas Neville Waul. Charles Robert Lee, Jr., **The Confederate Constitutions** (Chapel Hill: University of North Carolina Press, 1963), pp. 45-47; Winkler, **Journal of Secession Convention,** pp. 45-85; Wooster, **Secession Conventions,** pp. 129-132; Wooten, **Comprehensive History,** II, pp. 103-107.

[26]The vote on the ordinance of secession occurred on February 23, 1861. The final totals were 44,317 for secession and 13,020 against. Wooster, **Secession Conventions,** p. 133.

[27]Procter, **Reagan,** p. 127; Reagan, **Memoirs,** pp. 106, 109; **Montgomery Weekly Post,** March 5, 1861.

[28]Procter, **Reagan,** p. 128; Confederate States of America, **Journal of the Congress of the Confederate States of America, 1861-1865** (Washington: Government Printing Office, 1904-1905), I, pp. 97-99.

[29]Walter Flavius McCaleb, "The Organization of the Post Office Department of the Confederacy," **American Historical Review,** XII (October, 1906), p. 67; Procter, **Reagan,** pp. 129-130; Ben H. Procter, "John H. Reagan and the Confederate Post Office Department," **Georgia Review, XI** (Winter, 1957), p. 391; Reagan, **Memoirs,** p. 109.

[30]McCaleb, "Organization of the Post Office," p. 67; Procter, "Reagan and the Post Office," p. 392; Procter, **Reagan,** p. 129; Reagan, **Memoirs,** p. 109.

[31]Ellis Merton Coulter, **The Confederate States of America, 1861-1865** (Baton Rouge: Louisiana State University Press, 1950), pp. 120-121; Jefferson Davis, **The Rise and Fall of the Confederate Government** (New York: Thomas Yoseloff, 1958), I, pp. 241-243; Rembert W. Patrick, **Jefferson Davis and His Cabinet** (Baton Rouge: Louisiana State University Press, 1944), pp. 45-48.

[32]McCaleb, "Organization of the Post Office," p. 67; see also Procter, "Reagan and the Post Office," p. 392; **Procter, Reagan, p. 129; Reagan, Memoirs,** p. 109; and **Richmond Enquirer,** December 20, 1861.

[33]Procter, **Reagan,** pp. 121-130; Reagan, **Memoirs,** p. 110.

[34]McCaleb, "Organization of the Post Office," pp. 67-68; Procter, "Reagan and the Post Office," p. 392; Procter, **Reagan,** pp. 120-130; Reagan, **Memoirs,** pp. 109-110.

[35]Reagan, "An Account of the Organization and Operations of the Post Office Department of the Confederate States of America, 1861 to 1865," p. 2, Microfilm in the Reagan Papers; Letter, Reagan to Roberts, March 6, 1861, in Roberts Papers.

[36]L. R. Garrison, "Administrative Problems of the Confederate Post Office Department," **Southwestern Historical Quarterly,** XIX (October, 1915-January, 1916), pp. 111-112; McCaleb, "Organization of the Post Office," p. 68; Procter, "Reagan and the Post Office," p. 393; Procter, **Reagan,** p. 130; Reagan, **Memoirs,** p. 124.

[37]Procter, **Reagan,** p. 130; **Richmond Enquirer,** December 24, 1861. Reagan's first assistants were J. L. C. Danner, J. C. Bach, and W. W. Lester.

[38]McCaleb, "Organization of the Post Office," p. 68; Procter, "Reagan and the Post Office," p. 393; Procter, **Reagan,** pp. 130-131; Reagan, **Memoirs,** pp. 124-125.

[39]Procter, **Reagan,** p. 131; **Richmond Enquirer,** December 24, 1861.

[40]Procter, **Reagan,** p. 131; **Richmond Daily Examiner,** May 3, 1861.

[41]Procter, **Reagan,** p. 131; **Richmond Enquirer,** December 24, 1861.

[42]Garrison, "Administrative Problems," p. 112; McCaleb, "Organization of the Post Office," p. 69; Procter, "Reagan and the Post Office," p. 393; Procter, **Reagan,** p. 131; Reagan, **Memoirs,** p. 125.

[43]Reagan, "Report of the postmaster-general to the President, April 29, 1861," pp. 2, 4, in Reagan Papers. There are several reports and they will hereafter be cited as Report with the appropriate date; Garrison, "Administrative Problems," p. 117; Procter, **Reagan,** p. 131.

[44]Report, April 29, 1861, p. 4; Report, November 27, 1861, pp. 21-24; Garrison, "Administrative Problems," pp. 118-123; Procter, **Reagan,** p. 131; **Richmond Enquirer,** March 19, 1861.

[45]James Muscoe Matthews (ed.), **The Statutes at Large of the Provisional Government of the Confederate States of America, From the Institution of the Government, February 8, 1861, to its Termination, February 18, 1862, Inclusive** (Richmond: R. M. Smith, 1864), pp. 34-35; Garrison, "Administrative Problems," p. 118; Procter, "Reagan and the Post Office," p. 394; Procter, **Reagan,** p. 131.

[46]For the fiscal year ending on June 30, 1860, the annual deficit of the United States Post Office had been $1,941,425.35. Report, April 29, 1861, p. 9; McCaleb, '"Organization of the Post Office," p. 73; Procter, "Reagan and the Post Office," p. 394; Procter, **Reagan,** p. 132; Reagan, **Memoirs,** p. 133.

[47]Postage rates for a letter weighing one-half ounce or less within a mailing distance of 500 miles was 5¢; for a distance over 500 miles, 10¢; and for letters exceeding the prescribed weight an additional single postage was levied. Matthews, **Statutes, C.S.A.,** pp. 34-35; Report, November 27, 1861, p. 6; Procter, **Reagan,** p. 132n.

[48]Report, April 29, 1861, pp. 9-12; **Richmond Daily Examiner,** May 23, 1861; Procter, "Reagan and the Post Office," p. 394; Procter, **Reagan,** p. 132; Reagan, **Memoirs,** pp. 134-135.

[49]Matthews, **Statutes, C.S.A.,** pp. 109-110; Procter, "Reagan and the Post Office," p. 394; Procter, **Reagan,** p. 132.

[50]Report, April 29, 1861, pp. 9-10; **Richmond Daily Examiner,** May 23, 1861; McCaleb, "Organization of the Post Office," p. 74; Procter, "Reagan and the Post Office," p. 394; Procter, **Reagan,** p. 132; Reagan, **Memoirs,** p. 135.

[51]Report, April 29, 1861, pp. 12-18; **Montgomery Daily Mail,** April 29, 1861; Robert C. Black, **The Railroads of the Confederacy** (Chapel Hill: University of North Carolina Press, 1952), pp. 52-54; Procter, "Reagan and the Post Office," pp. 394-395; Procter, **Reagan,** pp. 132-133; Reagan, **Memoirs,** pp. 133-134.

[52]Circular, "A Proclamation by the Post-Master General of the Confederate States of America," May 13, 1861, in Reagan Papers; **Richmond Daily Examiner,** May 20, 1861; Garrison, "Administrative Problems," p. 113; McCaleb, "Organization of the Post Office," p. 72; Procter, "Reagan and the Post Office," p. 395; Procter, **Reagan,** pp. 133-134.

[53]Garrison, "Administrative Problems," p. 114; McCaleb, "Organization of the Post Office," p. 73; Procter, "Reagan and the Post Office," p. 395; Procter, **Reagan,** p. 134; Reagan, **Memoirs,** pp. 132-133.

[54]Garrison, "Administrative Problems," p. 237; Procter, "Reagan and the Post Office," p. 396; Procter, **Reagan,** p. 136.

[55]Garrison, "Administrative Problems," p. 237; Procter, **Reagan,** p. 136.

[56]Report, November 27, 1861, pp. 13-18; Report, December 7, 1863, p. 11; Procter, **Reagan,** p. 136.

[57]Report, November 27, 1861, pp. 13-18; Report, February 28, 1862, pp. 3-4; Report, December 7, 1863; pp. 10-11; Garrison, "Administrative Problems," pp. 236-242; Procter, "Reagan and the Post Office," pp. 396-397; Procter, **Reagan,** p. 136.

[58]Garrison, "Administrative Problems," pp. 243-247; see also Report, February 28, 1862, p. 16; Report, November 7, 1864, p. 9; **Richmond Daily Examiner,** July 26, 1861; Procter, **Reagan,** p. 138.

[59]**Richmond Daily Examiner,** September 16, 1861; August 14, 1863.

[60]**Ibid.,** October 4, 1861.

[61]Coulter, **Confederate States,** pp. 130-131.

[62]Procter, "Reagan and the Post Office," p. 397; Procter, **Reagan,** p. 138.

[63]Garrison, "Administrative Problems," pp. 232-235; Patrick, **Davis and His Cabinet,** pp. 286-289; Procter, "Reagan and the Post Office," p. 398; Procter, **Reagan,** p. 138; Reagan, **Memoirs,** pp. 158-159.

[64]Garrison, "Administrative Problems," p. 132.

[65]**Ibid.,** pp. 125-141; Patrick, **Davis and His Cabinet,** pp. 289-292; Procter, "Reagan and the Post Office," p. 398; Procter, **Reagan,** p. 138; Reagan, **Memoirs,** p. 159.

[66]**Richmond Daily Examiner,** August 17, 21, 1863.

[67]James Muscoe Matthews (ed.), **Public Laws of the Confederate States of America** (Richmond: R. M. Smith, 1864), pp.. 269, 276-277; Report, December 7, 1863, p. 12; Procter, **Reagan,** p. 139.

[68]Matthews, **Public Laws, C.S.A.,** p. 184; John Nathan Cravens, **James Harper Starr: Financier of the Republic of Texas** (Austin: Daughters of the Republic of Texas, 1950), pp. 136-143; Procter, "Reagan and the Post Office," p. 398; Procter, **Reagan,** p. 139.

[69]Procter, **Reagan,** pp. 139-140.

[70]**Ibid.,** pp. 145-146; Patrick, **Davis and His Cabinet,** p. 335.

[71]Davis, **Rise and Fall,** II, pp. 437-438; Douglas Southall Freeman, **R. E. Lee** (New York: Charles Scribner's Sons, 1934), III, p. 19; John Beauchamp Jones, **A Rebel War Clerk's Diary at the Confederate States Capital,** ed. by Howard Swiggert (New York: Old Hickory Bookshop, 1935), I, p. 266; Procter, **Reagan,** pp. 147-149; Reagan, **Memoirs,** pp. 121-122, 150-152.

[72]For a complete account of the flight of the Confederate cabinet see Alfred Jackson Hanna, **Flight into Oblivion** (Richmond: Johnson Publishing Co., 1938); also see Joseph T. Durkin, **Stephen R. Mallory: Confederate Navy Chief** (Chapel Hill: University of North Carolina Press, 1954), pp. 338-343; Davis, **Rise and Fall,** II, pp. 678-702; Francis R. Lubbock, **Six Decades in Texas; or Memoirs of Francis Richard Lubbock, Governor of Texas in War Time, 1861-1863,** ed., by C. W. Raines (Austin: B. C. Jones and Company, 1900), pp. 554-572; Patrick, **Davis and His Cabinet,** pp. 345-357; Procter, **Reagan,** pp. 154-161; Reagan, **Memoirs,** pp. 196-221.

[73]Lubbock, **Six Decades,** pp. 572-577; Procter, **Reagan,** pp. 165-167; Reagan, **Memoirs,** pp. 220-222; Alexander H. Stephens, **Recollections: His Diary When a Prisoner at Fort Warren, Boston Harbour, 1865,** ed. by Myrta Lockett Avary (New York: Doubleday, Page and Company, 1910), pp. 110-126.

[74]Letter, Reagan to President Andrew Johnson, May 28, 1865, in Reagan Papers; Reagan, **Memoirs,** pp. 225-226, 271-285; Procter, **Reagan,** pp. 169-170.

[75]Letter, Reagan to Major General Hooker, August 11, 1865, in Reagan Papers; **Dallas Weekly Herald,** October 14, 1865; Reagan, **Memoirs,** pp. 286-295; Procter, **Reagan,** pp. 172-173.

[76]**Dallas Weekly Herald,** November 11, 1865; Stephens, **Recollections,** pp. 531-532; Procter, **Reagan,** p. 174.

[77]Reagan, **Memoirs,** pp. 228-234; Stephens, **Recollections,** pp. 532-535; Procter, **Reagan,** pp. 174-176.

[78]Procter, **Reagan,** p. 176.

[79]For a complete account of Reagan's career following the Civil War see **Ibid.,** pp. 177-301.

Louis Trezevant Wigfall

by

GEORGE C. WIRSDORFER

Batteries of Confederate-controlled Fort Moultrie aimed shot and shell at the skiff carrying the small party toward Fort Sumter. Still the boat never swerved from her course, and officers commanding the batteries inferred that Wigfall must have been in it. Louis Trezevant Wigfall, aide to General P. G. T. Beauregard, was being rowed to the Federal fort during the bombardment in order to induce its commander, Major Robert Anderson, to surrender. Embarking with three Negro oarsmen and a coxswain, Private William Gourdin Young, brandishing only his sword to which he had tied his cambric handkerchief, Wigfall made his way across the bay on the unauthorized mission. He almost lost his life when a thirty-two pound ball struck the water within five yards of the skiff. Upon reaching Fort Sumter (located midway in Charleston Harbor), Wigfall made his way to an open porthole on the town side of the fort. With the aid of a loose piece of timber which he placed beneath the opening in the fort, he swung himself from a protruding gun into the embrasure. The heat was intense, fire was raging, and the smoke was insufferable with shells exploding above. Working his way to a group of soldiers, Wigfall inquired for Major Anderson. Upon locating the Federal commander, Wigfall offered him terms of unconditional surrender and said he would raise the white flag even if Anderson did not. The major finally accepted the terms, and the battle of Fort Sumter was over.[1]

This daring episode was but one of many in the tumultuous life of Louis Trezevant Wigfall, United States senator, Confederate brigadier general and Confederate senator from Texas. He was, however, not a native Texan, being born in the Edgefield District of South Carolina on April 21, 1816, the son of Levi Durand and Eliza (Thompson) Wigfall.[2] After attending the 1834-1835 session of the University of Virginia, young Wigfall enrolled at South Carolina College (now the University of

South Carolina), receiving his B.A. degree in 1837. He found time to serve in the Seminole War (1836-1842) as a sergeant, gaining valuable military experience. After being admitted to the bar in 1839, Wigfall established himself in Edgefield Village.[3]

Wherever Wigfall went he attracted devoted followers, but also stirred bitter opposition.[4] While in Edgefield he was elected colonel of the Seventh Regiment of the South Carolina Militia, serving from August 15, 1839 to July 16, 1845. He raised the regiment from an inefficient body of soldiers to a well-drilled and effective regiment—one of the best in the brigade.[5] During this time he also became involved in a bitter political feud with the politically and socially important Brooks family that led to the killing of young Thomas Bird and the inflicting and receiving of a wound in a duel with Preston Smith Brooks. Brooks subsequently was elected a congressman from South Carolina and gained dubious fame in 1856 for the caning of Senator Charles Sumner of Massachusetts on the floor of the Senate. Finding the atmosphere in Edgefield hostile, Wigfall moved to Texas.[6] He never again fought a duel but still was a "firm believer in the *code duello* as a factor in the improvement of both morals and the manners of a community."[7]

Meanwhile Wigfall and his second cousin, Charlotte Maria Cross, the daughter of George Warren Cross of Charleston, married on November 15, 1841. To this marriage were born five children; three, Francis Halsey, Louise Sophia, and Fanny, reached maturity.[8]

In 1845, through the influence of General James Hamilton of South Carolina, who was one of the early friends of the Republic of Texas, a law partnership was arranged between Wigfall and Judge William B. Ochiltree; and soon after, early in 1846, the South Carolinian came to Texas. Remaining in Galveston a short time and then residing in Nacogdoches for a brief period, Wigfall finally settled in Marshall in 1848, forming a law partnership with Ochiltree and T. J. Jennings.[9]

Politically, Wigfall was an ardent Democrat of the Calhoun states' rights school. He had contended in 1844 that South Carolina could submit neither to the protective tariff nor to the exclusion of Texas from the Union and therefore favored secession. He attended and served on the resolutions committee in Edgefield during June, 1844, at a "Great Texas Meeting" which called for the annexation of the Lone Star State.[10] In 1846, Wigfall opposed the Mexican War, defending John C. Calhoun's contention that the war would accentuate the slavery controversy.[11]

The acquisition of territory following the war with Mexico brought the slavery dispute to a crisis, and Wigfall hoped that South Carolina would act to unite the Southern States. If South Carolina refused to take the initiative to lead the South in the slavery crusade, he hoped that Texas would pick up the gauntlet. As a member of the Texas House of Representatives in 1850 Wigfall led the unsuccessful opposition to the cession of the disputed Santa Fe region, fearing that it would make "free soil" territory out of land that should belong to the slave state of Texas.[12] He felt the North was dependent upon the South to maintain manufacturing and comercial systems and that the North would accept any compromise. If the Union was doomed, however, Wigfall thought it might as well dissolve then as later, for the South was in the strongest position that the region could hope to attain.[13]

Wigfall was one of the organizers of the Democratic Party in Texas. He was adamantly opposed to the Know-Nothing Party with which Sam Houston, his political and personal enemy, was affiliated. The bitter gubernatorial race of 1857 saw Wigfall's efforts on the part of Governor Hardin R. Runnels against Houston crowned with success. During the same election Wigfall was chosen by the voters of Harrison County to represent them in the Texas State Senate. He was recognized as the leader of the "Southern-rights" Democrats in the Texas State Senate, and served as chairman of the State Affairs Committee as well as a member of the committees on the Judiciary, Internal Improvements, and Privileges and Elections. The support of the "Wigfall faction" of the Democratic Party in 1859 for the revival of the African slave trade and secession from the Union were two of the reasons for Houston's victory in the gubernatorial race. At this time the voters of the state were not prepared for such a radical move. This did not, however, prevent Wigfall's election to the United States Senate in 1859.[15]

By the death of J. Pinckney Henderson in 1858 a vacancy was created in the Texas representation in the United States Senate. According to one state political leader, the election of

Wigfall was due to the resentment throughout the South against John Brown's raid at Harper's Ferry, and there were indications that this opinion was shared by many. To elect him, however, a party caucus was necessary.[16] Since Wigfall at the time was a member of the state senate, it became necessary to reinterpret Section 24, Article III of the Bill of Rights of the Texas Constitution of 1845 which referred to the ineligibility of a member of the legislature to hold any other office.[17] The Texas House Committee on the Judiciary investigated the matter and found Wigfall eligible; and he was elected by the Texas Legislature on December 5, 1859. It is said that Governor Houston exclaimed when he heard his arch rival had been elected a senator: "Thank God this country is so great and strong that it can bear even that."[18]

Wigfall took his seat in the United States Senate on January 4, 1860, where he soon became well-known for his debating ability. In regard to Wigfall's forensic talent, William L. Yancey, later a fellow Confederate senator, stated: "Few members could match him in colloquy. He was original, prompt, aggressive and possessed of a most poignant wit."[19] His style of oratory, though brilliant and full of imagery, was analytical. At times the Senate went into an uproar over his colorful, caustic language. Though possessed of a venomous tongue, he also had a striking sense of humor and generous qualities of heart. As a commanding speaker he was erect and powerful in physique, featured by "a straight, broad brow, . . . a mouth coarse and grim, yet full of power, a square jaw, . . . eyes of wonderful depth and light, . . . flashing, fierce, yet calm."[20]

In the Senate Wigfall continued his extremist states' rights philosophy, making many powerful appeals on its behalf. He contended that the Federal government should protect slave property in the territories. His attack on Andrew Johnson's Homestead Bill was based on the fear of "free soil" in the territories.

As one of the authors of the "Southern Address" signed December 14, 1860, Wigfall urged secession and the organization of the Confederacy. It was signed by about one-half of the Southern senators and representatives. This address preceded every state ordinance of secession and was the official beginning of the Confederate States of America.[21]

Wigfall seemed to have been the only senator, besides Iverson of Georgia, who was against all compromises to hold the Southern States in the Union. By refraining from voting, he helped on January 16, 1861, to kill the Crittenden Compromise, one of the last hopes for saving the Union.[22]

In Texas a secession convention met in January, 1861, and authorized the submission of an ordinance of secession to Texas voters on February 23. Prior to the voting, however, on February 5, the convention elected Wigfall and six other delegates to represent the people of Texas at Montgomery, Alabama, where delegates of those states that had seceded were meeting to write a constitution and establish a provisional government.[23]

Wigfall, however, chose to remain in Washington. Using the subterfuge of awaiting official notification of the secession of Texas, Wigfall remained in the United States Senate to be in a position where he could keep advised of the movements of the National government and communicate them to the secession leaders.[24]. After President James Buchanan dismissed the Southerner, Secretary of War John B. Floyd, Wigfall wired to South Carolina saying that such a move meant war.[25] Upon hearing Abraham Lincoln's inaugural address, he further predicted war and urged the Confederacy to take the forts, Sumter (South Carolina) and Pickens (Florida), before reinforcements could reach them.[26]

In his last address to the United States Senate on March 2, 1861, Wigfall stated his belief that an amendment providing for the right of secession might bring the Gulf States back into the Union, if the protection of slaves as property was provided. However, at the close of the session he challenged: "We have dissolved the Union; mend it if you can; cement it with blood. . . ."[27] Wigfall never did resign his seat in the Senate, and was ultimately expelled from that august body on July 11, 1861.[28] However, Wigfall had left Washington on March 23, first going to Baltimore where he established a recruiting station for the Confederacy, and endeavoring to help Ben McCulloch buy arms for a mounted regiment in Texas. The ex-senator then proceeded to Richmond to visit the Virginia legislature, finally going to Charleston, South Carolina, on April 1.[29]

It was during his stay in Charleston that the Fort Sumter episode occurred. Wigfall did not receive the credit he felt he deserved for engineering Major Anderson's surrender and was very upset with Anderson's uncomplimentary account of the fall of Sumter. Showing his bitterness, Wigfall was heard to remark:

> Catch me risking my life for him [Anderson] again. He might have been man enough to tell the truth to those New Yorkers, however unpalatable to them a good word for us might have been. We did behave well to him.[30]

A short time after the fall of Sumter, Wigfall was on his way to Montgomery where he arrived finally on April 24, 1861, to attend the second session of the Provisional Congress of the Confederacy which convened on the twenty-ninth.[31] During the session Wigfall took the constitutional oath, which was administered by the President, and was placed on the Committee of Foreign Relations.[32] There is no record of the debates held in the Congress, for most of the work was done behind closed doors and the proceedings were not published. It was reported that although Wigfall said little he always attended the meetings.[33] Adjourning on the twenty-first of May, the Congress was scheduled to meet again at Richmond on the twentieth of July. The disunionists of 1861 did not measure up to the generation of Calhoun and Polk, but they were able to conduct a national government and devise a foreign policy.[34]

Wigfall found himself a favorite of the people by being an uncompromising defender of the South. Often called upon to speak wherever he journeyed, he was, it seemed, in his glory:

> Twelve years ago there had been scant hope of success for his Southern Rights Doctrine, but now he was considered first orator and statesman of Texas, and among the first in the Confederacy. His speeches were even complimented in the North. He served the Confederate government on many occasions in important ways which were not made known because of the belligerent attitudes of affairs. Perhaps it was simply an over supply of bravado, but there was nothing he would not undertake for "the cause."[35]

Wigfall had intended to travel to Texas directly from Montgomery after the second session of the Confederate Provisional Congress, but President Jefferson Davis called upon the Texan to accompany him to Richmond.[36] Both were received with great enthusiasm and were called upon to speak at every station. Upon returning to Texas, Wigfall addressed troops in Marshall, explaining they were raw troops, not well trained, but able to meet those which Lincoln would send to fight them. In closing he told the recruits: "The people of the South are with you. Pray God, I cross not your border [Texas] until freedom is secured."[37]

Wigfall returned to Richmond just prior to the battle of Manassas (July 21, 1861) but did not accompany President Davis to the battlefield site due to a disagreement. The Texan would not permit an open break with the President at that time, however, for he believed that "before the country is strong and settled in her new career, it would be disastrous for us, the head men, to engage in a row among ourselves.[38] For the purpose of securing information before the battle, it was reported that he made a trip to Washington, shaving off his whiskers and going through the city as a coal driver.[39]

Wigfall was commissioned colonel of the First Texas Infantry Battalion (later regiment) on August 28, 1861.[40] The eleven companies of the First Texas Regiment had marched to Virginia separately and were then organized by Wigfall, Lieutenant Colonel Hugh McLeod, and Major A. T. Rainey.[41] During September and October of 1861 the First Texas was quartered at Camp Wigfall (named for its commander), located near the present site of Quantico Marine Base at Dumfries, Virginia.[42] Wigfall was promoted to the rank of brigadier general on October 21, 1861, and given command of the three Texas regiments then in Virginia (the 1st, 4th, and 5th Texas Infantry) and the 18th Georgia Infantry Regiment.[43] Thus was formed the famous Texas Brigade with Wigfall as its first commander. The Texas Brigade spent a relatively inactive fall and winter guarding the Potomac Line. The Texans fortified their campsite on Powells Run (on the river some twenty-five miles south of Washington) against a possible Union overland drive on Richmond by constructing embrasures for artillery between Dumfries and Occoquan Creek. While stationed here it appeared that Wigfall divided the major part of his time between drilling his men and nipping on a jug of applejack. Near the campsite of the Texans was Cockpit Point, a location where the Potomac

River was relatively narrow. It was not unusual to see the tents and campfires of the Federals or to hear an evening concert by their bands, and for the pickets along the shoreline to exchange shots, taunts and threats.[44] This nearness of the enemy coupled with Wigfall's bacchanal habits caused at least one soldier to complain:

> If there is anything else that I have a right to complain of in common with every member of the brigade, it is of the vagaries and hallucinations of the brilliantly astute politician now in command of the brigade. They have been so frequent as to become monotonous. Old Sam Houston must have known whereof he spake when he dubbed him "Wiggletail." Whether it be due to constitutional nervousness, or to that by the apple-jack and kindred liquid refreshments of which he is said to be so fond, he has kept us from last month, and particularly since the Christmas holidays began, in a state of almost constant apprehension. He sees a Yankee in every shadow, hears one approaching in every breeze that rustles and clinks together the ice-crusted boughs of the pine trees under which the cabin selected for the brigade headquarters stands, and no sooner sees or hears one that he takes alarm and orders the long roll sounded by the drummer he keeps close at hand for just such emergencies.[45]

After two or three of these false alarms the commanders of the Fourth and Fifth Texas, Colonels Hood and Archer, disregarded the long roll and refused to call their men out until Wigfall had sent direct orders to do so. Beside this problem, Wigfall's men complained of his tendency to keep them close to camp, as reflected in another soldier's letter:

> I think that Wigfall will make an able and efficient commander. But he has one great fault. He loves whiskey too well. He has been drunk several times since we came here. But I think that he will be brave enough for any emergency. He says that the name of Texas shall never be disgraced by him nor his battalion. We cannot get out of camp without a pass from Wigfall and he has cursed so many of the boys about asking him for a pass, that we are all getting afraid of him.[46]

Wigfall's family later joined him at the Cockpit Point campsite, and his daughter recorded her memories of the occasion:

> My father's headquarters were at the little village tavern, where he spent some happy weeks, going out every afternoon to see the dress parade of the Regiments and wandering by the lovely Occoquan river, where the big cannons guarded the shores from the enemy's approach.[47]

Other visitors frequented the campsite to watch the Texans parade. Mrs. Mary Chesnut, a friend of the Wigfall family, commented on Wigfall's drilling: "How that redoubtable Wigfall did rush those poor Texans about. He maneuvered and marched them until I was weary for their sakes. Poor fellows! It was a hot afternoon, the thermometer in the nineties."[48] On one occasion President Davis presented a "Lone Star" flag, made by Mrs. Wigfall, to the Texans. In accepting the flag the gallant Wigfall was in fine rhetorical form. "I will lead them," he said, "where the battle's wreck lies the thickest and death's brief pang the quickest."[49] But Wigfall was never to lead the Texans into battle for he was still very much interested in politics, and had never resigned his seat in the Provisional Congress. Thus he wore two hats—the kepi of a Confederate general and the high silk top hat of a Confederate senator.

In Texas, the legislature met in regular session on November 4, 1861, and elected Wigfall and W. S. Oldham as senators to the Permanent Congress of the Confederacy. Wigfall was elected on the first ballot with only three votes cast against him.[50] When the Texas Brigade went into winter quarters, Wigfall officially resigned his command, February 20, 1862, and returned to Richmond for the meeting of Congress.[51]

The permanent constitution of the Confederacy went into effect on February 18, 1862, and on that day the senators-elect were called to order by Vice-President Alexander Stephens in the senate chamber of the state capitol. The vice-president administered the oath of office to those present. This did not include Wigfall who was late in arriving.[52] On the twenty-first the senators drew for the length of their terms with the four-year term falling to Wigfall and Oldham receiving one of six years.[53] Wigfall served on at least three committees: Foreign Affairs, Military Affairs and Territories.[54] The new Confederate Congress had to face many serious problems during its first session; but, since it often met in secret, it is impossible to know exactly what was said or done.

After the Federal inactivity during the second half of 1861, the spring of 1862 brought a series of disasters for Confederate arms. The events were reflected in the stringent measures which came out of the secret sessions at Richmond. The writ of *habeas corpus* was suspended by Congress; martial law was declared in various cities, and the first conscription act was passed. To make things more unfortunate, there was constant dissension in the Congress.[55]

On February 27, 1862, Wigfall, acting for the Committee on Military Affairs, reported a bill out of committee to authorize the suspension of the writ of *habeas corpus* in certain cases. He said that the condition of the country was so bad that it was necessary to declare martial law in certain areas and the provisions of the bill were intended particularly to meet cases involving the safety of cities. While the Senate soon adopted the bill in secret session, it was, however, the middle of April before the House of Representatives passed the act.[56]

One of the foremost problems confronting the Permanent Congress was that of conscription. When Congress convened at Richmond on February 18, 1862, two things required its immediate attention. First, it was necessary to introduce uniformity into military services in spite of the strenuous objections of the state governments. Second, large numbers of recruits had to be secured from a populace whose ardor for the war was cooling.[57] On the first of April in 1862 Wigfall introduced a bill for raising an army in the service of the Confederacy and proposed rules for its organization and regulation.[58] He spoke in favor of conscription, in spite of the fact that he had formerly threatened that King Cotton would easily humble the North, and the world, if need be, in the defense of states' rights. He said he had always been, and still was, a states' rights man but that the Confederacy as a whole was waging war and that for the time being all necessary centralized power should be given to the Confederate government. The Richmond government, he declared, was the agent of all the states, and exercised only such powers as had been delegated to it by the states. No state had the right to make war, raise armies, or conclude treaties of peace. These rights were expressly conferred upon the Confederate government. Moreover, there were no limitations to these powers. The voluntary system of which so much had been said was extra-constitutional if not unconstitutional. By relying on it alone, the country would be without an adequate army. If anyone should say that all this was "anti-Republican," he could reply that it was the doctrine of Washington, Jefferson and other illustrious men.[59] To exemplify his certainty, he declared that if it were not constitutional anyone might "spit in his face and call him a horse."[60]

Two weeks later on April 16, 1862, the Congress passed the first conscription act in American history.[61] While Wigfall voted for the bill, Oldham, the other Texas senator, voted against it on the grounds that Congress did not have the power to draft persons into military service. This controversy concerning constitutionality coupled with an exemption act for professional reasons and a clause allowing the employment of substitutes caused the conscription act to destroy much of the cooperatoin of the state governments and their people.

Another prime issue in which Wigfall was involved was the formation of the Supreme Court. Actual organization of the Supreme Court was considered in 1862 and again in January, 1863.[62] Wigfall desired that a Supreme Court be established. He believed that there should be some tribunal to decide questions between the various states and the Richmond government.[63] Attributing the destruction of the Union primarily to the superior intellect of the members of the old Supreme Court, he did not deem it necessary to have men of superior talent on the Court for:

> Had Chief Justice Marshall been a man of bad character, or inferior intellect, the old Union would still be in existence but his unimpeachable character, his great intellect enabled him to fasten his principles of Nationality to our institutions. The supreme court of Georgia, without a dissenting voice, has said that Judge Marshall spent his life writing against the Kentucky and Virginia Resolutions. Had Mr. Marshall tended the small business of his court the Union would not now be disrupted.[64]

Wigfall did not think, however, that the Constitution required the organization of the high court. He believed that Sections Forty-five and Forty-six of the Confederate Statute Book of 1861 would give the Supreme Court jurisdiction over the state courts. This he considered to be unconstitutional; and, as he had said in the beginning, he would not vote for a Supreme Court as long as these sections of the statute remained valid.[65] Because of a lack of particular need for such a judicial body and the probable division of Congress on the matter, the measure was postponed time and again.[66] Wigfall, true to his nature, took part in every discussion of the Senate, approving or disapproving, according to his personal feelings.

Well-liked by most people, Wigfall was considered an invaluable man to the cause. It was therefore most unfortunate for the Confederacy that from the beginning his relationship with President Davis was strained. In Washington, before the war when both served in the United States Senate, and at Montgomery there had been a close relationship between them; but as the war progressed and nerves grew taut their friendship faltered, and they seemed to take opposite sides on every question. The breach between Davis and Wigfall must have been noticeable to the public at an early date for Mrs. Chesnut notes it in her diary as early as June, 1861. The true cause for this break between fast friends is not known. Davis severed what little friendship remained by dealing Wigfall a sharp rebuke for the Texas senator's criticism of a presidential favorite, General Theophilus Hunter Holmes.

The alienation became a real break in November of 1862 when Davis was considering the appointment of a new secretary of war. Of his three considerations, James A. Seddon, Joseph E. Johnston, and Gustavus W. Smith, Seddon seemed to be most acceptable; and the appointment was offered him. No statement concerning the matter was published since Davis feared that, should Seddon decline, the others would not accept because the portfolio had not been offered to them first. On the same evening, Wigfall, interested in the matter as a key member of the Senate Committee on Military Affairs, called upon the President at which time they discussed the matter at length without Davis ever mentioning what he had done. In the morning papers Wigfall read of Seddon's appointment and acceptance. Wigfall, vexed and offended by what he deemed the President's lack of confidence in him, denounced Davis bitterly in the Senate, not particularly for the appointment of Seddon but for everything in general. The President sent John H. Reagan, a Confederate cabinet member from

Texas, to call upon the senator, saying that he had not intended any disrespect or a lack of confidence in him and that it was no time for friends to quarrel. Though Wigfall seemed appeased by the explanation, he continued his denunciation of Davis until the fall of the Confederacy.[67]

Joseph E. Johnston, one of the South's great generals, proved to be another factor for disagreement between Wigfall and the President. Wigfall wanted Johnston to command the Army of the West, but Davis was determined that Braxton Bragg retain that command. Johnston finally did succeed to the command of the Army of Tennessee during the early months of the Atlanta Campaign in 1864. However, in the midst of the campaign, President Davis intervened and replaced Johnston with John B. Hood after William Hardee had declined the position. This replacement roused Wigfall to the greatest anger, and he denounced the President, lauded Johnston, and begged Hood not to accept the command. He declared that no man could fight under the conditions imposed by Davis, and accused the President of admitting a spy to his office to view the campaign plans.[68] He believed that Davis was incapable of handling both the job of the President and of the Commander-in-Chief at the same time. According to the Texas senator:

> It is [was] impossible for Davis to attend to the Civil duties of his office and command the Army at the same time. Napoleon never attempted such a thing. The commander must be in the field.[69]

Later Wigfall exhibited the fear that Davis was losing his mind:

> Has it ever occurred to you that Davis's mind is becoming unsettled? No sane man would act as he is doing. I fear that his bad health and bad temper are undermining his reason and that the foundation is already sapped. God only knows what is to become of us with such a man at the head of the government.[70]

By the spring of 1864, Wigfall, convinced that Davis' poor judgment would ruin the country unless he could be controlled, sought to free General Robert E. Lee from direction by the President. He proposed that the Confederate Constitution be amended in order to deprive the President of his power as commander-in-chief and vest this power in an officer appointed and removable only by joint action of the President and Senate. Largely through Wigfall's efforts, in February of 1865 Lee became commander of all the Confederate armies. So earnest was Wigfall's conviction that the only chance of success was in a radical change of policy that he never realized that he was hindering rather than promoting the end he so fervently desired.[71]

Late in the summer of 1864, it became imperative for Wigfall to journey to Texas. Mrs. Wigfall accompanied him despite the difficulties. The crossing of the Mississippi River, then held by Federal forces was deemed to be most hazardous. An ambulance, drawn by mules, was obtained for the journey; and the couple left Jackson, Mississippi, on July 29.[72] The trip home was made with comparative ease considering the times with the enormous mosquitoes of the Louisiana swamps and corduroy roads presenting more of a problem than did the Mississippi crossing.[73]

On October 26, Wigfall was well-received when he addressed a large gathering of Austin citizens. His speech was a repetition of his usual arguments with a defense of the course pursued by the Confederate Congress.[74]

The return trip to Richmond proved to be dangerous. The road to the Mississippi through Louisiana was reported impassable to any conveyance due both to the large number of Federal soldiers present in the state and the fall rains. But somehow the mule-drawn ambulance of the Wigfalls arrived at the Mississippi River just south of Vicksburg without incident, largely because it was under the protection of an officer with an escort of ten men. The Mississippi itself was infested with Federal gunboats which lay in plain sight ready to fire a shot in any direction. After the ambulance wheels were secured in two large logs hollowed out in the center, the mules swam across, pulling the ambulance after them. The crossing was made at night with the gunboats looming on all sides. Mrs. Wigfall's only comment on the frightening journey was that the "mules would snort; and made such a dreadful noise that we expected every moment the gunboats would hear and send a shot across our bows."[75] The papers reported their capture, but several days later came word that they had crossed the river safely and were on their way to Richmond.

Wigfall's return was so delayed that the second session of the Second Confederate Congress (November 7, 1864-March 18, 1865) was well under way before he arrived back in Richmond.[76] The reverses of the Confederacy were acknowledged, but ultimate defeat was not contemplated, nor discussed as a possibility. Many, including the senator, continued their support by investing their gold in Confederate bonds. By some means Mrs. Wigfall's mother had succeeded in sending through the lines $1,000 in gold which was immediately changed for Confederate currency. Wigfall felt that he would not be true to his country if he admitted, even to himself, that Confederate money was not as "good as gold."[77]

As the end of the Confederacy drew near it revealed a triangle of bitter feelings in all affairs among the President, the Congress, and the state governments. The last weeks of the Congress were consumed with arguments concerning the utilization of slaves in the army and other desperate measures not contemplated in better times. Wigfall was one who strongly indicated the objections to the arming of the slaves. On the last day of the Congress, resolutions were heard on the subject.[78] Even in the face of defeat the South insisted upon protection of its slaves and their positions as chattel property in society.

Congress adjourned on March 18, 1865, apparently with more pride in its victories over Davis than in the military laws it had enacted. The abundance of able and ambitious leaders had proved a liability rather than an asset to the Confederate cause.[79] Wigfall himself, from whom so many had hoped for so much, had been more of a destructive than a constructive factor in the Confederate Senate.[80]

It is ironical to note that during the disintegration of the Confederacy the state of Texas was considering a new senator. Wigfall's term was to end in 1865, and the feelings of the people had changed. Tired of war and weary for peace, they did not glory in his radical beliefs. They turned against him almost completely, condemning his speeches and showing annoyance at his antagonism toward the President. Some denied that he had been warmly received on his journey in 1864. The man considered as the best choice to replace him was Governor Pendleton Murrah, who had "less radical notions and no finely spun theories of Democratic government."[81]

Wigfall reflected the eminence of the decline: "It is all over; the game is up," he said after Congress adjourned.[82] He made arrangements to return to Texas, for it "was only a short distance from Mexico, if they wanted to hang him."[83] A week before the evacuation of Richmond, the senator and his family began their journey, hoping to reach the Rio Grande.[84] At Raleigh they learned of the evacuation of Richmond and the surrender at Appomattox. From North Carolina they journeyed to the home of ex-Senator Benjamin H. Hill in La Grange, Georgia.

After Johnston's surrender on April 26, it became necessary, in order to escape arrest, that Wigfall conceal his identity. He still hoped to join E. Kirby Smith in Texas and make one last stand for the Confederacy. For that purpose he shaved his beard and procured a parole of a private soldier. After securing a large covered wagon and four mules to transport his family and their belongings, he took his place among some paroled Texans as an escort for the wagon. They traveled as country people, exciting little attention because it was a common sight at the time. Although the Wigfalls possessed only worthless Confederate money, a friend had given them a large box of tobacco which was as good as specie for trading purposes. Nothing stopped them until they reached Montgomery, Alabama, where they saw the first Federal pickets. It was decided that the family should separate since it would not be safe for the senator to travel by the usual methods through towns. He continued with the soldiers while his family remained with friends in Montgomery.[85]

Finally reaching his home in Marshall, Wigfall was cared for by the Negroes who had been his slaves. With their aid he was able to escape through the lines to England.[86]

As with many Confederate leaders who had fled to England, Wigfall found himself in London without money and without work. While little is known of his adventures there it is understood that he practiced law in that British city and participated in various business ventures. Wigfall's son, Francis Halsey, who had fled to Europe with his family, returned to New Orleans and Arkansas to seek work in insurance and to assist his father in securing English investments in Colorado mines.

Wigfall, in 1872, sailed back to Baltimore, Maryland, where

he resided with his daughter Louise (Mrs. D. Giraud Wright) for several months. Longing, however, to reestablish his law practice in his beloved Texas, he returned to Galveston in January of 1874. Shortly thereafter on February 18, 1874, the outspoken Texan, suffering from an undisclosed illness, quietly died.[87]

NOTES

[1]Mrs. D. Giraud Wright, **A Southern Girl in '61** (New York: Doubleday, Page and Co., 1905), pp. 45-46.

[2]Trinity Episcopal Church Records, Edgefield, South Carolina, University of Texas, Archives, Louis T. Wigfall Collection.

[3]Walter Prescott Webb (ed.), **The Handbook of Texas,** 2 vols., (Austin: The Texas State Historical Association, 1952), II, p. 906.

[4]Sarah Agnes Wallace, "Confederate Exiles in London, 1865-1870: The Wigfalls," **The South Carolina Historical and Genealogical Magazine,** LII (April, 1951), p. 74.

[5]Editorial in the Edgefield **Advertiser,** July 30, 1845, University of Texas, Archives, Louis T. Wigfall Collection.

[6]Letter, D. C. Ray to C. W. Lord, June 9, 1925, University of Texas, Archives, Louis T. Wigfall Collection; letter, J. P. Carroll lto James H. Hammond, November 1, 1840, University of Texas, Archives, Louis T. Wigfall Collection.

[7]Mrs. D. Giraud Wright, **A Southern Girl in '61,** p. 31.

[8]Letter, F. H. Wigfall to Mrs. D. G. Wright, April 11, 1892, University of Texas, Archives, Louis T. Wigfall Collection.

[9]"Death of General Louis T. Wigfall," ('appeared in the Galveston **News,** February 19, 1874), University of Texas, Archives, Louis T. Wigfall Collection.

[10]News item in the Edgefield **Advertiser,** July 30, 1845, University of Texas, Archives, Louis T. Wigfall Collection.

[11]Webb (ed.), **The Handbook of Texas,** II, p. 906.

[12]**Ibid.**

[13]News item in the **Texas Republican** (Marshall), May 30, 1850.

[14]Beverly Josephine Seehorn, "Louis Trezevant Wigfall, A Confederate Senator" (unpublished Master's thesis, Southern Methodist University, 1930), pp. 5-13.

[15]Webb (ed.), **The Handbook of Texas,** II, p. 907.

[16]Eugene C. Barker (ed.), **Readings in Texas History** (Dallas: The Southwest Press, 1929), p. 462.

[17]Dudley G. Wooten (ed.), **A Comprehensive History of Texas, 1685 to 1897** (Dallas: William G. Scarff, 1898), II, p. 57.

[18]Mary Boykin Chesnut, **A Diary from Dixie** (Boston: Houghton Mifflin Co., 1950), p. 76.

[19]John Witherspoon DuBose, **The Life and Times of William Lowndes Yancy** (New York: Peter Smith, 1942), II, p. 676.

[20]Dumas Malone (ed.), **Dictionary of American Bibliography**, 21 vols. (New York: Charles Scribner's Sons, 1936), XX, p. 188, quoting W. H. Russell, **My Diary North and South, 1863**, I, p. 907.

[21]Seehorn, "Louis Trezevant Wigfall, A Confederate Senator," p. 44.

[22]Webb (ed.), **The Handbook of Texas**, II, p. 907.

[23]Rupert Norvel Richardson, **Texas the Lone Star State** (Englewood Cliffs, New Jersey: Prentice-Hall, Inc., 1958), p. 185.

[24]Daniel Wait Howe, **Political History of Secession** (New York: G. P. Putnam's Sons, 1914), pp. 547-548.

[25]**The War of Rebellion: Official Records** (Washington: Government Printing Office, 1880-1901), Series I, Vol. 1, p. 252.

[26]Malone (ed.), **Dictionary of American Biography**, XX, p. 188.

[27]U. S. Congress, Senate, Senator Louis T. Wigfall speaking against H. J. Res. to amend the U. S. Constitution, 36th Congress, 1st Session. March 2, 1861. **Congressional Globe.** Vol. XXX, Pt. 2, p. 1373.

[28]Marcus J. Wright and Harold B. Simpson, **Texas in the War 1861-1865** (Hillsboro, Texas: Hill Junior College Press, 1965), p. 97.

[29]**The War of Rebellion: Official Records** (Washington: Government Printing Office, 1880-1901), Series I, Vol. 1, pp. 276-278.

[30]Chesnut, **A Diary from Dixie**, p. 46.

[31]Mrs. G. Giraud Wright, **A Southern Girl in '61**, p. 49.

[32]U. S. Congress, **Journal of the Congress of the Confederate States of America** (Washington: Government Printing Office, 1904-1905), I, pp. 159-169.

[33]News item in the Austin **State Gazette**, June 1, 1861.

[34]Seehorn, "Louis Trezevant Wigfall, A Confederate Senator," p. 59.

[35]Seehorn, "Louis Trezevant Wigfall, A Confederate Senator," p. 59.

[36]Mrs. D. Giraud Wright, **A Southern Girl in '61**, p. 49.

[37]News item in the **Texas Republican** (Marshall), June 22, 1861.

[38]Chesnut, **A Diary from Dixie**, p. 73.

[39]News item in the **Texas Republican** (Marshall), July 27, 1861.

[40]Marcus J. Wright and Harold B. Simpson, **Texas in the War 1861-1865, p. 97.**

[41]Mrs. A. V. Winkler, **The Confederate Capital and Hood's Texas Brigade** (Austin: Eugene Von Boeckmann, 1894), p. 31.

[42]Harold B. Simpson, "Whip the Devil and His Hosts," **Chronicles of Smith County, Texas,** VI (Fall, 1967), p. 2.

[43]W. L. Leigh, "General Confederate Officers from Texas," **Confederate Veteran,** XX (August, 1912), p. 391.

[44]Harold B. Simpson, **Gaines' Mill to Appomattox** (Waco, Texas: Texian Press, 1963), p. 59.

[45]J. B. Polley, **A Soldier's Letters to Charming Nellie** (New York: Neale Publishing Co., 1908), pp. 17-18.

[46]Hugh Irwin Power, Jr., "Texas at War—The Letters of Private James Hendrick, Army of Northern Virginia" (unpublished paper, Confederate Research Center, Hillsboro, Texas, 1964).

[47]Mrs. D. Giraud Wright, **A Southern Girl in '61,** pp. 74-75.

[48]Chesnut, **A Diary from Dixie,** p. 98.

[49]Article within University of Texas, Archives, Mrs. E. M. Schiwetz Civil War Collection.

[50]Seehorn, "Louis Trezevant Wigfall, A Confederate Senator," p. 65.

[51]Harold B. Simpson, Gaines' **Mill to Appomattox,** p. 66.

[52]U. S. Congress, **Journal of the Congress of the Confederate States of America,** II, p. 6.

[53]**Ibid.,** p. 14.

[54]"Proceedings of the First Confederate Congress," **Southern Historical Society Papers,** ILIV (June, 1923), pp. 45-47.

[55]Seehorn, "Louis Trezevant Wigfall, A Confederate Senator," pp. 67-69.

[56]U. S. Congress, **Jaurnal of the Congress of the Confederate States of America,** II, p. 179.

[57]Seehorn, "Louis Trezevant Wigfall, A Confederate Senator," p. 75.

[58]U. S. Congress, **Journal of the Congress of the Confederate States of America,** III, p. 114.

[59]Seehorn, "Louis Trezevant Wigfall, A Confederate Senator," p. 76.

[60]E. Merton Coulter, **The Confederate States of America, 1861-1865,** Vol. VII of **A History of the South,** ed. by Wendell Holmes Stephenson and E. Merton Coulter (10 vols.; Baton Rouge, Louisiana: Louisiana State University Press and the Littlefield Fund for Southern History of the University of Texas, 1950), p. 314.

[61]U. S. Congress, **Journal of the Congress of the Confederate States of America,** II, p. 176.

[62]**Ibid.,** II, pp. 23, 51, 94, 336, 365; III, pp. 36-37.

[63]News item in the Richmond **Examiner,** September 26, 1862.

[64]Seehorn, "Louis Trezevant Wigfall, A Confederate Senator," p. 83, citing a news item in the Richmond **Examiner, January 23, 1863.**

[65]Seehorn, "Louis Trezevant Wigfall, A Confederate Senator," p. 84, citing a news item in the Richmond **Examiner,** January 29, 1863.

[66]U. S. Congress, **Journal of the Congress of the Confederate States of America,** III, pp. 176, 223, 225, 730, 745, 755.

[67]Francis Lubbock, **Six Decades in Texas,** edited by C. W. Raines (Austin: Ben C. Jones and Co., 1900), pp. 161-162.

[68]Mrs. D. Giraud Wright, **A Southern Girl in '61,** p. 181.

[69]Letter, Louis T. Wigfall to C. C. Clay, Jr., December 11, 1862, University of Texas, Archives, Louis T. Wigfall Collection.

[70]Letter, Louis T. Wigfall to C. C. Clay, Jr., August 13, 1863, University of Texas, Archives, Louis T. Wigfall Collection.

[71]Webb (ed.), **The Handbook of Texas,** II, p. 907.

[72]Mrs. D. Giraud Wright, **A Southern Girl in '61,** pp. 180-181.

[73]Mrs. D. Giraud Wright, **A Southern Girl in '61,** pp. 203.

[74]News item in the Austin **State Gazette,** October 26, 1864.

[75]Mrs. D. Giraud Wright, **A Southern Girl in '61,** pp. 206-207.

[76]U. S. Congress, **Journal of the Congress of the Confederate States of America,** IV, p. 3.

[77]Mrs. D. Giraud Wright, **A Southern Girl in '61,** pp. 220-22.

[78]U. S. Congress, **Journal of the Congress of the Confederate States of America,** IV, pp. 726-731.

[79]Albert Burton Moore, **Conscription and Conflict in the Confederacy** (New York: The Macmillan Co., 1924), p. 353.

[80]Chesnut, **A Diary from Dixie,** p. 467.

[81]News items in the Austin **State Gazette,** May 3, 1865, April 12, 1865; news item in the **Texas Republican** (Marshall), May 3, 1865.

[82]Chesnut, **A Diary from Dixie,** p. 373.

[83]**Ibid.**

[84]Mrs. D. Giraud Wright, **A Southern Girl in '61,** p. 242.

[85]**Ibid.,** pp. 244-246.

[86]**Ibid.,** pp. 16-17.

[87]Webb (ed.), **The Handbook of Texas,** II, p. 907.

Illustrations

JOHN ROBERT BAYLOR
1822 — 1894

— Plate 1 —

EDWARD CLARK
1815 — 1880

— Plate 2 —

RICHARD W. "DICK" DOWLING
1838 — 1867

— Plate 3 —

JOHN BELL HOOD
1831 — 1879

— Plate 4 —

FRANCIS RICHARD LUBBOCK
1815 — 1905

— Plate 5 —

JOHN BANKHEAD MAGRUDER
1810 — 1871

— Plate 6 —

PENDLETON MURRAH
Date of birth unknown — 1865

— Plate 7 —

WILLIAMSON SIMPSON OLDHAM
1813 — 1868

— Plate 8 —

JOHN H. REAGAN
1818 — 1905

LOUIS TREZEVANT WIGFALL
1816 — 1874

— Plate 10 —

Bibliography

JOHN ROBERT BAYLOR

PRIMARY SOURCES

NEWSPAPERS

Alta California, January, 1861-July, 1865.
Albuquerque Rio Abaja Press, January, 1861-December, 1862.
Austin Daily Statesman, February 9, 1894.
Austin State Gazette, January, 1861-December, 1862.
Colorado Republican and Rocky Mountain Herald, January, 1861.
Dallas Morning News, February 9, 1894.
Denver Rocky Mountain Herald, January, 1861-December, 1862.
Harper's Weekly, January, 1861-December, 1862.
Houston Tri-Weekly Telegraph, January, 1861-December, 1862.
Mesilla Times, January, 1861-December, 1862.
New Orleans Daily Picayune, January, 1861-December, 1862.
New York Times, January, 1862-December, 1865.
New York Daily Tribune, January, 1862-December, 1862.
Richmond Daily Enquirer, January, 1861-July, 1865.
Richmond Daily Examiner, January, 1861-July, 1865.
Sacramento Daily Union, January, 1861-December, 1865.
San Antonio Daily Ledger and Texan, January, 1861-December, 1862.
San Antonio Herald, January, 1861-December, 1862.
San Francisco Bulletin, January, 1862-December, 1862.
Santa Fe New Mexican, January, 1861-December, 1862.
Santa Fe Weekly Gazette, January, 1861-December, 1862.

PUBLIC DOCUMENTS

Confederate States: **Journal of the Congress of the Confederate States of America, 1861-1865.** 7 vols. Senate Documents, 58th Cong., 2d Sess. Washington: Government Printing Office, 1904-1905.

————————. **Official Reports of Battles, as Published by the Order of the Confederate Congress at Richmond.** New York: Charles B. Richardson, 1963.

Richardson, James D. (comp.) **A Compilation of the Messages and Papers of the Confederacy Including the Diplomatic Correspondence, 1861-1865.** 2 vols. Nashville: United States Publihsing Company, 1905-1906.

Russell, John T. (comp.) **Official Register of New Mexico Volunteers Called into Service of the United States under President's Proclamation of May 3, 1861.** Santa Fe: Santa Fe Gazette Office, 1862.

State of Texas. **Confederate Military Affairs 1861-1865. Papers Pertaining to Military Affairs in Texas During the Civil War.** Texas State Library, Archives Division, Austin, Texas.

State of Texas. Muster Rolls: **Second Texas Regiment Mounted Rifles,** War Department Collection of Confederate Records. National Archives, Washington, D. C.

Winkler, Ernest W. (ed.). **Journal of the Secession Convention of Texas, 1861.** Austin: Austin Printing Company, 1912.

United States. House of Representatives. **Miscellaneous Documents.** 78th and 37th Cong., 2d Sess. Washington: Government Printing Office, 1862.

————————. **Journal Executive Proceedings,** 37th and 38th Cong., December 1, 1858 to August 6, 1861. Vol. XIII, Washington, Government Printing Office, 1887.

————————. **Reports of Committees of the Senate of the United States of the Thirty-Seventh Congress.** 4 vols. Washington: Government Printing Office, 1863.

__________. Interior Department, Bureau of Indian Affairs. **Reports of the Commissioner of Indian Affairs for the Years 1862, 1863, 1864 and 1865.** (Separate volumes for each year.) Washington: Government Printing Office, 1863, 1864, 1865, 1866.

__________. **The War of the Rebellion: A Compilation of the Official Records of the Union and Confederate Armies.** Four series, 128 vols. Washington: Government Printing Office, 1880-1900.

__________. Cowles, Calvin D. (comp.) **Atlas to Accompany the Official Records of the Union and Confederate Armies.** Washington: Government Printing Office, 1891-1896.

__________. Utley, Robert M. **Fort Davis National Historic Site, Texas Historical Handbook Number Thirty-Eight.** Washington: Government Printing Office, 1965.

__________. Utley, Robert M. **Fort Union National Monument, New Mexico.** Historical Handbook Number Thirty-five. Washington: Government Printing Office, 1962.

BOOKS

Johnson, Robert Underwood, and Clarence Clough Buel, **Battles and Leaders of the Civil War.** 4 vols. New York: The Century Company, 1884-1888. Reprinted by Thomas Yoseloff in 1956.

Jones, John B. **A Rebel War Clerk's Diary,** Earl Schenk Miers (ed.). New York: Sagamore Press, Inc., 1958.

McKee, Captain James Cooper. **Narrative of the Surrender of a Command of U. S. Forces at Fort Fillmore, New Mexico in July, 1861.** Boston: John A. Lowell Company, 1886.

Noel, Theophilus. **A Campaign from Santa Fe to the Mississippi: Being a History of the Old Sibley Brigade from Its First Organization to the Present Time, Its Campaigns in New Mexico, Arizona, Texas, Louisiana and Arkansas in the Years 1861-2-3-4.** Shreveport: Shreveport News Printing Establishment, 1865.

__________. **Autobiography and Reminiscences of Theophilus Noel.** Chicago: Theo. Noel Company Print, 1904.

OTHER

Darrow, Caroline Baldwin. "Recollections of the Twiggs Surrender," **Battles and Leaders of the Civil War,** I, 33-39.

Hunter, Marvin J. "John Robert Baylor, 1822-1895," **Frontier Times,** Vol. 6, No. 12 (September, 1929), 482-486.

Pettis, George H. "The Confederate Invasion of New Mexico and Arizona," **Battles and Leaders of the Civil War,** II, 103-111.

Teel, Trevanion T. "Sibley's New Mexican Campaign, Its Objectives and the Causes of Its Failures," **Battles and Leaders of the Civil War,** II, 700.

SECONDARY SOURCES

BOOKS

Appleton's American Cyclopedia and Register of Important Events of the Year 1861. New York: D. H. Appleton and Company, 1866.

__________. **Cyclopedia of American Biography.** 6 vols. New York: D. H. Appleton and Company, 1888.

Bancroft, Hubert H. **History of Arizona and New Mexico, 1530-1888.** San Francisco: The History Company, 1890.

Callahan, James M. **The Diplomatic History of the Southern Confederacy.** Baltimore: John Hopkins Press, 1901.

Coan, Charles F. **A History of New Mexico.** 3 vols. Chicago: The American Historical Society, Inc., 1925.

BIBLIOGRAPHY

Colton, Ray. C. **The Civil War in the Western Territories. Arizona, Colorado, New Mexico, Utah.** Norman: University of Oklahoma Press, 1959.

Evans, Clement A. (ed.). **Confederate Military History.** 12 vols. Atlanta: Confederate Publishing Company, 1899.

Farish, Thomas Edwin. **History of Arizona.** 8 vols. San Francisco: Filmer Brothers Electrotype Company, 1915-1918.

Ganaway, Loomis M. **New Mexico and the Sectional Controversy, 1846-1861.** Albuquerque, University of New Mexico Press, 1944.

Greeley, Horace. **The American Conflict: A History of the Great Rebellion in the United States of America, 1860-1861.** 2 vols. Hartford: O. D. Case and Company, Vol. I, 1864; Vol. II, 1866.

Heyman, Jr., Max. L. **Prudent Soldier, A Biography of Major-General E. R. S. Canby, 1817-1873.** Glendale: The Arthur Clark Company, 1959.

Horgan, Paul. **Great River—The Rio Grande in North American History.** 2 vols. New York: Rinehart and Company, 1954.

Hunt, Aurora. **The Army of the Pacific.** Glendale: The Arthur Clark Company, 1951.

Johnston, William P. **The Life of Albert Sidney Johnston.** New York: D. Appleton and Company, 1878.

Keleher, William A. **Turmoil in New Mexico, 1846-1868.** Santa Fe: The Rydal Press, 1952.

Lossing, Benson J. **Pictorial Field Book of the Civil War.** 3 vols. Philadelphia: G. W. Childs Company, 1866-1868.

Miller, Francis Trevelyn (Editor-in-Chief), and Lanier, Robert S. (Managing Editor). **The Photographic History of the Civil War.** 10 vols. Original edition published by the Patriot Publishing Company, Springfield, Massachusetts, in 1911. New edition with Introduction by Henry Steele Commager. New York: Thomas Yoseloff, 1957.

Mills, W. W. **Forty Years at El Paso, 1858-1898.** Chicago: W. B. Conkey Company, 1901.

Moat, Louis Shepheard (ed.). **Frank Leslie's History of the Civil War.** New York: Mrs. Frank Leslie, Publisher, 1890:

Moore, Frank (ed.). **The Rebellion Record: A Diary of American Events.** 12 vols. New York: D. Van Nostrand Company, 1862-1868.

Sloan, Richard E., and Ward R. Adams, **History of Arizona.** Phoenix: Record Publishing Company, 1930.

Trevis, James H. **Arizona in the '50's.** Albuquerque: University of New Mexico Press, 1954.

Twitchell, Ralph Emerson. **The Leading Facts of New Mexico History.** 5 vols. Cedar Rapids, 1911-1917.

Webb, Walter Prescott, and Carroll, H. Bailey (eds.). **The Handbook of Texas.** 2 vols. Austin: The Texas State Historical Association, 1952.

Whitford, William Clarke. **Colorado Volunteers in the Civil War: The New Mexico Campaign in 1862.** Denver: The State Historical and Natural History Society, 1906.

OTHER

Anderson, Hattie M. "With the Confederates in New Mexico—Memoirs of Hank Smith," **Panhandle-Plains Historical Review,** Vol. II (1929), 65-97.

Barker, William J. "Forgotten War For the West," **Denver Post,** November 6 and 13, 1949.

Bloom, Lansing B. (ed.). "Confederate Reminiscences of 1862," **New Mexico Historical Review,** Vol. V (July, 1930), 315-324.

Boyd, Le Roy. "Thunder on the Rio Grande, the Great Adventure of Sibley's Confederates for the Conquest of New Mexico and Colorado," **Colorado Magazine,** Vol. XXIV (July, 1949), 131-140.

Connell, F. S. "The Confederate Territory of Arizona from Official

Sources," **New Mexico Historical Review,** Vol. XVII (April, 1942), 148-163.

Gilbert, Benjamin F. "The Confederate Minority in California," **California Historical Society Quarterly,** Vol. XX (June, 1941), 154-170.

Hayes, A. A. "The New Mexican Campaign of 1862," **Magazine of American History,** Vol. XV (February, 1886), 171-184.

Hoffman, Edna Evans. "The Civil War in Arizona," **Arizona Highways,** Vol. XXXVIII, No. 6 (June, 1962), 30-38.

Hunsaker, William J. "Lansford W. Hastings' Project for the Invasion and Conquest of Arizona and New Mexico for the Southern Confederacy," **Arizona Hitsorical Review,** Vol. IV (July, 1931), 5-12.

☆ ☆ ☆

EDWARD CLARK

PRIMARY SOURCES

Clark Papers. The Clark Papers, consisting of approximately 100 pieces, include miscellaneous letters of the Clark family; a brief diary belonging to Edward Clark; family Bible; a file from William E. Bergin of the Department of the Army, Office of the Adjutant General, relating to Clark's military record. The Clark Papers, the property of O. H. Clark, Edward Clark's grandson, Marshall, Texas, are now loaned to the Marshall Historical Museum, Marshall, Texas.

PUBLIC DOCUMENTS

The War of the Rebellion: A Compilation of the Official Records of the Union and Confederate Armies. 70 vols., in 128; Washington: Government Printing Office, 1880-1901.

Winkler, William (ed.). **Journal of the Secession Convention of Texas, 1861.** Austin, Texas: Austin Printing Company, 1912.

BOOKS

Barr, Amelia E. **All the Days of My Life, An Autobiography. An Autobiography.** New York: D. Appleton and Company, 1913.

Blessington, J. P. **The Campaigns of Walker's Division.** New York: Lange, Little and Company, 1875.

Davis, Jefferson. **The Rise and Fall of the Confederate Government.** In 2 vols. Richmond: Garrett and Massie, Inc., 1938.

Day, James M. (ed.) **House Journal of the Ninth Legislature Regular Session.** Waco: Texian Press, 1964.

Johnson, Robert, and Clarence Buel (eds.),. **Battles and Leaders of the Civil War.** Vol. I. New York: Thomas Yoseloff, Inc., 1954.

NEWSPAPERS

Dallas Herald, November 23, 1859; July 31, 1861; November 20, 1861; January 13, 1866.

Standard, July 29, 1861.

Texas State Gazette (Austin), June 22, 1861; December 8, 1860; April 12, 1865.

Texas Republican (Marshall), August 1, 1855; June 8, 1861.

BIBLIOGRAPHY

SECONDARY SOURCES

BOOKS

Bolton, Paul. **Governors of Texas.** Corpus Christi: The Corpus Christi **Caller-Times,** 1947.

Brown, John Henry. **History of Texas from 1865 to 1892.** St. Louis: Becktold and Company, 1893.

Daniel, L. E. **Personnel of the Texas State Government With Sketches of Representative Men of Texas.** San Antonio: Maverick Printing House, 1892.

DeShields, James T. **They Sat in High Places, The Presidents and the Governors of Texas.** San Antonio, Texas: The Naylor Company, 1940.

Evans, Clement. **Confederate Military History.** Vol. XI. New York: Thomas Yoseloff Company, 1962.

Felgar, T. R. "Texas In the War for Southern Independence." Unpublished Ph.D. dissertation, University of Texas, 1935.

Hicks, John D. **The Federal Union.** Second edition. Cambridge: Riverside Press, 1952.

Johnson, Frank W. **Texas and Texans.** Edited by Eugene Barker and Ernest Winkler. Vol. I. Chicago: The American Historical Society, 1914.

Johnson, Ludwell H. **Red River Campaign: Politics and Cotton in the Civil War.** Baltimore: The John Hopkins Press, 1958.

Lubbock, Francis R. **Six Decades In Texas or Memoirs of Francis Richard Lubbock.** Edited by C. W. Raines. Austin: Ben C. Jones Printer, 1900.

Moore, Walter B. **Governors of Texas.** Dallas: The Dallas **Morning News,** 1947.

Nunn, William C. **Escape From Reconstruction.** Fort Worth: Leo Potishman Foundation, Texas Christian University, 1956.

Richardson, Rupert. **Texas the Lone Star State.** Second edition. Englewood Cliffs, N. J.: Prentice-Hall, Inc., 1960.

Simpson, Harold B. **Gaines' Mill to Appomattox.** Waco, Texas: Texian Press, 1963.

Thrall, Homer S. **A Pictorial History of Texas.** Revised edition. New York: N. D. Thompson Publishing Company, 1885.

Texas Historical Foundation. Centennial Commemoration. **Red River Campaign.** (April 4, 1964.)

Webb, Walter P., and Carroll, Bailey (eds.). **The Handbook of Texas.** 2 vols. Austin, Texas: Texas Historical Association, 1952.

Williams, Alfred M. **Sam Houston and the War of Independence in Texas.** Boston: Houghton Mifflin Company, 1893.

Wooster, Ralph A. **The Secession Convention of the South.** Princeton, N. J.: Princeton University Press, 1962.

PERIODICALS

Clark, Marjorie (ed.). "A Mexican War Letter," **Southwestern Historical Quarterly,** XLVII (January, 1944), 326-327.

Elliott, Claude. "Union Sentiment in Texas 1861-1865," **Southwestern Historical Quarterly,** L (April, 1947), 449-477.

Graham, Philip (ed.), "Texas Memoirs of Amelia Barr," **Southwestern Historical Quarterly,** LXIX (April, 1966), 473-498.

Ramsdell, Charles W. "The Texas State Military Board, 1862-1865," **Southwestern Historical Quarterly,** XXVII (April, 1924), 253-275.

Sandbo, Anna Irene. "First Session of the Secession Convention," **Southwestern Historical Quarterly,** XVIII (October, 1914), 162-194.

Wooster, Ralph A. "An Analysis of the Texas Know-Nothings," **Southwestern Historical Quarterly,** LXX (January, 1967), 414-423.

☆ ☆ ☆

RICHARD W. "DICK" DOWLING

GUIDES AND BIBLIOGRAPHIC AIDS

Boatner, Mark Mayo. **The Civil War Dictionary.** New York: David McKay Company, Inc., 1956.
Handlin, Oscar, **et al.**, eds. **Harvard Guide to American History.** Cambridge, Massachusetts: Belknap Press of Harvard University Press, 1954.
Hartwell, Mary A., comp. **Checklist of United States Public Documents, 1789-1909.** Vol. I. 3d ed. revised. Washington, D. C.: Government Printing Office, 1910.
Webb, Walter P., **et al.**, eds. **The Handbook of Texas.** 2 vols. Austin, Texas: The Texas State Historical Association, 1952.
Winkler, Ernest W., and Friend, Llerena, eds. **Check List of Texas Imprints, 1861-1876.** Austin, Texas: The Texas State Historical Association, 1963.

PRIMARY SOURCES

NEWSPAPERS

Clarksville Standard. September, 1863.
Dallas Herald. September-October, 1863.
Galveston News. September-October, 1863.
Houston Telegraph. December, 1857-September, 1867.
Houston Tri-Weekly Telegraph. September-October, 1863.
New York Times. September, 1863.

PUBLIC DOCUMENTS

Official Records of the Union and Confederate Navies in the War of the Rebellion. 31 vols. Washington, D. C.: Government Printing Office, 1894-1927. Series I, Vol. XIX; Series I, Vol. XX.
The War of the Rebellion: A Compilation of the Official Records of the Union and Confederate Armies. 128 vols. Washington, D. C.: Government Printing Office, 1880-1901. Series 1, Vol. I; Series I, Vol. XV; Series I, Vol. XXVI, Part I.

SCHOLARLY JOURNALS

Drummond, John A. "The Battle of Sabine Pass." **Confederate Veteran,** XXV (August, 1917), 364-365.
Hagy, P. S. "Military Operations of the Lower Trans-Mississippi Department, 1863-64." **Confederate Veteran,** XXIV (December, 1916), 545-549.

BOOKS

Buel, Clarence Clough, and Robert Underwood Johnson, eds. **Battles and Leaders of the Civil War.** Vols. III and IV. New ed. New York: Thomas Yoseloff, Inc., 1956.
Davis, Jefferson. **The Rise and Fall of the Confederate Government.** Vol. II. New York: D. Appleton and Company, 1911.
Ford, John Salmon. **Rip Ford's Texas.** Edited by Stephen B. Oates. Austin, Texas: University of Texas Press, 1963.
Kellersberger, Getulius. **Memoirs of an Engineer in the Confederate Army in Texas.** Translated by Helen H. Sundstrom. Austin, Texas: Privately Published, University of Texas Library, 1957.

Lubbock, Francis R. **Six Decades in Texas; or, Memoirs of Francis Richard Lubbock, Governor of Texas in War Time, 1861-1863.** Edited by C. W. Raines. Austin, Texas: B. C. Jones and Co., 1900.

Richardson, James D., comp. **A Compilation of the Messages and Papers of the Confederacy, Including the Diplomatic Correspondence, 1861-1865.** 2 vols. Nashville, Tennessee: United States Publishing Company, 1906.

Welles, Gideon. **Diary of Gideon Welles.** Vol. I. Boston and New York: Houghton Mifflin Company, 1887.

Wright, Marcus J., comp. **Texas in the War 1861-1865.** Edited by Colonel Harold B. Simpson. Hillsboro, Texas: The Hill Junior College Press, 1965.

SECONDARY SOURCES

MANUSCRIPTS

Jackson, Vivian Gladwin. "A History of Sabine Pass." Unpublished M.A. thesis, University of Texas, 1930.

NEWSPAPERS

Dallas Morning News. April 23, 1902.

Port Arthur News. August 25-September 1, 1963.

SCHOLARLY JOURNALS

Barr, Alwyn. "Sabine Pass, September, 1863." **Texas Military History,** II (February, 1962), 17-22.

__________. "Texas Coastal Defense, 1861-1865." The **Southwestern Historical Quarterly,** XLV (July, 1961), 1-31.

"Commemorating the Battle of Sabine Pass." **Confederate Veteran,** XXXII (December, 1924), 456-457.

Fitzhugh, Lester N. "Saluria, Fort Esperanza, and Military Operations on the Texas Coast, 1861-1864." **The Southwestern Historical Quarterly,** LXI (July, 1957), 66-100.

Muir, Andrew Forest. "Dick Dowling and the Battle of Sabine Pass." **Civil War History,** IV (December, 1958), 394-428.

Oates, Stephen B. "John S. 'Rip' Ford: Prudent Cavalryman, C.S.A." **The Southwestern Historical Quarterly,** LXIV (January, 1961), 289-314.

Rullman, Elizabeth. "Dick Dowling and His Forty-Three Irishmen." **Frontier Times,** XVI (July, 1939), 421-425.

Simpson, James B. "The Battle of Sabine Pass." **Frontier Times,** XXI (August, 1944), 419-422.

Warner, C. A. "Texas and the Oil Industry." **The Southwestern Historical Quarterly,** L (July, 1946), 1-24.

Young, Jo. "The Battle of Sabine Pass." **The Southwestern Historical Quarterly,** LII (April, 1949), 398-409.

BOOKS

Andrews, J. Cutler. **The North Reports the Civil War.** Pittsburgh: University of Pittsburgh Press, 1955.

Brown, John Henry. **History of Texas from 1685 to 1892.** Vol. II. St. Louis: L. E. Daniell, 1892-1893.

Dyer, Frederick H., comp. **A Compendium of the War of the Rebellion.** 3 vols. New ed. New York: Thomas Yoseloff, Inc., 1959.

Evans, Clement A. (ed.), **Confederate Military History.** Vol. XI. Atlanta, Georgia: Confederate Publishing Company, 1899.

Farragut, Loyall. **The Life of David Glasgow Farragut, Embodying His Journal and Letters.** New York: D. Appleton and Company, 1879.

Lossing, Benson J. **The Pictorial Field Book of the Civil War in the Unit-**

ed States of America. Vol. III. Hartford, Connecticut: T. Belknap, 1874.

Mahan, Alfred T. **The Navy in the Civil War.** Vol. III. **The Gulf and Inland Waters.** Subscription edition. New York: Charles Scribner's Sons, 1885.

Pray, Mrs. R. F. **Dick Dowling's Battle: An Account of the War Between the States in the Eastern Gulf Region of Texas.** San Antonio, Texas: The Naylor Company, 1936.

Sackett, Frances Robertson. **Dick Dowling.** Houston, Texas: Gulf Publishing Company, 1937.

Scharf, John Thomas. **History of the Confederate States Navy: From Its Organization to the Surrender of Its Last Vessel.** New York: Rogers and Sherwood, 1887.

Simpson, Harold B. "Sabine Pass," **Battles of Texas.** Waco, Texas: Texian Press, 1967.

Wooten, Dudley Goodall (ed.). **A Comprehensive History of Texas, 1685-1897.** Vol. II. Dallas, Texas: W. G. Scarff, 1898.

Wortham, Louis J. **A History of Texas: From Wilderness to Commonwealth.** Vol. IV. Fort Worth, Texas: Wortham-Molyneaux Company, 1924.

☆ ☆ ☆

JOHN BELL HOOD

PRIMARY SOURCES

NEWSPAPERS

Dallas **Herald,** June 24, July 22, 1865.

New Orleans **Times,** April 30, 1868.

PUBLIC DOCUMENTS

Appointment Register. Records Group #109, National Archives, Washington, D. C.

Headquarters, 8th Army, **General Order #14,** November 13, 1857. National Archives, Washington, D. C.

Post Returns, Fort Mason, Texas, 1851-1861, National Archives, Washington, D. C. (Microfilm of the **Post Returns** of Fort Mason, Texas, are available at The Confederate Research Center, Hillsboro, Texas.)

United States Secretary of War, **Annual Report,** 1857, 35th Congress, 1st Session, House Executive Document 2, p. 56.

United States War Department. **The War of the Rebellion: Official Records of the Union and Confederate Armies.** 128 vols. Washington, D. C., 1880-1901.

BOOKS

Amann, William F. (ed.). **Personnel of the Civil War.** 2 vols. New York: Thomas Yoseloff, 1961.

Barziza, Decimus et Ultimus. **The Adventures of a Prisoner of War.** R. Henderson Shuffler (ed.). Austin, University of Texas Press, 1964.

Davis, Nicholas A. **The Campaign From Texas to Maryland.** Richmond: Presbyterian Committee of Publication of the Confederate States, 1863.

Fletcher, William Andrew. **Rebel Private, Front and Rear.** Bell Irvin Wiley (ed.). Austin: University of Texas Press, 1954.

Glover, Robert W. (ed.). **Tyler to Sharpsburg: The War Letters of Robert H. and William H. Gaston.** Waco: W. M. Morrison, 1960.

Hamilton, Sgt. D. H. **History of Company M, First Texas Volunteer Infantry, Hood's Brigade.** Waco: W. M. Morrison, 1962.
Hood, John Bell. **Advance and Retreat.** New Orleans: P. G. T. Beauregard, 1880.
James, Mrs. John Herndon. **I Remember.** San Antonio: Naylor Co., 1938.
Johnson, Robert Underwood and Clarence Clough Buel (eds.). **Battles and Leaders of the Civil War.** 10 vols. New York: The Century Co., 1884-87.
Polk, J. M. **The North and South American Review.** Austin: Von Boeckmann-Jones Co., 1912.
Polley, J. B. **A Soldier's Letters to Charming Nellie.** New York: Neale Publishing Co., 1908.
__________. **Hood's Texas Brigade.** New York: Neale Publishing Co., 1910.
Reagan, John H. **Memoirs.** New York: The Neale Publishing Co., 1906.
Robertson, Jerome B. (comp.). **Touched With Valor. The Civil War Papers and Casualty Reports of Hood's Texas Brigade.** Harold B. Simpson (editor). Hillsboro: Hill Junior College Press, 1964.
Stevens, Judge John W. **Reminiscences of The Civil War.** Hillsboro: Hillsboro Mirror, 1902.
Todd, Geo. T. **First Texas Regiment.** Harold B. Simpson (ed.). Waco: Texian Press, 1963.
West, John C. **A Texan in Search of a Fight.** Waco: J. C. West, 1901.
Winkler, Mrs. A. C. **Confederate Capital and Hood's Brigade.** Austin: Eugene Von Boeckmann, 1894.
Wright, Mrs. Giraud. **A Southern Girl in '61.** New York: Doubleday, 1905.

SECONDARY SOURCES

PUBLIC DOCUMENT

Biographical Dictionary of The American Congress, 1774-1961. Washington: USGPO, 1961.

MANUSCRIPTS

Campbell, Gerald Douglas. "The Texas Brigade in the Pennsylvania Campaign of 1863." Unpublished Master's thesis, Department of History, Southwest Texas State Teachers College, 1959.
Reese, Morgan M., "John Bell Hood and the Texas Brigade." Unpublished Master's thesis, Department of History, Southwest Texas State Teachers College, 1941.
Simpson, Harold B. "General John Bell Hood—Southern Thunderbolt." Presentation given before the Civil War Round Table of Wiesbaden, Germany on March 12, 1956. Mimeographed in 100 copies.
Stennis, Rene Lee, "Hood's Texas Brigade in the Army of Northern Virginia." Unpublished Master's thesis, Department of History, Southern Methodist University, 1938.

SCHOLARLY JOURNALS

Adamoli, Giulio. "New Orleans in 1867," **Louisiana Historical Quarterly,** Vol. 6 (April), 1923, pp. 270-80.
Englehardt, H. T., "A Note on the Death of John Bell Hood," **The Southwestern Historical Quarterly.** Vol. LVII, No. 1 (July, 1953), pp. 91-93.
Simpson, Harold B., "Foraging With Hood's Brigade From Texas to Pennsylvania," **Texana,** Vol. I, No. 3 (Summer, 1963), pp. 258-76.
__________. "Hood's Texas Brigade at Appomattox," **Texana,** Vol. III, No. 1 (Spring, 1965), pp. 1-19.
__________. "The Recruiting, Training and Camp Life of a Company of Hood's Brigade in Texas, 1861." **Texas Military History,** Vol. 2, No. 3 (August, 1962), pp. 171-192.

__________. "West Pointers in the Texas Confederate Army," **Texas Military History,** Vol. 6, No. 1 (Spring, 1967), pp. 55-88.

__________. (ed.) "Whip the Devil and His Hosts, The Civil War Letters of Eugene O. Perry," **Chronicles** (of Smith County, Texas), Vol. 6, No. 2 (Fall, 1967), pp. 10-15+.

POPULAR JOURNALS

Crimmins, Col. M. L., "General John Bell Hood," **Frontier Times,** Vol. 10, No. 6 (March, 1933), pp. 241-47.

Hunter, J. Marvin. "Battle With Indians on Devil's River," **Frontier Times,** Vol. 3, No. 6 (March, 1926), pp. 12-15.

__________. "General John B. Hood's Victory," **Frontier Times,** Vol. 4, No. 7 (April, 1927), p. 16.

__________. "John Bell Hood: A Great Soldier," **Frontier Times,** Vol. 21, No. 6 (March, 1944), pp. 235-36.

O'Connor, Richard, "Anne's Curse," **Life,** October 25, 1948, pp. 25-30.

Rust, H. G., "Desperate Fight on Devil's River," **Frontier Times,** Vol. 21, No. 4 (January, 1944), pp. 140-43.

Simpson, Harold B., "No One Ever Sees the Backsides of My Texans," **Civil War Times Illustrated,** Vol. 4, No. 6 (October, 1965), pp. 34-39.

BOOKS

Boatner, Mark M., III, **The Civil War Dictionary.** New York: David McKay Company, Inc., 1959.

Brackett, G. Albert, **History of the United States Cavalry.** New York, 1865.

Chilton, Frank B. **Official Minutes of Hood's Texas Brigade Monument Dedication and Thirty-ninth Annual Reunion.** Houston: F. B. Chilton, 1911.

Collier, Captain Calvin L. **They'll Do To Tie To: 3rd Arkansas Infantry Regiment, CSA.** Little Rock: Major Thomas D. Warren, 1959.

Coulter, E. Merton, **The Confederate States of America, 1861-1865.** Baton Rouge: Louisiana State University Press, 1950.

Cullum, George W. **Biographical Register of the Officers and Graduates of the U. S. Military Academy, West Point,** New York... 3 vols. New York, 1907.

Dyer, John P. **The Gallant Hood.** Indianapolis: Bobbs-Merril, 1950.

Everett, Donald E. (ed.). **Chaplain Davis and Hood's Texas Brigade.** San Antonio: Principia Press of Trinity University, 1962.

Freeman, Douglas Southall. **Lee's Lieutenants.** 3 vols. New York: Charles Scribner's Sons, 1944.

Golson, Josephine Polley. **Bailey's Light.** San Antonio: Naylor, 1950.

Hall, Charles B. **Military Records of the General Officers of the Confederate States of America.** New York, 1898.

Harwell, Richard Barksdale. **Songs of the Confederacy.** New York: Broadcast Music, Inc., 1951.

Henry, Robert Selph. **The Story of the Confederacy.** Indianapolis: Bobbs-Merrill, 1936.

Herr, John K. and Edward S. Wallace. **The Story of the U. S. Cavalry.** Boston: Little, Brown, 1953.

Johnson, Sid S. **Texans Who Wore the Gray.** n.p., 1907.

Laswell, Mary (ed.). **Rags and Hope: The Memoirs of Val C. Giles, Four Years With Hood's Brigade. Fourth Texas Infantry, 1861-1865.** New York: Coward-McCann, 1961.

Miller, Francis Trevelyan (ed.) **The Photographic Histtory of the Civil War.** 10 vols. New York: The Review of Reviews, 1911.

O'Connor, Richard. **Hood: Cavalier General.** New York: Prentice-Hall, 1949.

Price, George F., **Across the Continent With the Fifth Cavalry.** New York: Antiquarian Press, 1959 (re-print).

Register of Graduates, United States Military Academy, 1802-1946. New York: The West Point Alumni Foundation, 1946.
Simpson, Harold B., **Gaines' Mill to Appomattox: Waco and McLennan County in Hood's Texas Brigade.** Waco: Texian Press, 1963.
__________. **The Marshall Guards: Company E, First Texas Infantry.** Marshall (Texas): The Port Caddo Press, 1967.
__________. "Fort Mason," **Frontier Forts of Texas.** Waco: Texian Press, 1966.
Warner, Ezra. **Generals in Gray.** Baton Rouge: Louisiana State University Press, 1959.
Webb, Walter P. (ed.). **The Handbook of Texas.** 2 vols. Austin: The Texas State Historical Association, 1952.
Wright, General Marcus J. **Arkansas in the War, 1861-1865.** Batesville (Ark.): The Independence County Historical Society, 1963.
Wright, Gen. Marcus J., **Texas in the War, 1861-1865,** Harold B. Simpson (ed.), Hillsboro (Texas): Hill Junior College Press, 1965.

LETTERS

Kenneth W. Rapp, Asst. Archivist, USMA to the author dated July 2, 23, 1965; September 13, 1965; September 20, 1966.

☆ ☆ ☆

FRANCIS RICHARD LUBBOCK

PRIMARY SOURCES

NEWSPAPERS

Dallas Morning News, Dallas, Texas, 1887, 1905.
Telegraph and Texas Register, Houston, Texas, 1837, 1838.
The Clarksville Standard, Clarksville, Texas, 1858, 1859, 1860, 1861, 1862, 1863, 1865.
The Daily Statesman, Austin, Texas, 1905.
The Dallas Weekly Herald, Dallas, Texas, 1862, 1874, 1887.
The Houston Daily Post, Houston, Texas, 1903.
The Texas State Gazette, Austin, Texas, 1837, 1855, 1857, 1858, 1862, 1863.
The Tri-Weekly State Gazette, Austin, 1862, 1863.

PUBLIC DOCUMENTS

The War of the Rebellion: A Compilation of the Official Records of the Union and Confederate Armies. Series I, Vols. IX, XIII, XIV, XV, XVI, XXXIV, and XXXVII; Series II, Vols. V and VIII; Series IV, Vols. I and II. Washington, D. C.: U. S. Government Printing Office, 1882-1901.

PAMPHLETS

Valedictory of Governor F. R. Lubbock to the Tenth Legislature, November 5, 1863. Austin: State Gazette Book and Job Office, 1863.

BOOKS

Davis, Jefferson. **The Rise and Fall of the Confederate Government.** Vol. II. New York: D. Appleton and Co., 1881.
Day, James M. (ed.). **State Journal of the Ninth Legislature of the State of Texas November 4, 1861-January 14, 1862.** Austin: Texas State Library, 1963.

Day, James M., and Dorman Winfrey (eds.). **Texas Indian Papers.** (Edited from original manuscripts in Texas State Archives.) Austin: Texas State Library, 1961.
Gammel, H. P. N. **The Laws of Texas 1822-1897.** Vols. II, IV, and V. Austin: Gammel Book Company, 1900.
Lubbock, Francis. **Six Decades in Texas or Memoirs of Francis Richard Lubbock, Governor of Texas in Wartime 1861-1863.** C. W. Raines (ed.). Austin: Ben C. Jones and Company, 1900.
Reagan, John H. **Memoirs.** Walter Flavius McCaleb (ed.). New York: The Neale Publishing Company, 1906.
Winkler, Ernest W. (ed.). **Journal of the Secession Convention of Texas, 1861.** Austin: Austin Printing Company, 1912.
——————. **Platforms of Political Parties in Texas.** Austin: University of Texas, 1916.
Wooten, Dudley G. (ed.). **A Comprehensive History of Texas.** Dallas: William G. Scarff, 1898.
Wright, Marcus J. (comp.), and Simpson, Harold B. (ed.). **Texas in the War, 1861-1865.** Hillsboro: The Hill Junior College Press, 1965.

OTHER SOURCES

Francis Richard Lubbock Bibliographical File, University of Texas Library, Austin, Texas.
Collections in University of Texas Archives.
James B. Barry Papers
Frank Brown Papers
Guy M. Bryan Papers
Civil War Miscellany
Coryell County Papers
John W. S. Dancy Papers
Jeremiah Y. Dashiel Papers
Adina De Zavala Papers
Katherine Elliott Essay
Benjamin C. Franklin Papers
Stephen C. Glasscock Papers
Thomas S. Henderson Papers
John W. Herndon Papers
James M. Hill Papers
Gideon Linceum Papers
Henry W. Raglin Papers
John H. Reagan Papers
Nathan G. Shelley Papers
Henry Smith Papers

SECONDARY SOURCES

MANUSCRIPTS

Flusche, Raymond Paul. **Francis Richard Lubbock.** Unpublished MA Thesis. Lubbock: Texas Tech, May, 1947.

MAGAZINES AND SCHOLARLY JOURNALS

"Governor Francis R. Lubbock," **Frontier Times.** J. Marvin Hunter (ed.). IX (December, 1931), p. 97.
Ramsdell, Charles W. "The Last Hope of the Confederacy," **Texas State Historical Association Quarterly,** XIV (1911), pp. 130-131.
Sandbo, Anna Irene. "Beginnings of the Secession Movement in Texas," **The Southwestern Historical Quarterly,** XVIII (1915), pp. 41-73.

BIBLIOGRAPHY

BOOKS

Barker, Eugene C., Charles Shirley Potts, and Charles W. Ramsdell. **A School History of Texas.** New York: Row Peterson and Company, 1928.

Barker, Eugene C. (ed.). **Texas History.** Dallas: The Southwest Press, 1929.

Biographical Encyclopedia of Texas. New York: Southern Publishing Company, 1880.

Bolton, Paul. **Governors of Texas.** Corpus Christi: Corpus Christi Caller-Times, 1947.

Chesnut, Mary Boykin. **A Diary From Dixie.** Isabella D. Martin and Myrta L. Avary (eds.). Gloucester: Peter Smith, 1961.

Daniel, L. E. **Personnel of the Texas State Government.** San Antonio: Maverick Printing House, 1892.

____________. **Types of Successful Men of Texas.** Austin: Eugene Von Boeckmann, 1890.

DeShields, J. T. **They Sat in High Place.** San Antonio: The Naylor Company, 1940.

Everett, Donald E. (ed.). **Chaplain Davis and Hood's Texas Brigade.** San Antonio: Principia Press of Trinity University, 1962.

Hanna, Alfred Jackson. **Flight Into Oblivion.** Richmond: Johnson Publishing Company, 1938.

Johnson, Frank. **A History of Texas and Texans.** E. C. Barker and E. W. Winkler (eds.). Vol. I. Chicago: American Historical Society, 1914.

Kittrell, Norman G. **Governors Who Have Been and Other Public Men of Texas.** Houston: Dealy-Adey-Elgin Company, 1921.

Malone, Dumas (ed.). **Dictionary of American Biography.** Vol. XI. New York: Charles Scribner's Sons, 1933.

McCraw, William. **Professional Politicians.** Washington, D. C.: The Imperial Press, 1940.

Meade, Robert Douthat. **Judah P. Benjamin—Confederate Statesman.** New York: Oxford University Press, 1943.

Moore, Albert Burton. **Conscription and Conflict in the Confederacy.** New York: The Macmillan Company, 1924.

Parks, Joseph Howard. **General Edmund Kirby Smith—CSA.** Baton Rouge: Louisiana State University Press, 1954.

Procter, Ben H. **Not Without Honor—The Life of John H. Reagan.** Austin: University of Texas Press, 1962.

Ramsdell, Charles W. **Reconstruction in Texas.** New York: Columbia University Press, 1916.

Richardson, Rupert N. **Texas the Lone Star State.** New York: Prentice-Hall, Inc., 1943.

The National Cyclopaedia of American Biography. Vol. IX. New York: James T. White and Company, 1907.

Thrall, H. S. **A History of Texas.** New York: University Publishing Company, 1876.

Webb, Walter Prescott (ed.). **The Handbook of Texas.** Vol. II. Austin: The Texas State Historical Association, 1952.

Wharton, Clarence R. **History of Texas.** Dallas: Turner Company, 1935.

____________. **Texas Under Many Flags.** Vol. II. Chicago: The American Historical Society, Inc., 1930.

Williams, Amelia W., and Barker, Eugene C. (eds.). **The Writings of Sam Houston 1813-1863.** Vol. II. Austin: The University of Texas Press, 1939.

Wilson, James Grant, and Fiske, John (eds.). **Appleton's Cyclopaedia of American Biography.** Vol. IV. New York: D. Appleton and Company, 1888.

☆ ☆ ☆

JOHN BANKHEAD MAGRUDER

PRIMARY SOURCES

MANUSCRIPTS

Dyer, Joseph Osterman. "History of Galveston." Original MS in Rosenberg Library, Galveston, Texas.

__________. "1830-1868—Supplemental History of Galveston." Original MS in Rosenberg Library, Galveston, Texas.

Ewell, Richard Stoddert. Papers. Typewritten copy of the originals [Library of Congress] in Rosenberg Library, Galveston, Texas.

Lee, St. George S. Congratulatory letter to General John Bankhead Magruder, January, 1863. Copy of the original given to author by Alice Murphy of the Houston **Post.**

Stuart, Ben C. "Galveston's Early Military Companies, Being a Brief Account of the Commands Serving on the Frontier during the Mexican and Civil War and the Organizations for Home Service." Original MS in Rosenberg Library, Galveston, Texas.

__________. "History of Galveston." Original MS in Rosenberg Library, Galveston, Texas.

NEWSPAPERS

Civilian. Galveston, Texas, 1860-1865.

Flakes Bulletin. Galveston, Texas, 1861-1865.

News. Galveston, Texas, 1860-1866.

Telegraph. Houston, Texas, 1861-1865, 1883.

PUBLIC DOCUMENTS

J.O.L.O. Record Book—Record of the Shipping Observers stationed on the Henley Building (Galveston) during the Civil War. Original in Rosenberg Library, Galveston, Texas.

Massie, J. C. Special Order to the Citizens of Galveston, May 23, 1862. Original MS in Rosenberg Library, Galveston, Texas.

Official Records of the Union and Confederate Navies in the War of the Rebellion. 31 vols. Washington, D. C.: Government Printing Office, 1894-1927.

Tucker, Philip C., III. In the Matter of the Confederate States of America vs. the Gunboat Steamship called the "Harriet Lane." Certified copy of the original by Philip C. Tucker, III, Commissioner of Prize, in Rosenberg Library, Galveston, Texas. (Typewritten.)

The War of the Rebellion: A Compilation of the Official Records of the Union and Confederate Armies. 130 vols. Washington, D. C.: Government Printing Office, 1880-1901.

SCHOLARLY JOURNALS

Smith, Rebecca W. and Marion Mullins (eds.). "Diary of H. C. Medford, Confederate Soldier, 1864," **Southwestern Historical Quarterly,** XXXIV (October, 1930 to January, 1931), pp. 106-140; pp. 203-230.

Tucker, Philip C., III. "The United States Gunboat **Harriet Lane," Southwestern Historical Quarterly,** XXI (April, 1918), pp. 360-380.

Winfrey, Dorman H. (ed.). "Two Battles of Galveston Letters," **Southwestern Historical Quarterly,** LXV (October, 1961), pp. 251-257.

BIBLIOGRAPHY

BOOKS

Debray, Xavier B. **A Sketch of the History of Debray's 26th Regiment of Texas Cavalry.** Austin: Eugene von Boeckman Book and Job Printer ,1884.

Dorsey, Sarah A. **Recollections of Henry Watkins Allen.** New York: M. Doolady, 1866.

Franklin, Robert M. **Story of the Battle of Galveston.** Galveston News (May 8, 1911).

Fremantle, Arthur James Lyon. **Three Months in the Southern States: April-June, 1863.** New York: John Bradburn, 1864.

North, Thomas. **Five Years in Texas; or What You Did Not Hear During the War from January 1861 to January 1866. A Narrative of His Travels, Experiences, and Observations, in Texas and Mexico.** Cincinnati: Elm Street Printing Colpany, 1871.

Raines, C. W. (ed.). **Six Decades in Texas or Memoirs of Francis Richard Lubbock: A Personal Experience in Business, War, and Politics.** Austin: Ben C. Jones & Company, Printers, 1910.

Semmes, Raphael. **Memoirs of Service Afloat, During the War Between the States.** Baltimore: Kelly, Piet & Company, 1869.

Sinclair, Arthur. **Two Years on the "Alabama."** Boston: Lee and Shepard Publishers, 1895.

Terrell, Alexander W. **From Texas to Mexico and the Court of Maximilian in 1865.** Dallas: The Book Club of Texas, 1933.

SECONDARY SOURCES

MANUSCRIPTS

"Blockades and Battles, 1861-1865." Unpublished MS in Rosenberg Library, Galveston, Texas. (Typewritten.)

Hayes, Charles Waldo. "The Island and City of Galveston." Unpublished MS in Rosenberg Library, Galveston, Texas. (Typewritten.)

Lockwood, Herbert. "The Skeleton's Closet," unclassified manuscript given to author by Alice Murphy of the **Houston Post.** (Typewritten.)

"Texas Horsemen of the Sea. In Galveston Harbor, January, 1863." Galley proof in Rosenberg Library, Galveston, Texas.

SCHOLARLY JOURNALS

Barr, Alwyn. "Texas Coastal Defense, 1861-1865," **Southwestern Historical Quarterly,** LXV (July, 1961), pp. 1-31.

Cumberland, Charles C. "The Confederate Loss and Recapture of Galveston, 1862-1863," **Southwestern Historical Quarterly,** LI (October, 1947), pp. 109-130.

Ellison, S. J. "Anglo-American Plan for the Colonization of Mexico," **Southwestern Social Science Quarterly,** XVI (September, 1935), pp. 42-52.

Harmon, George D. "Confederate Migration to Mexico," **Hispanic American Historical Review,** XVII (1937), pp. 458-487.

Hill, Lawrence F. "The Confederate Exodus to Latin America," **Southwestern Historical Quarterly,** XXXIX (July, 1935 to April, 1936), pp. 100-134; pp. 161-199; pp. 309-326.

Marvin, David F. "The **Harriet Lane,**" **Southwestern Historical Quarterly,** XXXIX (July, 1925), pp. 15-20.

Ramsdell, Charles W. "Texas from the Fall of the Confederacy to the Beginning of Reconstruction," **The Quarterly of the Texas State Historical Association,** XI (January, 1908), pp. 199-219.

Rippy, J. Fred. "Mexican Projects of the Confederates," **Southwestern Historical Quarterly,** XXII (April, 1919), pp. 291-317.

Rister, Carl C. "Carlota, A Confederate Colony in Mexico," **Journal of Southern History,** XI (February, 1945), pp. 33-50.
Trexler, H. A. "The Harriet Lane and the Blockade of Galveston," **Southwestern Historical Quarterly,** XXV (October, 1931), pp. 109-123.

BOOKS

Evans, Clement A. **Confederate Military History.** 12 vols. Atlanta: Confederate Publishing Company, 1899.
Farber, James. Texas C.S.A. New York: The Jackson Company, 1947.
Henderson, George Francis Robert. **Stonewall Jackson and the American Civil War.** 2 vols. New York: Longmans, Green, and Company, 1903.
Nunn, William C. **Escape from Reconstruction.** Fort Worth: Manney Company, 1956.
Parks, Joseph Howard. **General Edmund Kirby Smith, CSA.** Baton Rouge: Louisiana State University Press, 1954.
Pray, Mrs. R. F. **Dick Dowling's Battle: An Account of the War Between the States in the Eastern Gulf Coast Region of Texas.** San Antonio: The Naylor Company, 1936.
Scharf, J. Thomas. **History of the Confederate States Navy from Its Organization to the Surrender of Its Last Vessel.** New York: Rogers and Sherwood, 1887.
Tolbert, Frank X. **Dick Dowling at Sabine Pass.** New York: McGraw-Hill Book Company, Inc., 1962.
Wooten, Dudley G. (ed.). **A Comprehensive History of Texas, 1685-1897.** 2 vols. Dallas: William G. Scarff, 1898.

PENDLETON MURRAH

PRIMARY SOURCES

MANUSCRIPTS

Brown, Frank. "Annals of Travis County and the City of Austin." Typed copy at the State Archives, from the war years to 1875.

NEWSPAPERS

Daily Telegraph (Houston), 1864. University of Texas Library.
Dallas Herald. 1863-1869. Texas Christian University.
Flakes Daily Bulletin (Galveston), 1865. University of Texas Library.
Flakes Tri-Weekly Bulletin (Galveston), 1865. Confederate Research Center, Hill Junior College.
Galveston Tri-Weekly News (Houston), 1864).
La Grange Patriot. 1863. University of Texas Library.
Tri-Weekly State Gazette (Austin), 1863, 1865. University of Texas Library.
Tri-Weekly Telegraph (Houston), 1865, University of Texas Library.

PUBLIC DOCUMENTS

Day, James M. (ed.). **House Journals.** Tenth Legislature of the State of Texas. Austin: Texas State Library, 1965.
Executive Correspondence. State Archives, Austin, Texas.
Gammel, H. P. N. (comp.). **Laws of Texas, 1822-1897.** Vol. V. Austin: Gammel Book Company, 1898.
Journal of the Congress of the Confederate States of America, 1861-1865. Vol. IV. Washington: Government Printing Office, 1905.
Messages of Governor Murrah to the Legislature of the State of Texas. Austin: State Gazette Book and Job Office, 1864.

BIBLIOGRAPHY

Statutes at Large of Confederate States of America. First Congress, Third Session.

War of the Rebellion: A Compilation of the Official Records of the Union and Confederate Armies. 128 vols. Washington: Government Printing Office, 1880-1901.

BOOKS

Appleton, D. (ed.). **The American Annual Encyclopaedia.** Vol. V. New York: D. Appleton and Co., 1872.

OTHER SOURCES

Letter from Vivian A. Mitchell to the Librarian of the University of Texas, July 19, 1962.

SECONDARY SOURCES

MANUSCRIPTS

Felgar, Robert Pattison. "Texas in the War for Southern Independence." Unprinted doctoral thesis, The University of Texas Library, 1934.

SCHOLARLY JOURNALS

Bourlan, Hal. "Bold Attempt to Rob the State Treasury at Austin," **Confederate Veteran.** Vol. XXXI (November, 1923), 415.

Holladay, Florence Elizabeth. "The Powers of the Commander of the Trans-Mississippi Department, 1863-1865," **Southwestern Historical Quarterly.** Vol. XXXI (January-April, 1918), 349-350.

BOOKS

Bancroft, Hubert Howe. **History of the North Mexican States and Texas.** Vol. II. San Francisco: The History Company: 1889.

Bolton, Paul. **Governors of Texas.** Corpus Christi: **Corpus Christi Caller-Times,** 1947.

Daniell, L. E. **Texas, The Country and Its Men.** Austin: Press of The City Printing Co., n.d.

DeShields, James T. **They Sat in High Place.** San Antonio: The Naylor Company, 1940.

Eby, Frederick. Education in Texas, Source Material. "Bulletin of the University of Texas," No. 184. Austin: The University of Texas, 1918.

Evans, Clement Anselm (ed.). **Confederate Military History.** Vol. XI. Atlanta: Confederate Publishing Company, 1899.

Jackson, Pearl Cashell. Texas **Governors' Wives.** Austin: E. L. Steck, 1915.

Kittrell, Norman G. **Governors Who Have Been and Other Public Men of Texas.** Houston: Dealy-Adey-Elgin Co., 1921.

Miller, Edmund Thornton. **A Financial History of Texas.** "Bulletin of the University of Texas," No. 37. Austin: University of Texas, 1916.

National Cyclopedia of American Biography. Vol. IX. New York: James T. White and Co., 1907.

Nunn, W. C. **Escape From Reconstruction.** Fort Worth: Leo Potishman Foundation, 1956.

Thrall, A. M. **A History of Texas.** New York: University Publishing Company, 1892.

Thrall, Homer S. **Pictorial History of Texas.** St. Louis: N. D. Thomas and Company, 1879.

Webb, Walter Prescott (ed.). **Texas Handbook.** Vol. II. Austin: Texas Historical Association, 1952.

Wooten, Dudley G. **A Comprehensive History of Texas.** Vol. II. Dallas: William G. Scarff, 1898.

Wortham, Louis J. **A History of Texas from Wilderness to Commonwealth.** Vol. IV. Fort Worth: Wortham-Molyneaux Co., 1924.

☆ ☆ ☆

WILLIAMSON SIMPSON OLDHAM

PRIMARY SOURCES

MANUSCRIPTS

Oldham, Williamson Simpson, **A History of a Journey from Richmond to the Rio Grande from March 30, until June 26, 1865, or The Last Days of the Confederate States with a Review of the Causes that Led to Their Overthrow.** (Manuscript in the Archives of the Library of the University of Texas).

NEWSPAPERS

Harper's Weekly (New York, 1860-1865).
Houston Daily Telegram (1868).
New York Times (1860-1865).
Texas Republican (1868).
Texas State Gazette (Austin, 1850-1861).

PUBLIC DOCUMENTS

War of the Rebellion, Official Records of the Union and Confederate Armies. 128 vols. Series I, Vols. 1, 22, 26, 34, 53; Series IV, Vols. 1, 3. Washington: U. S. War Dept., (1880-1901).

PAMPHLETS

Oldham, Williamson S. "Rights of the South in Opposition to 'Squatters Sovereignty'." **Speech** delivered August 27, 1856, at Austin, Texas. (Archives of the University of Texas.)
Oldham, W. S. **Speech** upon the Bill to Amend the Conscript Laws made in the Senate, September 4, 1862. (Archives of the University of Texas.)
Oldham, W. S. **Speech on Finances** delivered in the Senate, December 3, 1863. (Archives of the University of Texas.)
Oldham, W. S. **Speech on the Resolutions of the State of Texas,** Concerning Peace, Reconstruction and Independence delivered in the Senate, January 30, 1865. (Archives of the University of Texas.)

SCHOLARLY JOURNALS

Day, James M. **Texas Senate and House Journal,** Ninth and Tenth First Called Session. Austin: Texas State Library, 1865.
Fontaine, Edward. "Hon. Williamson S. Oldham." **De Bow's Review.** Vol. XXXVII, pp. 864-880. New Orleans: After the War Series, 1866-1870.
Journal of the Congress of the Confederate States of America, 1861 to 1865. 7 vols., Vols. 1, 2, 4. Washington: Government Printing Office, 1904-1905.
Journal of the House of Representatives of the General Assembly of Arkansas, 1838, 1842, 1848.
Winkler, E. W., ed. **Journal of the Secession Convention of Texas, 1861.** Austin: Austin Publishing Company, 1912.

BIBLIOGRAPHY

BOOKS

Brown, John Henry. **History of Texas from 1685 to 1892.** Vol. 2. St. Louis: L. E. Daniell, 1892.
Foote, Henry S. **Bench and Bar of the South and Southwest.** St. Louis: Soule, Thomas & Wentworth, 1876.
Lynch, James D. **The Bench and Bar of Texas.** St. Louis: Nixon Jones Printing Co., 1885.
North, Thomas. **Five Years in Texas or What You Did Not Hear During the War.** Cincinnati: Elm Street Printing Co., 1871.
Stephens, Alexander H. **Constitutional View of the War Between the States.** Chicago: Zeigler, McCurdy & Co., 1870.
"Texas." **Appleton's Annual Cyclopaedia.** 42 vols., Vol. 2. New York: D. Appleton and Company, 1872.
Thrall, Homer S. **A Pictorial History of Texas.** St. Louis: N. D. Thomas and Co., 1879.

SECONDARY SOURCES

MANUSCRIPTS

King, Alma Dexta. "The Political Career of Williamson Simpson Oldham." (Master's Thesis, University of Texas Archives, 1929.)

NEWSPAPERS

Dallas Herald (1861-1865).

SCHOLARLY JOURNALS

King, Alma Dexta. "The Political Career of Williamson Simpson Oldham." **Southwestern Historical Quarterly.** Vol. XXXIII. Austin: Texas State Historical Association, 1930.
Oldham, Williamson Simpson. "Colonel John Marshall." **Southwestern Historical Quarterly.** Vol. XX. Austin: Texas Historical Association, 1917.
Ramsdell, Charles W. "The Confederate Government and the Railroads." **American Historical Review.** Vol. XXII. 1916.
Terrell, A. W. "Recollections of General Sam Houston." **Southwestern Historical Quarterly.** Vol. XVI. Austin: Texas State Historical Association, 1913.
Wooten, Dudley G. **A Comprehensive History of Texas.** 2 vols., Vol. 2. Dallas: William G. Scarff, 1898.
Wortham, Louis J. **A History of Texas.** 5 vols., Vol. III. Fort Worth: Wortham-Molyneaux Co., 1924.
Wright, Marcus J., and Simpson, Harold B. **Texas in the War 1861-1865.** Hillsboro: Hill Junior College Press, 1965.
Yearns, Wilfred B. **The Confederate Congress.** Athens: The University of Georgia Press, 1960.

BOOKS

Eaton, Clement. **A History of the Southern Confederacy.** New York: The McMillan Co., 1954.
Farber, James. **Texas, C.S.A.** San Antonio: The Jackson Company, 1947.
Fulmore, Z. T. **History and Geography of Texas as Told in County Names.** Austin: S. R. Fulmore, 1926.
Henderson, Harry M. **Texas and the Confederacy.** San Antonio: Naylor Company, 1955.
Johnson, F. W. **Texas and Texans.** 5 vols., Vols. I, II. Chicago: The American Historical Society, 1914.
Malone, Dumas, ed. **Dictionary of American Biography.** 22 vols., Vol. XIV. New York: Charles Scribner and Sons, 1934.

Nunn, W. C. **Escape from Reconstruction.** Fort Worth: Texas Christian University, 1956.
Ownsley, Frank L. **States Rights in the Confederacy.** Massachusetts: Peter Smith, 1961.
Pope, William F. **Early Days in Arkansas.** Little Rock: 1895.
Ramsdell, Charles W. **Behind the Lines in the Southern Confederacy.** Baton Rouge: Louisiana State Union Press, 1944..
Schwab, John C. **The Confederate States of America, 1861-1865.** New York: 1901.
Speer, Ocie. **Texas Jurists.** Dallas: By author, 1936.
Thomas, David Y. **Arkansas in War and Reconstruction.** Little Rock: Arkansas Division of the United Daughters of the Confederacy, 1926.
Williams, Amelia W., and Barker, E. C., eds. **Writings of Sam Houston.** Vols. III, IV, VI, VIII. Austin: University of Texas Press, 1942.
"Williamson Simpson Oldham." **Handbook of Texas.** Vol. 2. Austin: Texas State Historical Association, 1952.

☆ ☆ ☆

JOHN H. REAGAN

PRIMARY SOURCES

MANUSCRIPTS

Reagan, John H. Papers, 1840-1905. Texas State Archives, Austin, Texas.
Roberts, Oran Milo. Papers, 1844-1895. University of Texas Archives, Austin, Texas.
Starr, James H. Papers. University of Texas Archives, Austin, Texas.

NEWSPAPERS

Dallas Weekly Herald, 1859-1865.
Montgomery Daily Mail, 1861.
Richmond Daily Examiner, 1861-1864.
Richmond Enquirer, 1861-1864.

PUBLIC DOCUMENTS

Confederate States of America. **Journal of the Congress of the Confederate States of America, 1861-1865.** 7 vols. Washington: Government Printing Office, 1904-1905..
Matthews, James Muscoe (ed.). **Public Laws of the Confederate States of America.** Richmond: R. M. Smith, 1864.
————. **The Statutes at Large of the Provisional Government of the Confederate States of America, From the Institution of the Government, February 8, 1861, to Its Termination, February 18, 1862, Inclusive.** Richmond: R. M. Smith, 1864.
The War of the Rebellion: A Compilation of the Official Records of the Union and Confederate Armies. 70 vols. Washington: Government Printing Office, 1880-1901.
Winkler, Ernest William, ed. **Journal of the Secession Convention of Texas, 1861.** Austin: Austin Publishing Co., 1912.

SCHOLARLY JOURNALS

Reagan, John H. "A Conversation with Governor Houston," **Quarterly of the Texas State Historical Association,** III (April, 1900), pp. 279-281.

BIBLIOGRAPHY

BOOKS

Davis, Jefferson. **The Rise and Fall of the Confederate Government.** 2 vols. New York: Thomas Yoseloff, 1958.

Jones, John Beauchamp. **A Rebel War Clerk's Diary at the Confederate States Capital.** Edited by Howard Swiggett. 2 vols. New York: Old Hickory Bookshop, 1935.

Lubbock, Francis R. **Six Decades in Texas; or, Memoirs of Francis Richard Lubbock, Governor of Texas in War Time, 1861-1863.** Edited by C. W. Raines. Austin: B. C. Jones and Company, 1900.

Reagan, John H. **Memoirs: With Special Reference to Secession and the Civil War.** Edited by Walter Flavius McCaleb. New York: Neale Publishing Company, 1906.

Stephens, Alexander H. **Recollections: His Diary When a Prisoner at Fort Warren, Boston Harbour, 1865.** Edited by Myrta Lockett Avary. New York: Doubleday, Page and Company, 1910.

SECONDARY SOURCES

MANUSCRIPTS

Good, Benjamin Harvey. "John Henninger Reagan." Unpublished Ph.D. dissertation, University of Texas, 1931.

Hudgins, Ellis Andres. "The Public Career of John H. Reagan." Unpublished Master's thesis, Baylor University, 1961.

Jeffcoat, Clifford R. "John H. Reagan." Unpublished Master's thesis, East Texas State Teachers College, 1951.

SCHOLARLY JOURNALS

Addington, Wendell G. "Slave Insurrections in Texas," **Journal of Negro History,** XXXV (October, 1950), pp. 419-434.

Eaton, Clement. "Mob Violence in the Old South," **Mississippi Valley Historical Review,** XXIX (December, 1942), pp. 351-370.

Garrison, L. R. "Administrative Problems of the Confederate Post Office Department," **Southwestern Historical Quarterly,** XIX (October, 1915-January, 1916), pp. 111-141, 232-250.

McCaleb, Walter Flavius. "The Organization of the Post Office Department of the Confederacy," **American Historical Review,** XII (October, 1906), pp. 66-74.

__________. "John H. Reagan," **Quarterly of the Texas State Historical Association,** IX)July, 1905), pp. 41-50.

Maher, Edward R., Jr. "Sam Houston and Secession," **Southwestern Historical Quarterly,** LV (April, 1952), pp. 448-458.

Procter, Ben H. "John H. Reagan and the Confederate Post Office Department," **Georgia Review,** XI (Winter, 1957), pp. 387-399.

Sandbo, Anna Irene. "Beginnings of the Secession Movement in Texas," **Southwestern Historical Quarterly,** XVIII (July, 1914), pp. 46-73.

__________. "First Session of the Secession Convention in Texas," **Southwestern Historical Quarterly,** XVIII (October, 1914), pp. 162-194.

White, William W. "The Texas Slave Insurrection of 1860," **Southwestern Historical Quarterly,** LII (January, 1949), pp. 259-285.

BOOKS

Black, Robert C. **The Railroads of the Confederacy.** Chapel Hill: University of North Carolina Press, 1952.

Coulter, Ellis Merton. **The Confederate States of America 1861-1865.** Baton Rouge: Louisiana State University Press, 1950.

Dietz, August. **The Confederate States Post Office Department: Its Stamps and Stationery.** Richmond: Dietz Press, 1948.

Dumond, Dwight Lowell. **The Secession Movement 1860-1861.** New York: The Macmillan Company, 1931.
Durkin, Joseph T. **Stephen R. Mallory: Confederate Navy Chief.** Chapel Hill: University of North Carolina Press, 1954.
Elliott, Claude. **Leathercoat: The Life History of a Texas Patriot.** San Antonio: Standard Printing Company, 1938.
Freeman, Douglas Southall. **R. E. Lee.** 4 vols. New York: Charles Scribner's Sons, 1934.
Friend, Llerena. **Sam Houston: The Great Designer.** Austin: University of Texas Press, 1954.
Hanna, Alfred Jackson. **Flight Into Oblivion.** Richmond: Johnson Publishing Co., 1938.
Kittrell, Norman G. **Governors Who Have Been, and Other Public Men of Texas.** Houston: Dealy-Adey-Elgin Co., 1921.
Lee, Charles Robert, Jr. **The Confederate Constitutions.** Chapel Hill: University of North Carolina Press, 1963.
Lynch, James Daniel. **The Bench and Bar of Texas.** St. Louis: Nixon-Jones Printing Company, 1885.
Meade, Robert Douthat. **Judah P. Benjamin: Confederate Statesman.** New York: Oxford University Press, 1943.
Nevins, Allan. **The Statesmanship of the Civil War.** New York: The Macmillan Company, 1953.
Patrick, Rembert W. **Jefferson Davis and His Cabinet.** Baton Rouge: Louisiana State University Press, 1944.
Procter, Ben H. **Not Without Honor: The Life of John H. Reagan.** Austin: University of Texas Press, 1962.
Ramsdell, Charles William. **Civil War and Reconstruction in Texas.** New York: Longmans, Green, and Company, 1910.
Strode, Hudson. **Jefferson Davis: American Patriot.** New York: Harcourt, Brace and Company, 1955.
__________. **Jefferson Davis: Confederate President.** New York: Harcourt, Brace and Company, 1959.
Thompson, William T. **Robert Toombs of Georgia.** Baton Rouge: Louisiana State University Press, 1966.
Wooster, Ralph A. **The Secession Conventions of the South.** Princeton: Princeton University Press, 1962.
Wooten, Dudley Goodall (ed.). **A Comprehensive History of Texas, 1685 to 1897.** 2 vols. Dallas: William G. Scarff, 1898.

LOUIS TREZEVANT WIGFALL

PRIMARY SOURCES

MANUSCRIPTS

Oldham, W. S. "The Last Days of the Confederate States, With a Review of the Causes That Led to Their Overthrow." Unpublished manuscript, University of Texas, Archives.

NEWSPAPERS

Austin **State Gazette.** April 12, 1865; May 3, 1865.
Clarksville **Northern Standard.** December 10, 1859.
Dallas **Herald.** January, 1859-November, 1861.
Texas **Republican** (Marshall). May, 1849-May, 1865.
Richmond **Examiner.** March 12, 13, 1862; September 26, 1862.

BIBLIOGRAPHY

PUBLIC DOCUMENTS

Journal of the Secession Convention of Texas, 1861. Edited by Ernest William Winkler. Austin: Austin Printing Co., 1912.

U. S. Congress. **Biographical Directory of the American Congress, 1774-1961.** Washington: Government Printing Office, 1961.

U. S. Congress. **Journal of the Congress of the Confederate States of America, 1861-1865.** 7 vols. Washington: Government Printing Office, 1904-1905.

U. S. Congress. Senate. Senator Louis T. Wigfall speaking against H. J. Res. to amend the U. S. Constitution, 36th Congress, 1st Session, March 2, 1861. **Congressional Globe,** Vol. XXX, Pt. 2, p. 1373.

The War of Rebellion: Official Records. (Publication directed by Elihu Root). Washington: Government Printing Office, 1880-1901.

OTHER SOURCES

University of Texas. Archives, W. S. Oldham Collection.
University of Texas. Archives, J. H. Reagan Collection.
University of Texas. Archives, Mrs. E. M. Schiwetz Civil War Collection.
University of Texas. Archives, Louis T. Wigfall Collection.

BOOKS

Chesnut, Mary Boykin. **A Diary from Dixie.** Boston: Houghton Mifflin Co., 1950.

Clay, Mrs. Virginia. **The Belle of the Fifties.** Edited by Ada Sterling. New York: Doubleday Page, 1904.

Everett, Donald E., ed. **Chaplain Davis and Hood's Texas Brigade.** San Antonio, Texas: Principia Press of Trinity University, 1962.

Fletcher, William Andrew. **Rebel Private.** Austin: University of Texas Press, 1954.

Houston, Sam. **The Writings of Sam Houston, 1813-1863.** Edited by Amelia W. Williams and Eugene C. Barker. Austin: University of Texas Press, 1938-1945.

Johnson, Robert Underwool and Clarence Clough Buel, eds. **Leaders and Battles of the Civil War.** New York: Thomas Yoseloff, Inc., 1956.

Lubbock, Francis. **Six Decades in Texas.** Edited by C. W. Raines. Austin: Ben C. Jones and Co., 1900.

Polley, J. B. **A Soldier's Letters to Charming Nellie.** New York: Neale Publishing Co., 1908.

Reagan, John H. **Memoirs.** Edited by Walter F. McCaleb. New York: Neale Publishing Co., 1906.

Stephens, Alexander H. **A Constituional View of the Late War Between the States.** St. Louis, Missouri: National Publishing Co., 1870.

Todd, George T. **First Texas Regiment.** Waco, Texas: Texian Press, 1963.

Winkler, Mrs. A. V. **The Confederate Capitol and Hood's Texas Brigade.** Austin: Eugene Von Boeckmann, 1894..

Wright, Mrs. D. Giraud. **A Southern Girl in '61.** New York: Doubleday, Page and Co., 1905.

SECONDARY SOURCES

MANUSCRIPTS

Lord, Clyde Willis. "The Ante-bellum Career of Louis Trezevant Wigfall." Unpublished Master's thesis, University of Texas, 1925.

Power, Hugh Irwin, Jr. "Texas at War—The Letters of Private James Henry Hendrick, Army of Northern Virginia." Unpublished paper, Confederate Research Center, Hillsboro, Texas, 1964.

Seehorn, Beverly Josephine. "Louis Trezevant Wigfall, A Confederate Senator." Unpublished Master's thesis, Southern Methodist University, 1930.

SCHOLARLY JOURNALS

Estill, Mary S. (ed.), "Diary of a Confederate Congressman, 1862-1863: F. B. Sexton." **Southwestern Historical Quarterly,** XXXVIII (April, 1935), 270-301; XXXIX (July, 1935), 33-65.

"General Topic: The Confederate Congress." **Confederate Veteran,** XXXV (July, 1927), 273.

King, Alma Dexta. "The Political Career of William Simpson Oldham." **Southwestern Historical Quarterly,** XXXIII (October, 1929), 112-113.

Leigh, W. L. "General Confederate Officers from Texas." **Confederate Veteran,** XX (August, 1912), 391.

"Proceedings of the First Confederate Congress." **Southern Historical Society Papers,** XLIV (June, 1923); XLV (May, 1925).

Rister, Carl Coke. "Carlota, A Confederate Colony in Mexico." **The Journal of Southern History,** XI (February, 1945), 33-50.

Sandbo, Anna Irene. "Beginnings of the Secession Movement in Texas." **Southern Historical Quarterly,** XVIII (July, 1914), 41-73.

__________. "The First Session of the Secession Convention." **Southwestern Historical Quarterly,** XVIII (July, 1914), 162-194.

Simpson, Harold B. "Whip the Devil and His Hosts." **Chronicles of Smith County, Texas,** VI (Fall, 1967), 12+.

Wallace, Sarah Agnes. "Confederate Exiles in London, 1865-1870: The Wigfalls." **The South Carolina Historical and Genealogical Magazine,** LII (April, 1951), 74+.

BOOKS

Barker, Eugene C. (ed.), **Readings in Texas History.** Dallas: The Southwest Press, 1929.

Boatner, Mark Mayo, III. **The Civil War Dictionary.** New York: David McKay Co., Inc., 1959.

Callahan, J. M. **The Diplomatic History of the Southern Confederacy.** Springfield, Mass.: Walden Press, 1957.

Catton, Bruce. **The Coming Fury.** Garden City, New York: Doubleday and Co., Inc., 1961.

Dowdey, Clifford. **Experiment in Rebellion.** Garden City, New York: Doubleday and Co., Inc., 1947.

DuBose, John Witherspoon. **The Life and Times of William Lowndes Yancey.** 2 vols. New York: Peter Smith, 1942.

Howe, Daniel Wait. **Political History of Secession.** New York: G. P. Putnam's Sons, 1914.

Johnson, Francis White. **A History of Texas and Texans.** Edited by Eugene C. Barker and Ernest William Winkler. 5 vols. New York: The American Historical Society, 1914.

Malone, Dumas (ed.). **Dictionary of American Biography.** 20 vols. New York: Charles Scribner's Sons, 1936.

Moore, Albert Burton. **Conscription and Conflict in the Confederacy.** New York: The Macmillan Co., 1924.

Richardson, Rupert Norval. **Texas the Lone Star State.** Englewood Cliffs, New Jersey: Prentice-Hall, Inc., 1958.

Simpson, Harold B. **Gaines Mill to Appomattox.** Waco: Texian Press, 1963.

The Texas Almanac. Galveston: Richardson and Company. The years 1861 to 1865.

Webb, Walter Prescott, ed. **The Handbook of Texas.** 2 vols. Austin: The Texas State Historical Association, 1952.

Wooten, Dudley G., ed. **A Comprehensive History of Texas, 1685 to 1897.** 2 vols. Dallas: William G. Scarff, 1898.

Wortham, Louis J. **A History of Texas.** 4 vols. Fort Worth, Texas: Wortham-Molyneaux Co., 1924.

Wright, Marcus J. (comp.) and Harold B. Simpson (ed.). **Texas in the War: 1861-1865.** Hillsboro, Texas: Hill Junior College Press, 1965.

Index

INDEX

— A —

Adams, Wirt: 162
Adams-Southern Express Co.: 165-166
Alabama: 43, 110
Allen, Henry: 32, 116
Anderson, Robert: 180
Arizona: 42-46

— B —

Bailey, George H.: 45-46
Ballinger, William: 133
Banks, N. P.: 30-31, 42-43, 45, 113-115, 130
Barnes, James W.: 129
Baron, Adele: 76
Baron, N. A., Jr.: 76
Barr, Amelia: 21
Baylor, George Wythe: 9
Baylor, John Robert: early life in Indian Territory and the Southwest, 1-2; mans West Texas forts, 3; plans New Mexico invasion, 3-4; invests Mesilla Valley, 5-6; anticipates fight at San Augustin Pass, 7-8; accepts Lynde's surrender, 8-9; proclamation to the people of Arizona, 10; appoints himself military governor, 10; sends force to Fort Stanton, 10; anticipates Federal attack, 11; friction with General H. H. Sibley, 11; confirmed as military governor, 12; commissioned brigadier-general, 12; extermination letter, 13-15; refusal to disavow extermination order, 14; authority to raise troops rescinded, 14; remains active in state military affairs, 15; elected to Congress, 15; military rank re-instated, 15; urges another attempt to take Arizona, 15; plan deemed impractical, 16; death, 16
Baylor, Dr. John Walker: 1
Bayou City: 105, 107
Bean, E. M.: 129
Bee, Hamilton: 32
Bell, H. H.: 109-110
Bell, John C.: 79
Bemiss, S. M.: 71
Benjamin, Judah P.: 86-88, 162
Bird, Thomas: 176
Bonnell, George W.: 77
Boone, Daniel: 56
Bragg, Braxton: 63, 187
Breckenridge, John C.: 19, 79
Brewster, H. P.: 162
Brooks, Preston Smith: 176
Brooklyn: 109
Brown, John: 157, 178
Brown, William: 95
Bryan, Guy M.: 132
Buchanan, James: 179
Buckner, Simon Bolivar: 70, 115-116
Burrell, Isaac: 105, 107
Byrd, William: 27

— C —

Calhoun, John C.: 177
Callaway, Richard: 56
Camp Colorado: 59
Canby, Edward: 115-116, 133
Camp Wood: 59
Cavallo: 108
Chambers, T. J.: 28, 81, 122, 124
Chesnut, Mary: 183, 186
Clark, Edward: campaign of 1859, 18; denies membership in Know-Nothing party, 18-19; elected lieutenant-governor, 19; inaugurated as lieutenant-governor, 19; supports secession, 20; his merits and demerits, 22; birth of, 22; marriage of, 22; delegate to constitutional convention of 1845, 23; member of the house of representatives, 23; member of state senate, 23; secretary of state, 23; Mexican War service, 23; citation for bravery at Monterrey, 23; governor of Texas, 23; asks for Confederate protection of frontier, 24; mobilizes state for Confederate cause, 24; troop levies, 26; issues proclamation for Texans to defend selves, 26; requests merchants to turn over ammunition to state, 26; inventory of guns requested, 26; requests more Confederate troops, 27; seeks clothing and blankets, 27; organizes clothing depots, 27-28; creates military board, 28; demands state prison make wool, 28; calls for state elections, August, 1861, 28; candidate for governor, 1861, 28-29; denounced in campaign, 29; defeated for governor, 29; joins Confederate army, 29-30; commands brigade, 30; action in Louisiana, 30; at Mansfield and Pleasant Hill, 30; wounded at Mansfield, 31;

wounded at Pleasant Hill, 32; discharged from army, 32; promotion to brigadier general unconfirmed, 32; flees to Mexico, 32; goes to Washington, D. C., for presidential pardon, 32; last days, 32-33, 79-81, 116, 148
Clark, M. H.: 96
Clements, Benjamin: 163
Clifton: 42-46, 105, 107-108
Committee on Public Safety: 21, 25, 145
Confederate Cotton Bureau: 126-127
Congress, Confederate States of America: 12-13, 47
Cook, Joseph J.: 38-39, 106, 111
Cooper, Samuel: 62-63
Crocker, Frederick: 42, 45-46
Crosby, Josiah: 2
Cross, Charlotte Maria: 176
Cross, George Warren: 176

— D —

Darby, John T.: 66-67
Davidson, John W.: 65
"Davis Guards": 37-41, 44-48
Davis, Jefferson: 12, 15, 47, 58, 64-65, 68, 70, 76, 82, 89, 93-94, 96-97, 109, 128-129, 146, 151, 153-154, 161-162, 168, 180-181, 186-187
Davis, Varina (Mrs.): 96
Deal, John: 66
DeWalt, K. B.: 129
DeWitt, C. C.: 129
Douglas, Stephen A.: 19, 79
Dowling, Benjamin R.: 37
Dowling, Felix Sabine: 48
Dowling, Mary: 36
Dowling, Mary Annie: 48
Dowling, Patrick: 41-42
Dowling, Richard W. "Dick": early life, 36-37; marriage, 37; member of Houston Light Arty. Co., 37; joins Jefferson Davis Guards, 37; assigned to Colonel "Rip" Ford's command, 38; sent to Lower Rio Grande, 38; returns to Houston, 1861, 38; artillery training, 38; participates in battle of Galveston, 39; commands cannon on **Josiah Bell,** 39-40; participates in surrender of **Morning Light,** 40; receives commendation for action off Sabine Pass, 40; mans defense positions at Sabine Pass, 40; maintains vigilence at Fort Griffin, 43; orders guns into action at Sabine Pass, 44; action of gun crews, 45; takes Crocker's surrender, 45; victory at Sabine Pass, 46; importance of victory to the South, 47; assigned to recruiting duty in Texas, 48; post-war career, 48; death, 48-49; 112.
Dowling, William: 36

— E —

Early, Jubal: 114, 116
Elias Pike: 108
Ellet, Henry T.: 162
Epperson, B. H.: 126

— F —

Farragut, David: 109-110
Flournoy, George M.: 143, 159
Floyd, John B.: 56, 179
Ford, John S. "Rip": 1, 38, 84
Fort Bliss: 4, 11
Fort Breckenridge: 8
Fort Craig: 3, 9-11
Fort Davis: 4, 10
Fort Griffin: 40-45, 47-48, 112-113
Fort Fillmore: 3-4, 6
Fort Inge: 11
Fort Jackson: 116
Fort Mason: 55-56, 59
Fort Quitman: 11
Fort Stanton: 10-11
Fort Sumter: 25
Fort Thorn: 10
Fortress Monroe: 97
Franklin, William B.: 42, 46
French, Richard: 57
French, Theodosia: 56

— G —

Galveston, battle of: 106-107
Gibbs, Alfred: 8
Gibbs, John: 127
Granger, Gordon: 133-134
Granite City: 42-45
Green, Nathan: 139
Green, Tom: 94
Gregg, John: 145
Griffin, W. H.: 42
Grimes, Jesse: 78

— H —

Halleck, Henry W.: 30, 42
Hampton, Wade: 66
Hamilton, James: 176
Hardee, William: 187
Hardeman, Peter: 8
Harmer, Josiah: 56
Harrell, J. E.: 163
Harriet Lane: 105-107; 109-110
Hart, Simeon: 2-3, 11

INDEX

Hatteras: 110
Hebert, P. O.: 83-84, 89, 103
Helm, Thomas: 13
Hemphill, John: 86, 145
Henderson, James Pinckney: 23, 78, 177
Hennan, Anna Marie: 70
Hennessy, Patrick: 37
Herbert, P. T.: 3
Hill, Benjamin H.: 190
Hindman, T. C.: 63, 116
Hogg, James S.: 98
Holmes, Theophiles Hunter: 186
Hood, James: 57
Hood, John Bell: fights Indians on Devil's River, Texas, 55; wounded at Devil's River, 56; commended for Devil's River fight, 56; early life, 56; personality, 57; West Point cadet, 57-58; assigned to 2nd U. S. Cavalry in Texas, 58; resigns commission, 60; joins Southern army, 61; reports to Lee at Richmond, 61; assigned to Magruder's command, 61; assigned to 4th Texas Infantry Regiment command, 61; commands Texas Brigade, 61; at Eltham's Landing and Gaines' Mill, 62; at Second Manassas and Antietam, 62; Jackson recommends for promotion to major-general, 62; at Fredericksburg, Suffolk, and Gettysburg, 62; wounded at Gettysburg, 62; wounded at Chickamauga, 63; praised for Chickamauga, 62; promoted to lieutenant-general, 64; assigned to Army of Tennessee, 64; commands corps in Atlanta campaign, 64; replaces Joseph E. Johnston, 64; Atlanta Campaign battles, 64; abandons Atlanta, 64; Tennessee Campaign, 64; routed at Nashville, 64; ordered to Texas to raise army, 65; surrenders at Natchez, 65; narrow escapes and wounds during war, 67-68; Hood's appraisal of the Texas Brigade, 69; post-war career, 70; marriage to Anna Marie Hennan, 70; death of wife and daughter, 71; Hood's death, 71-72; 114, 182, 187
Hood, John W.: 56-57
Hood, Luke: 56
Hood, Olivia: 57
Hood's Texas Brigade: 66, 68-68, 95, 183
Hood, William: 57
Houston, Sam: 18-19, 21, 23, 77-80, 109, 143, 148-149, 161, 177

— J —

Jackson, Stonewall: 62, 67, 104
Jennings, T. J.: 176
John F. Carr: 108
Johnson, Amos: 44-45
Johnson, Andrew: 32, 168-169, 178
Johnston, Albert Sydney: 9, 82
Johnston, Joseph E.: 63, 186-187, 190
Johnston, William Preston: 95, 97
Josiah Bell: 39-40
Juarez, Benito: 116

— K —

Kirk, Annie: 140
Knights of the Golden Circle: 20

— L —

Law, Richard L.: 107-108
Lecompte: 108
Lee, George Washington Custis: 95
Lee, Robert E.: 58-59, 61, 95, 114-115, 132, 168, 187
Lewis, Joseph F.: 163
Lincoln, Abraham: 79, 179
Longstreet, James: 62-63, 70
Loughery, R. W.: 124
Lubbock, Francis (Frank): 18-19; 28-29; early life, 76-78; elected lieutenant-governor, 78; candidate for governor, 80; elected governor, 81; description of, 81; journeys to Richmond, 82; meets with Davis, 82; inaugural address, 82-83; calls for new frontier defense policy, 84; calls for munitions manufacture, 84; Confederate manpower problem, 84; calls for more efficient state military organization, 85; frontier regiment created, 86; military board created, 86; carries out bond exchange plan with Richmond, 86; approves use of state penitentiary for clothing manufacture, 87; issues proclamation for 15,000 volunteers, 87; misunderstanding over troop levies, 88; assures Davis of Texas support, 89; participates in governors' conference on defense plan, 89; desires change in military commanders, 89; authorized to use manpower draft, 90; faces opposition to draft, 90; places Austin County under martial law, 90; praises Magruder's victory at Galveston, 91; asks for impressment of slave

labor, 91; desires more frontier protection, 91; praises Texas military contribution, 91-92; calls for more troops, 92; chairman of governor's conference, 93; receives suggested alliance between Texas and France, 93; refuses to run for second gubernatorial term, 93; valedictory message, 93-94; enters army on staff of Magruder, 94; transfers to Tom Green's command, 94; reassigned to headquarters of Trans-Mississippi Department, 94; battle experience, 94; appointed aide-de-camp to President Davis, 95; departs for Richmond, 95; associates on President's staff, 95; flees Richmond, 95; captured, 96; taken to Fortress Monroe, 96-97; released, 97; post-war career, 97-98; death, 98; 109, 124, 127
Lubbock, Henry Thomas Willis: 76, 107
Lubbock, Tom: 82
Luckett, Phillip N.: 111
Lynde, Isaac: 4-7

— M —

Magoffin, James W.: 2
Magruder, John Bankhead: 14, 32, 39, 43-44, 47-48, 61, 89-92, 94; named to command District of Texas, New Mexico and Arizona, 104; early life, 104; appointed colonel in Confederacy, 104; commands troops on Virginia peninsula, 104; victorious at Big Bethel, 104; appointed brigadier-general, 104; commander at Yorktown, 104; slows Federal advance on Richmond, 104-105; promoted to major-general, 105; participates in Seven Days' Battle, 105; extraordinary courage at Malvern Hill, 105; transferred to Texas, 105; expected to retrieve loss of Galveston, 105; directs battle of Galveston, 106-107; arranges three hours truce with Federals, 107-108; achieves victory at Galveston, 109; hero of the hour, 109; returns to Houston headquarters, 110; unable to secure supplies, 111; confronted with mutiny, 111; frustrated by reduction of forces, 111; much of command transferred, 112; commends Dowling on victory, 112-113; confronted with mutiny over food, 114; commands District of Arkansas, 115; returns to Texas, 115; appeals to troops to continue struggle, 115; surrenders, 116; flees to Mexico, 116; named chief of colonization land office by Maximilian's government, 116; returns to United States, 116-117; lectures on war experiences, 117; death, 117; 127, 129-130
Mallory, Stephen: 162
Mary Boardman: 108
Mays, R. E.: 10
Medford, H. C.: 114
Menninger, Christopher: 162
"Milam Guards": 77
Miller, W. D.: 163
Moore, Isaiah N.: 9
Moore, Thomas: 32, 116
Morning Light: 40
Murrah, Pendleton: 32, 93-94, 116; elected governor (1863), 122; obscurity as a state personality, 122; marries Sue Ellen Taylor, 123; elected to state legislature (1857), 124; conflict over Confederate impressment act, 125; concerned over Confederate Cotton Bureau, 126; announces policy of non-impressment of cotton, 126; offers alternate plan of purchasing cotton, 126; orders Military Board to cease purchase of cotton, 127; opposes impressment of transportation, 127; views on slave impressment, 127; objects to confiscation and impressment of Texas cattle, 127-128; attempts to restore law and order in Texas, 128; opposes Confederate draft of state militia, 128; recommends frontier defense companies be exempt from draft, 129; desires state troops be organized into brigades before entering Confederate service, 130; follows acts of Confederate Congress, 130; haunted by financial insolvency of Texas, 130; suggests issue of treasury warrants be stopped, 131; health deteriorates, 131; family tragedy, 132; encourages Texans to maintain hope, 132; finally ad-

mits defeat, 132-133; pleads with lawmen to maintain order, 133; calls for special session of state legislature, 133; tries to avoid Federal occupation, 133-134; flees to Mexico, 134; dies at Monterrey, Mexico, 134; 189

— Mc —

McCulloch, Ben: 2, 24, 179
McCulloch, Henry E.: 86
McLaws, Lafayette: 62
McLeod, Hugh: 181
McKee, James C.: 5-6
McKernan, Michael, 44, 46
McKinney: Thomas J.: 132
McKessick, Mary Vance: 139-140
McNally, C. H.: 6

— N —

Neptune: 105-107
Nicholas (Mescalero-Apache chief): 4, 10-11

— O —

Ochiltree, William B.: 20, 145, 148, 176
Odlum, Benjamin D.: 36
Odlum, Elizabeth Anne: 37
Odlum, Frederick H.: 37, 41, 43-44, 47
Offutt, Henry St. George: 163
Oldham, Williamson Simpson: early life, 139; associate justice of Supreme Court of Arkansas, 140; moves to Texas, 140; death of wife, 140; remarries, 140; co-owner and editor of **Texas State Gazette** (Austin), 141; prepares digest of Texas statutes, 142; advocates secession, 143; moves from Austin to Brenham, 143; attends Secession Convention, 144; votes for Ordinance of Secession, 145; elected delegate to Montgomery Convention, 145; takes seat in Confederate Congress, 145; appointed member on Judiciary and Naval Affairs Committee, 146; named commissioner to Arkansas, 146; returns to Texas, 148; writes Clark to prepare Texas for invasion, 148; appointed to Committee on Territories, 148; elected to Confederate Senate, 149; champions states rights and free trade, 149; opposes Wigfall on conscription, 150; desires Texas frontier regiment be free from conscription, 151; opposes investing power in provost-marshal, 151-152; objects to suspension of habeas corpus, 152-53; appointed to committee to assess resources of Confederacy, 153; leaves Confederate capital after Davis, 153-154; flees to Mexico, 154; goes to Canada, 154; pardoned, 154; post-war life, 154; death, 154; 183
Osterhaus, Peter J.: 116
Owasco: 105-106, 108

— P —

Pease, E .M.: 23
Pemberton, John C.: 167-168
Polk, Leonidas: 57
Porter, David D.: 114
Porter, Sarah E.: 98
Preston, Sally "Buck": 66-68
Preston, William: 116
Price, Sterling: 115-116

— R —

Rainey, A. T.: 181
Randal, Horace: 30, 32
Raymond, James H.: 132
Reagan, Elizabeth: 158
Reagan, John H.: 20, 86, 95-96, 145; early life, 158; leaves U. S. Congress, 159; elected delegate to state Secession Convention, 160; asks for Houston's cooperation, 160; named by Secession Convention to confer with Houston, 161; named Postmaster General in Confederate cabinet, 161-162; entices workers away from U. S. Post Office Department, 163; organized Confederate Post Office Department, 163; takes measure to cut expenses and increase revenue, 164; overhauls mail route system, 164; opposibine Pass, 40; mans defense positions at Sabine Pass, 40; ET tion of railroads, 165; loses battle with express companies, 165-166; wages fight with editors and publishers, 166; guards against encroachment of other government agencies, 166; harmony not always rule in his own department, 166-167; establishes Trans - Mississippi Post Office Department, 167; ill at ease in Richmond Society, 167; participates in decision to invade

North, 167-168; flees Richmond, 168; sent to Federal prison, 168; pardoned, 169; post-war years, 169; death, 169; 186
Rector, Henry M.: 88
Renshaw, William B.: 39, 105, 108, 110
Reynolds, Thomas C.: 32, 116
Rhodes, Robert: 45
Richardson, T. G.: 67
Roberts, Oran M.: 97, 144, 146, 159-160
Robertson, Jerome B.: 144
Robertson, Sterling C.: 128
Rogers, W. P.: 159
Runnels, H. R.: 18, 78, 177

— S —

Sabin, C. B.: 154
Sachem: 42-46; 105, 108
Saxon: 108
Sayers, Joseph D.: 97
Schwartzman, Gustaf: 163
Schofield, John: 64
Scott, Lue: 98
Scott, Winfield: 56
Scurry, William R.: 3, 107-108, 141
Secession Convention: 21, 80, 85, 144-45, 159-160
Second U. S. Cavalry: 58-59
Seddon, James A.: 16, 186
Semmes, Rapheal: 110
Shelby, Joseph: 116, 134
Shepard, James E.: 144
Sherman, William T.: 64, 168
Sibley, Henry H.: 11-12
Smith, Ashbel: 133
Smith, E. Kirby: 31-32, 93-95, 112, 115-116, 125-127, 132-133, 190
Smith, Gustavus W.: 186
Smith, Leon: 43-44, 46, 105-106, 108
Smith, Niles H.: 45-46
Star of the West: 25
Starr, James H.: 167
Steele, Frederick: 115
Stephens, Alexander: 161, 183
Stevenson, C. L.: 63
Stewart, A. P.: 63
Stockdale, Fletcher: 134
Sumner, Charles: 176

— T —

Taylor, Richard: 31, 115
Taylor, Sue Ellen: 123
Taylor, Zachary: 95
Terrell, A. W.: 134
Terry, B. F.: 82
Terry's Texas Rangers (8th Texas Cavalry): 82
Theron, B.: 93
Toombs, Robert: 162
Twiggs, David E.: 2, 24-25, 56

— U —

Uncle Ben: 40, 43, 45-46

— V —

Van Dorn, Earl: 1, 4, 10, 25
Velocity: 40

— W —

Wainwright, Jonathan: 105
Waite, C. A.: 24
Walker, John G.: 115
Walker, L. P.: 147-148; 162
Waller, Edwin: 6-7
Watkins, Oscar M.: 39-40
Waul, T. N.: 145
Wayne, Mad Anthony: 56
Weitzel, Godfrey: 42
West, Charles S.: 132
Westfield: 105, 107-108, 110
Wharton: John A.: 94
Wheeler, "Fighting Joe": 97
White, George W.: 142, 154
Wigfall, Eliza (Thompson): 175, 183, 188
Wigfall, Francis Halsey: 190
Wigfall, Levi Durand: 175
Wigfall, Louis T.: 20, 61, 86, 145, 149-150; attempts to induce surrender of Fort Sumter, 175; early life, 175-176; marries, 176; immigrates to Texas, 176; forms law partnership at Marshall, 176; helps to organize Democratic party in Texas, 177; elected to U. S. Senate, 177-178; coauthor of Southern address urging secession, 178; elected as delegate to Montgomery Convention, 179; predicts war, 179; recommends protection of slaves as property, 179; expelled from U. S. Senate, 179; attends Provisional Congress of Confederacy, 180; accompanies President Davis to Richmond, 180-181; commissioned colonel, 181; promoted to brigadier-general and to command of Texas Brigade in Virginia, 181-182; complaints of soldiers, 182; elected to Confederate Senate, 183; member of Military Affairs Committee, 184; backs conscription, 185; aids in

promoting Supreme Court, 185-186; strained relations with Jefferson Davis, 186-187; sought to free Robert E. Lee from direction of Davis, 187-188; returns to Texas, 188; returns to Richmond, 188; objects to arming slaves, 189; flees capital, 190; reaches Texas without arrest, 190; escapes to England, 190; last days and death, 190

Wigfall, Louise: 66-67, 191
Wilcox, Cadmus: 116
Wood, John Tyler: 95
Wortham, W. B.: 98

— Y —

Yancey, William L.: 178
Young, W. C.: 25-26